Legendary Lawman:
The Story of Quick Draw
Jelly Bryce

By Ron Owens

TRADE PAPER PRESS

Turner Publishing Company
200 4th Avenue North • Suite 950
Nashville, Tennessee 37219
(615) 255-2665
www.turnerpublishing.com

Legendary Lawman: The Story of Quick Draw Jelly Bryce

ISBN: 978-1-63026-368-3

Printed in the United States of America
10 11 12 13 14 15 16 17—0 9 8 7 6 5 4 3 2

Table of Contents

About the Author

After serving more than 30 years with the Oklahoma City Police Department, Ron Owens recently retired as a Captain commanding the Criminal Intelligence Unit. Born in Oklahoma City and a graduate of the University of Central Oklahoma, he spent his first 18 years on the force as a Patrolman and Detective including 8 years in Homicide, 11 years as a Hostage Negotiator on the Tactical Team and other assignments in Narcotics, Sex Crimes and Forgery.

He is a member of the Fraternal Order of Police, the Oklahoma Sheriffs and Peace Officers Association, the Oklahoma Historical Society, Oklahombres, the Sons of Confederate Veterans, the Sons of Union Veterans of the Civil War and the First Families of the Twin Territories.

His first two books, OKLAHOMA JUSTICE, a history of the first century of the OCPD, and OKLAHOMA HEROES, a tribute to slain Oklahoma officers, were also published by Turner Publishing and he contributed to their volume TO SERVE AND PROTECT.

He currently lives in Oklahoma City near his son and new granddaughter.

Abbreviations

ASAC—Assistant Special Agent in Charge. The second-in-command of a FBI field office.

FBI—Federal Bureau of Investigation. The primary investigative law enforcement agency of the U.S. Department of Justice. Originally, it was the United States Bureau of Investigation from 1909 to 1933. The name was changed to the United States Division of Investigation in the summer of 1933 and to the Federal Bureau of Investigation on July 1, 1935. For the sake of simplicity, this organization is referred to as the FBI throughout this work.

OCPD—Oklahoma City Police Department.

OCSO—Oklahoma County Sheriff's Office.

OHP—Oklahoma Highway Patrol, first organized in 1937.

OP—Office of Preference. The first choice(s) of Field Offices or resident agencies where a FBI agent requests to be stationed.

OSBI—Oklahoma State Bureau of Investigation, the first force of state-commissioned criminal investigators for the state of Oklahoma. Started as the Oklahoma Bureau of Criminal Identification and Investigation in 1925. Name changed to the Oklahoma State Bureau of Investigation in 1957.

OSP—Oklahoma State Penitentiary in McAlester, Oklahoma.

OSPOA—Oklahoma Sheriff and Peace Officers Association.

SA—Special Agent, the basic title for agents of the FBI.

SAC—Special Agent in Charge. The top supervisor of a FBI field office.

Acknowledgements

From start to finish, this was an investigation. Only in the movies and on TV are the successful ones done by one person. Unfortunately, there was no screenwriter for this investigation so it, like this book, is non-fiction. As a result, there is plenty of credit and lots of thanks to go around.

To retired FBI Special Agent Don Kyte, thanks for the contacts and three decades of trust and friendship. Yes, Don, it really is a family. Like most, a little dysfunctional at times but still a family. And no, I don't know why I persist in telling you things you already know except it's a habit by now.

To Sue Brunts, Secretary of the Retired Police Officers Association of Oklahoma and Hillary Robinette of the Society of Former Special Agents of the FBI, for helping put the word out.

To the late K.O. Rayburn, the Grand Old Man of the Oklahoma Council for Law Enforcement Education and Training (CLEET), thanks for the contacts. There isn't a law enforcement officer in the state of Oklahoma today that hasn't benefited from his efforts and, whether they know it or not, those benefits have been passed down to every citizen in their dealings with law enforcement.

To Delona Sue Bryce, Lila Dawson and Raymon P. Kasbaum, Delf Bryce's surviving relatives, who assisted me, thanks for helping to humanize and personalize the man. I have tried to do him justice.

To former FBI Special Agents Charlie Brunner, Cary Carlton, John Curtis, Cartha "Deke" DeLoach, Donald V. Eberle and his most gracious wife Jean, Gordon Jackson, Ray Kissiah, Maurice J. Kelly, Jim McGuire, Judge Edwin L. Mechem, Joe Pearson, George Robb, Bertie Sapp, Donald Sloat, Laird K. Smith and Jim Worrell. Thanks for the memories, the networking and your careers in law enforcement. Even those of you who couldn't help very much, tried. I have never talked or corresponded with a more interesting group of very good men.

I don't know much about private industry but from my experiences in law enforcement service, it's usually the civilian support staff including clerks, secretaries, stenographers, technicians and executive assistants who provide the bedrock foundation that keeps the place running while the folks with the badges have all the fun. Thanks to former FBI employees Velma Beyer, Virginia Buckley, Bob Calhoun, Bob Gentry, Doug Hilbert, Pauline McNally, Betty Miller, Dorothy Muirhead, Geneva Newkumet, Kay Orr, Agnes Tichy and Robert Warren for their unique insights into this aspect of the Bryce saga.

To retired OCPD Chief Robert V. Wilder, the late Assistant Chief W.A. "Ace" Williams, the late Major Jack Mullenix, Major Ken Nash, Major J.C. McCrite and his lovely wife Joan (a niece of Smokey Hilbert), the late Captain Gene Goold, Lt. Chris Walker, Lt. Bill Mead, Lt. Don Ayers, Lt. Don Cochran and Sgt. Jack Garrette. If they needed to, the OCPD could field an entire shift of the toughest damned old senior citizens you ever saw.

Thanks for some of the more esoteric assistance to John Bennett, Elmo Black, Steve Black, Ann Bradburn, Bill Buchanan, Ed Clark, Leon Cleary, Bruce Duncan, Bob Graham, Sam Harris, Roy Jinks, Karen Johnson, Leroy Jones, Golden Kennedy, Jarvis Littlefield, Darrell Nightingale, Margaret Evett O'Pry, Nyda Robinson, Lloyd Rosell, Charles Ryan, Linda Stephens, Susie Stephens and Tom Tate.

Also included here are a certain number who requested anonymity which is a shame since some of them provided some of the most interesting information. But I gave you my word and I'll keep it in perpetuity.

As usual, if there are any inaccuracies, misinterpretations or criticism attached to this work, they are mine alone.

Ron Owens
Oklahoma City, Oklahoma
August 22, 2000

Preface

This book suffers from several shortcomings that I profoundly regret.

I began the research for this book in August of 1999. Unfortunately, that was 93 years after Jelly Bryce was born, 71 years after he joined the Oklahoma City Police Department, 65 years after he joined the FBI, 41 years after he retired and 25 years after his death. This lapse in time is one of the causes for one of those shortcomings. That is also reflected in the fact that most of the people who knew Jelly Bryce personally or worked with or for him are in their eighth or ninth decades now. Time passes, flesh weakens and memories fade. Several of those who assisted me in my research have passed away before this book was published.

Oddly enough, I despised history in my early education and most especially Oklahoma history. Part of that was the rebellion of a headstrong boy against being force-fed certain courses. Another part was uninspiring teachers. I never had a history course or a history teacher who interested me until I was a sophomore in college. By then I was deeply involved in another major course of study that interested me more so the die was cast. I have paid for my late developing interest in history many times over in regrets for missed opportunities.

I deeply regret that during the years 1969-1977, while I was a young patrolman running around the streets of Oklahoma City in a black and white police car, putting bad people in jail and having more fun that I ever deserved, I never took the time to check into my law enforcement heritage. Had I done just a little background into the legacy I had inherited, I could have taken a few hours to drive to Mountain View and talk with Jelly Bryce or to McAlester to talk with Clarence Hurt. I don't know what makes me think that either of these legendary lawmen would have opened up to a slick-sleeved young patrolman for the sake of posterity but I sure would have liked to have had the opportunity.

Another shortcoming is caused by ingrained reticence. The year after Jelly Bryce's death, Sanford J. Ungar published a book about the FBI during which he was given unprecedented access to FBI facilities and personnel. In it, he quoted the Assistant Special Agent in charge of a major FBI field office as saying "For me, it would be impossible to be totally candid with you, because for twenty-two years I was taught to be guarded...I don't think I can be totally candid with anybody, because of my training. I have to be very concerned about what I say...I can't even be candid with my wife..."

Such was the tradition during the era of J. Edgar Hoover's directorship of that organization and it is very uniformly exemplified by nearly all who were members during that era. It is not limited to the FBI. In my own law enforcement career, I would soon learn that all professional law enforcement officers accumulate a stockpile of such knowledge and secrets. Some are shared only with trusted colleagues, some only with those who were present for the events and some you take to the grave with you.

For all his gregariousness among his professional colleagues and his showmanship during his firearms demonstrations, Delf Bryce was basically a very close-mouthed, private man. A man who stringently separated his personal and professional lives. He was also a man of honor and integrity, a man who honored trusts that were placed in him. An inveterate keeper of secrets.

Typically, over the years of his career in law enforcement, the number of people he trusted dwindled. They were almost exclusively law enforcement officers. He may have occasionally shared some amusing or interesting information with his wives and children but I suspect these were minimal. He couldn't have revealed too much without making the dangers of his job apparent and, like many officers, I'm sure he downplayed those dangers to his family. Probably more than most because he needed to more than most. A man of determined will, strong personality, ample ego and iron self-control, he doesn't appear to have been the kind of man who needed to share his stresses much. He internalized them.

He would only take a few drinks and completely relax in very select company. Those were the very few people he trusted implicitly who could identify with the things he saw and heard in his job, and what he thought and felt as a result.

Smokey Hilbert was one of these. So were Mickey Ryan, H.V. Wilder and Lee Mullenix. No doubt he also had trusted friends in the FBI but these were the men who trained him, working long days and nights with him from his first days as a police officer. These were the men who had gone through the doors with him, ducked bullets with him, watched his back while he watched theirs. It is almost impossible to describe the kind of bond and trust that develops between people who have shared those experiences to those who have not. In keeping with its ultimate goal of survival, it has a primal nature.

That is why many officers develop relationships with their partners that is as close, and sometimes closer, as those with their spouses and children. Like most people, law enforcement officers usually care deeply about their families. Also like most people, they are rarely called upon to risk their lives for them. But with two partners on the street level of police work in a large city, voluntarily taking that kind of risk can be an almost daily occurrence. Like the verse says, greater love hath no man.

Also complicating matters was the fact that Bryce had a self-deprecating way of expanding his own legend while simultaneously playing it down. When he was telling "war stories" to some people, they couldn't be absolutely certain whether he was embellishing them or just telling them what they wanted to hear.

Another problem that arose was an equal reticence among some of his relatives. Although I contacted both of his sons, both refused to cooperate with or assist me. By way of explanation, the older son based his refusal on the fact that he intended to one day write his own book about his famous father in spite of the fact that, by his own admission, he "didn't know (his) dad very well." Although he didn't specifically say so, I got the impression he felt that anything he gave me for inclusion in this volume would detract from his own intended book. The second son would give no reason for his refusal. Various other relatives proved not only uncooperative but obstructionist. A few did cooperate but they were a distinct minority.

Another problem was what I interpret as an unnecessary and destructive (from a strictly historical point of view) redaction of FBI files (see the Afterword Section).

Ideally, all the information in this book would have come from Jelly Bryce's mouth directly to my ear. Unfortunately, that was not possible. Therefore we have to settle for second, third or fourth best. Whenever possible, the incidents recounted here are those from people who actually witnessed the events, official records of the OCPD, the FBI, those reported in the news media and, lastly, from those who were told by those actually present. When there were conflicting stories, they were judged in the foregoing manner and the most likely one is what appears here.

Jelly Bryce deserved a better, more comprehensive biography than this. I wish I could have given it to him and to you.

At any rate, this will probably be the best book you have ever read about Jelly Bryce—because it is the only one that exists so far. Maybe the people who could make it better will do so for the next author to take up this quest.

I

Dawn In The Last Frontier –
Oklahoma Territory

When the settlement of the American frontier was beginning, towns tended to spring up near rivers. Later, they tended to follow the railroads. The difference whether a town would blossom into a city, remain a town or disappear altogether often depended on where a railroad chose to build their tracks. Such was the case when the final frontiers of the wild west, Oklahoma and Indian Territories, were settled.

It all began with a land run into central Oklahoma Territory on April 22, 1889. The settlement and partitioning of Indian lands was scheduled to continue for another dozen years, consisting of another four land runs and two lotteries.

In early April of 1899, the Chicago, Rock Island and Pacific Railroad finished building its line 51 miles west of Chickasha, Oklahoma Territory, in the northern part of the Kiowa-Comanche-Apache reservation. Since the federal government prohibited white settlement on Indian lands and that area was not scheduled to be opened to white settlement until 1901, settlers migrated to a location north of the Washita River, two miles from the railroad's terminus. This town, initially only a store and post office established on October 14, 1893, was called Oakdale.

The store's goods came more than 50 miles by wagon from El Reno and more settlers followed them. A tent city, unofficially dubbed "City of the Woods", sprang into being. A quarter section of land (160 acres) was soon purchased from one of the owners of the Oakdale store for a town site and some officials from the railroad company came out from Topeka, Kansas, to view the end of their line. Much as it is today, the gently undulating hills were a verdant green interspersed with red ochre scars of tilled earth with wild sunflowers growing by the roadsides. The story is told that after viewing their newly finished 144-foot-long depot, station house and water tanks, their eyes were naturally drawn to the northern edge of the bordering Wichita Mountains and one of them suggested "Let's call this place Mountain View." Thus was it informally known until the name of the local post office was officially changed on October 9, 1900, and Mountain View, Oklahoma Territory, became a real place.

A century after its founding, the town is still home to barely more than a thousand souls. As Delf Bryce would later joke, the second tallest structure in town is still the single water tower, later surpassed only by the twin grain elevators. The "downtown" area is barely three blocks long and is quintessential small-town America. The kind of place where drivers in passing cars automatically wave to complete strangers, cars and homes are frequently left unlocked with impunity, people sleep with their windows open on hot summer nights and children can still walk to school, alone and unmolested.

Fel Albert Bryce was born in the northeast Texas town of Gilmer, Upshur County, about 100 miles due east of Dallas, on March 25, 1884. His parents soon relocated to Alvord, some 40 miles north of Fort Worth, and he attended grade school there. In 1897, Fel came with his brother and sister-in-law to Oakdale, Oklahoma Territory. The hardy family made the nearly 300-mile journey by wagon, transporting a dismantled cotton gin while the teenaged boy rode a horse the entire distance. Once settled in their new home and finding themselves happy there, they notified the rest of the family who relocated with them. The boy finished his formal education at the Oakdale School and began making ends meet by working on cattle drives to Pampa, Texas, and delivering mail locally.

The opening of the Kiowa-Comanche-Apache reservation by lottery in July of 1901 drew still more settlers to the Mountain View area but a defining calamity struck the town in May of 1903. Massive rainfalls—the local newspaper likened it to "the ocean being turned upside down"—engorged the aptly named Rainy Mountain Creek and the Washita River. Both overflowed their banks, merged and formed a stretch of flood waters eight miles wide. The entire business section of the town was inundated under several feet of water.

After the waters ebbed, a coalition of businessmen rapidly set about arranging for the purchase of a new town site on the south side of the river. Since that land was Indian land, it literally took an Act of Congress to get it approved but, miraculously even for those simpler times, that was achieved in fairly short order. The residents then began a unique experience—dismantling what was left of the town and moving it a mile and a half across the Washita River from the southeastern part of present-day Washita County into the northeastern part of Kiowa County.

Buildings were sawed into sections and moved in portions. A hardware salesman who visited the town at the time found the rear half of a store on its original lot while the front half had been moved to the new town site. He wrote to a friend that he had visited the longest hardware store in the world because it was a mile and a half from the front door to the back door. Forever embedded in children's memories would be riding on beds and sofas as they slid back and forth across wooden floors in half a house, wagons full of rocks hitched behind it to slow its slide down hillsides.

God's trials and tribulations were not through with Mountain View because another defining disaster struck the new town site on the afternoon of November 4, 1905. A tornado hit the town, damaging $100,000 worth of property, injuring at least 18 people and killing seven, one of them a baby boy born during the storm.

One of the buildings destroyed was the two-story school. This after all the trouble of removing the upper story, transporting it across the river and re-assembling the building. Funds were raised and a new six-room brick schoolhouse was raised. All the grades were in the same building and the first graduating class of six matriculated in the spring of 1906. By 1909, a growing student body necessitated a separate high school. A new one was built next to the grade school. The larger, taller, more spacious two-story building

Winnie and Fel Bryce (photo courtesy of D.S. Bryce)

was built of brick with a large attic, basement and the town's first auditorium. Sometimes their graduating class would only consist of a single student but they had their separate high school. In later years, their sports teams would be dubbed the Mountain View Tigers.

In the year before Oklahoma became a state, life was still primitive and hard in Mountain View. Clothes were washed on corrugated wash boards in tubs filled with river or well water, meals were cooked on wood or coal-burning stoves, clothes were ironed with flat irons heated on the stoves, ice was delivered by wagon, milk by horse-drawn two-wheeled cart and dispensed with a quart-sized dipper, eggs were literally a dime a dozen and calico was sold for a nickel a yard. Improvements would come but slowly. The town wouldn't install a sewer system until 1928 and Main Street wouldn't be paved until two years after that. Until then, it was outhouses, dust in the drought and mud in the deluge.

In between the floods and cyclones, the hard-working young Fel Bryce had fallen in love. Maggie Meek had been born on December 6, 1889, in the town of Purcell in the old Chickasaw Nation of Indian Territory. With the opening of the Kiowa-Comanche-Apache lands, her family had relocated 75 miles west to Mountain View. Eventually, she met and was courted by the industrious, handsome young Fel Bryce.

Mrs. Lila Bryce Dawson
September 1999, age 87

Because they had to, kids grew up faster on the early Oklahoma prairie. Circumstances forced girls to become women and boys become men earlier than today. Maggie Meek married her 21-year-old suitor on December 3, 1905, three days before her sixteenth birthday. Fel continued with his odd jobs to support his new family and, after finishing her own education, Maggie began teaching in Mountain View's grade school.

Fel and Maggie Bryce's first child and only son was born on a Thursday, December 6, 1906, Maggie's seventeenth birthday. In pre-statehood Oklahoma, more children were born in their homes than in hospitals. Formal birth certificates were a rarity or non-existent. The story goes that the boy was originally named Jacob Adolphus Bryce after his two grandfathers, Jacob Bryce and Delf Adolphus Meek, both of whom allegedly doted on the boy. Adolphus' foreign-sounding and somewhat intimidating middle name naturally led to him being known to his intimates as "Delf." Although many who knew him from early childhood would call the boy "Jake" all his life, he seemingly was always called "Delf" within the family. Nevertheless, the Oklahoma State Department of Health does not have a birth certificate on file under either name.

Later in life, he apparently wished to change his name to honor both his grandfather and father so he adopted the name Delf Albert Bryce. This was apparently done without official court action, as were many other things in those days. Confusions in spelling contributed to the enigma. His high school graduation photo which hangs in the hallways of Mountain View High School today is labeled "Delph A. Bryce." The confusion with his dual names would continue into his majority. In the 1929 Annual of the Oklahoma City Police Department, the first one in which he is listed, his photograph is identified as "D.A. Bryce" but in the narrative of his arrests, he is identified as "J.A. Bryce."

The Bryce's second child was born on March 27, 1912. A daughter, she was named Lila. She and her older brother became inseparably close. In a nursing home eighty-seven years later, many of her memories dimmed by the passing years, she would still smile beatifically at the mention of his name, calling him "a prince of a brother." An official FBI photograph of him occupies a place of honor on her wall.

She recounts an old family story saying that her brother actually cut his teeth on a gun. Her father had an old pistol and "when Delf was a boy, they let him teethe on Daddy's unloaded pistol. They propped him up with pillows there in the crib and let him go after it."

In the early days after statehood, wild game was plentiful in western Oklahoma and it would probably have been unusual for any family not to have supplemented their larder by hunting. It was still dangerous country, also. The people shared their space with rattlesnakes, water moccasins, copperheads, wolves, coyotes and cougars. It would probably have been unusual for most boys in the area not to have had some training and familiarity with firearms from an early age but young Delf Bryce was seen as a prodigy from an earlier age than most. His family encouraged his talents.

He had his first .22 rifle by the age of ten, a hand pumped air rifle preceded that and he also became familiar with using a shotgun. His primary benefactor was his maternal grandfather, Delf Meek. He became the boy's primary supplier of ammunition and encouraged him to practice his marksmanship. Bryce once saved over one hundred dollars he earned by shining shoes. He bought one pair of pants and spent the rest on ammunition. Considering the economy of those days, that would buy a great deal of ammunition. With this supply, he practiced a lot and refined his natural talents.

From an early age, he had phenomenal eyesight and eye-hand coordination far beyond the normal. Still in grammar school, he was the only ten-year-old kid walking the streets of Mountain View, unsupervised, with a rifle or air rifle and "No one thought anything about it," his sister said. A friend from Bryce's childhood, Leah Reimer said "—us kids would try to scare game up out of the brush and Delf would shoot whatever flew up with his rifle—he never missed—he was a perfect shot." By the fourth grade, Bryce was shooting rabbits on the run and quail on the wing with a rifle. He often practiced in a creek bed near his home. He would tie a string around an empty soda pop bottle and, tying it to a tree limb, set it swinging. But he wouldn't aim at the bottle. That was too easy a target. He'd aim at the string.

He was a common sight riding his bicycle in the area of Saddle Mountain, a small hamlet 18 miles south of Mountain View. Entrepreneurial at an early age, Bryce would shoot eagles (obviously long before those birds were federally protected) and sell the feathers to the local Indians. In the manner of the old ways, they would use them to decorate their now-ceremonial war bonnets and shields.

Fel Bryce was an active man who believed in public service to his community and was described by all who knew him as a "model citizen." He was an active member of the First Methodist Church and taught Sunday school every week. He served on the Mountain View Board of Education for five years and later served as president of the local Chamber of Commerce for a number of years. For a time, he owned a general store in town where his son worked in addition to his other chores at home. Fel also operated a wholesale gas company and delivered gas to nearby communities like Saddle Mountain. Also well known for his hobby of doing very high quality leatherwork, Fel made and sold stock whips and quirts. One of those whips, of beautiful but utilitarian workmanship, is today displayed in a museum in Saddle Mountain near a display honoring his more famous son.

The only things allowed to interrupt the boy's childhood diversions of shooting, hunting and fishing were his education and illness. For all his outdoors activities, Bryce's childhood was punctuated with bouts of influenza, chicken pox, whooping cough, typhoid fever, measles and mumps. Occasionally sickly but basically hardy, he began grammar school in Mountain View in 1913.

As Bryce neared the end of his elementary education, a major tragedy was visited upon the family. On February 21, 1921, his mother died from pneumonia at the age of 31. The local newspaper noted that his father's parents came in from Wilson in Carter County to be with the family in their grief.

Maggie Meek Bryce was buried in Mountain View Cemetery with Reverend J.D. Kidd of the First Methodist Church officiating at the services. Sprays of flowers were sent from the Mountain View School and separate bouquets came from the students in her third and seventh grade classes.

The following year, Delf graduated from grammar school with a grade average of 88.

Following World War I, the U.S. Army began holding Civilian Military Training Camps (CMTC's) for young men. In the southwest region which covered Texas, Oklahoma, Colorado, New Mexico and Arizona, it was under the direction of the U.S. Army's Eighth Corps headquartered at Fort Sam Houston in San Antonio, Texas. For thirty days every summer, 3,000 young men were given "an outing at government expense" at whichever of four military posts was closest to their homes. The four posts were Camp Travis, Texas, Fort Sill, Oklahoma, Fort Logan, Colorado, and Fort Huachuca, Arizona. It was a combination of a boys camp, part-time military school and military recruitment device.

The young men's transportation expenses to and from the military camps was paid for them and their food, clothing and living quarters furnished without charge. With the intent of "keeping boys out of mischief", the camps promoted the ideals of "loyalty, patriotism, citizenship, good morals and a clean, healthy life." They offered instruction in athletics and the fundamentals of military training including firearms. The boys were not required to enlist but were subjected to military-style discipline. Disobedience was punished by returning the boys to their homes.

Encouraging a long-term commitment, the course was divided into four graduated and progressive levels, patriotically named for the colors of our national flag and intended to be taken in successive years. The Basic Red Course was open to young men 17 to 25 years of age. It consisted of training in military fundamentals but no specific instruction in any particular branch of the service.

The Advanced Red Course covered basic instruction in a branch of the student's choice. The branches covered were Infantry, Cavalry, Field Artillery, Coast Artillery, Engineers, Signal Corps and the Air Service.

The White Course was open to 18 to 26-year-olds who had graduated from the previous year's Advanced Red Course. It prepared the students to become non-commissioned officers in the Organized Reserves or the National Guard.

The Blue Course was open to 19 to 27-year-olds who had graduated from the previous year's White Course. It prepared candidates to become officers in the Organized Reserve Corps.

Indicative of the fact that this wasn't your average boys camp, World War I veterans were accepted into the courses up to age 35. While learning their military fundamentals, smooth-cheeked boys were rubbing elbows with combat-scarred veterans of the trenches of

France.

Delf Bryce attended his first CMTC at Fort Sill in the summer of 1922 at the age of 15. How he got in under the official age limit is not known. In fact, he had attended two of the camps before he ever reached the minimum published age of 17. Although his attendance is documented in his FBI background investigation, the records of the specific courses taken cannot be located today. It could be considered a natural progression that he took the Infantry course with its emphasis on field crafts and marksmanship with small arms. With his years of practice and familiarity as well as his natural talents, he could have naturally been expected to excel in the latter course. He allegedly won first place in both rifle and pistol courses and then won the national rifle championship at Camp Perry, Ohio, although neither Camp Perry's records nor those of the sponsoring National Rifle Association can verify it. He would faithfully attend every succeeding camp through the summer of 1926 after he graduated from Mountain View High School.

Oddly enough, particularly in view of his future profession and adventures, the winter after his first CMTC, Bryce was shot in the peaceful hamlet of his birth.

The Mountain View News reported that about 4 P.M. on the chilly Sunday afternoon of February 11, 1923, two local Mountain View boys, C.E. Sumner Jr. and Wordy Sohn, were involved in some apparently innocent horseplay near the Morris Filling Station. What made it turn from innocent to deadly was the .22 caliber target rifle that the boys were scuffling over. The gun accidentally discharged just as 16-year-old Delf Bryce was passing by the gas station. The bullet struck him in the left side of the chest, passed through and lodged just under the skin of his back.

The wounded boy was taken to the doctor's office where the bullet was removed and he was then taken home. The local weekly newspaper reported "At first, he was considered to be in a dangerous condition but he is rapidly getting straightened out. No blame is to be laid on the other boys as they were not aware the gun would go off—they were in the act of putting it up and as all boys will do, were scuffling over it, the gun going off and striking Delf who was passing by at the time."

The report was accurate in its prediction of Bryce's complete recovery after Doctor Hathaway removed the projectile. Most of the rest of it was a repetition of a fabrication, "as all boys will do." Bryce later told trusted friends, the kind boys trust not to divulge their secrets to the authorities or parents, the true story. The boys were in a barn that didn't belong to them and where they shouldn't have been. They were shooting pigeons in the rafters when the accident occurred. The Sumner boy was the one who actually shot him.

The most incredible fact was yet to come. In all the harrowing adventures to follow in the next half century, no other bullet would ever touch him.

II
The Extended Family

Winnie Preskitt was born on January 7, 1896, in Wilbarger County, Texas. The county's meandering northern border was the same Red River that formed the southern border of Oklahoma Territory. When she was two years old, her parents, J.T. and Lucinda Preskitt, moved 150 miles northwest to the territorial town of Norman.

By all accounts, there was nothing unusual or extraordinary about her childhood and adolescence. After less than a decade of statehood, hard times in Oklahoma still made kids grow up faster. Three months after her eighteenth birthday, Winnie married Henry Kasbaum in April of 1914.

Their first child, Mildred, was born in 1917. Their second was a boy, born in June of 1921, and was named Raymon. The name was always pronounced "Raymond" but the "d" was left off of the spelling. In later years, when Raymon asked his mother why she did that, she gave him a direct answer—"Because that's the way I wanted it." Tragically, he never got to know his father. Henry Kasbaum died in February of 1922.

It must have been a daunting prospect for a 26-year-old widow with two pre-school aged children to face a man's world that had only allowed women to vote for the past two years. What would she do? Winnie Kasbaum was the kind of woman who was up to the task.

She entered the University of Oklahoma and earned a degree in education. Newly graduated teachers go where the jobs are and this time, the job was in Mountain View. Winnie relocated her family 70 miles to the west and began teaching school. Six lives were about to coincide and Raymon Kasbaum was about to gain a peer group that didn't frown on unusual names.

She was 29, he was 41. Despite the slight disparity in their ages, Fel Bryce and Winnie Kasbaum had a lot in common. Widow and widower had lost their spouses less than a year apart. Both were native Texans whose families had relocated them to Oklahoma Territory in their youths. Each had two children, one of each sex. Fel's son Delf was in his last year of high school and daughter Lila had just turned thirteen. Winnie's daughter Mildred was eight and her son Raymon was four. Mildred had few memories of her father and

Raymon had none.

Courtship can be like sharp objects—more dangerous for the young and immature. They need not be long, drawn-out affairs to be conducted properly, particularly when the parties involved are two moral, intelligent, mature adults. After an abbreviated courtship, Fel Bryce and Winnie Kasbaum were married in the Gotebo Methodist Church seven miles west of Mountain View on November 11, 1925, a couple of weeks before Delf Bryce played his last high school football game. Both had taken the marriage vows once before, promising to keep the sanctity of the marriage until death did them part. They had both kept those vows and now were taking them again. They would keep them this time also.

Not only was the marriage successful, so was the melding of the families. Fel Bryce—"as good a man as there ever was" in his stepson's words—became a true father to Mildred and Raymon Kasbaum, the only one the boy ever knew. With that example set, how could the children treat each other any way other than as true siblings? They all became as close as true brothers and sisters, remaining so throughout their lives. Raymon and Lila became especially close and Raymon always looked upon Delf as his older brother. The "step" was all but forgotten.

Bryce's younger sister, Lila (Bryce) Dawson, remembers her older brother playing quarterback on his high school football team as well as being a member of the track team but you couldn't prove it (or disprove it) by reading The Mountain View Times.

In the decade of the Roaring Twenties, Mountain View's local newspaper was a once-weekly affair that usually consisted of from eight to ten pages. Small headlines like "Grandma Kirk Passed Away Tuesday" and the local market report dominated the front page. Farther back were ads for horses, cattle, chickens, feed and farm implements for sale. Other ads proclaimed the virtues of Wintersmith's Chill Tonic, Carter's Little Liver Pills, St. Joseph's Liver Regulator and Vaseline Carbolated Petroleum Jelly.

The sports reporting, at least for the local high school football team, usually consisted of a couple of column-inches at best but at least it was usually on the front page. The football season started in late September or early October and was over by Thanksgiving. An irregular schedule featured opponents from schools in small neighboring towns like Apache, Hollis, Hydro, Tuttle, Elk City, Hinton, Snyder, Hobart, Anadarko and Carnegie. Occasionally teams from Grandfield, Sentinel High and Port High came to town for a game.

Competing with the very limited student bodies of smaller town schools, they fielded nine players instead of the usual eleven. Rules for replacements, substitutions and two-platoon football were in the future. The boys played both offense and defense.

The 1923 team finished with a 5-1-3 record. Unusually for a small town, no individual accomplishments were mentioned by name in the paper. At the end of the season, all the members of the team were listed but Delf Bryce wasn't among them for that year. Unfortunately they didn't list them at all for the next two years which would have been Bryce's Junior and Senior years.

The 1924 team played more games and did better, winning six, tying three and losing only two games. The statistics of the 1925 team were seemingly less impressive at 4-2-3 but, in nine games, they held four of their opponents scoreless and only 35 points were scored against them all season. In addition to an impressive defense, their offense improved as the season went along. In their last two games, they outscored their opponents 137-10, finishing with a 104-3 trouncing of Apache. In one of their more boastful statements, the local paper said "our boys like to have ran themselves down—making touchdowns almost at will." Considering the final score, one wonders why they even bothered with the "almost."

A photograph exists of the 1925 Mountain View nine. They are wearing dress slacks and their letter sweaters with a large "M" on their chests. They are also wearing their "game faces", not a hint of a smile in the lot. Each sweater has stripes on the upper left sleeve.

Mountain View Ball Team, 1926. Delf Bryce, Ralph Gibson, Orvil Withrow, Willis Worley, Jimmy Tidmore, Maurice Fariss, Harold Baublets, Frazier Fariss, Lee Mason. (photo courtesy of Schoonmaker Publishers)

Eight of them have two stripes and one has a single stripe. Possibly this denotes the number of years they have been awarded their letter in football. The boys are also stair-stepped from left to right in the photo, ranging from the shortest and slimmest to the tallest and stockiest. The first one on the left, sporting two stripes on his sleeve, is Delf Bryce.

It has been reported that Delf Bryce was an all-state football player. An examination of the lists of both the large and small city all-state football teams of 1925 as printed in The Daily Oklahoma on November 29 and December 6, 1925, do not list his name or that of any other Mountain View player.

Mountain View was building a new high school on First Street on the eastern edge of the town. It would include a gymnasium, a larger auditorium and a new home economics department but Delf Bryce would never be a student there. Nevertheless, his photo still hangs on the wall there along with the other nine boys and four girls in his graduating class.

Athletics behind, he went back to the academics, evidently successfully. On May 20, 1926, he graduated from Mountain View High School with a B average.

Although the town of Seminole, Oklahoma, was platted in the same year Delf Bryce was born, 1906, it wasn't incorporated as a

Mt. View: gradeschool on left and high school on right. (photo courtesy of Schoonmaker Publishers)

city until the day after Christmas in 1924. From a recorded population of 206 in the year of Oklahoma's statehood, 1907, it gradually increased to 854 by the time of the 1920 census. It seemed to be destined to be a small Oklahoma hamlet forever.

By 1926, although periodic drilling for oil had been going on in the area for more than a dozen years, most wells had been busts and the best of them had been major disappointments. Two months after Delf Bryce graduated from high school, in July of 1926, the Garland Independent Fixico No. 1 well became the first well to tap one of the greatest oil fields in the world. It erupted into a gusher producing 10,000 barrels of oil a day and Seminole became Oklahoma's newest boom town.

People were seemingly drawn from everywhere and, before the summer was over, the population had boomed to over 15,000. Without a paved road in sight, summer rains turned the town into "a mass of mud, mules, men and drilling equipment."

After graduating from high school, Bryce moved to Seminole. It was a little over a hundred miles almost due east of Mountain View as the crow flies but the roads of the day would have made the trip a little over 125 miles. He spent the next year working in a grocery store. Given what we know of his personality now, the boredom and repetition of it must have been stultifying.

III
State Game Ranger

At its inception, Oklahoma Territory was a cornucopia of fresh game. Spanish conquistadors, Indians, cowboys, Boomers and Sooners had been living off of the land for centuries. When the first Territorial government was established in 1890, it took them some time to realize that some form of regulation was necessary for the burgeoning new land.

The first game and fish laws were passed by the legislature in 1895 but provided for no central administrative office or method of enforcing the new laws. Local, county, and township officers were empowered to enforce them, encouraged by receiving half of each fine as their pay. The new laws prohibited killing wild game and insectivorous birds except during special hunting seasons established for quail, prairie chicken, turkey, dove and plover.

In 1903, the Territorial Game and Fish Protective Association was formed to enforce the Game Marketing Act. Marketing game became illegal and railway and express companies were fined heavily for shipping game animals. Six years later, Oklahoma had become a state and the Association petitioned the legislature for a more permanent and organized form of administration. In 1909 the State Game and Fish Department was created with the hiring of a State Game Warden and eight salaried employees including a supervisor and the first six game wardens. The first hunting license cost $1.25. In the first four years, it created $94,000 in revenue.

In 1913, the Department was disbanded and the money put into a fund for the new state capitol building. Protests from sportsmen resulted in the department being re-established in 1915. The 1925 State Legislature established the Oklahoma State Game and Fish Commission. For the first time, fishing licenses were issued and protection was established for fur bearing mammals.

After a year in Seminole, Delf Bryce was ready for a change. A change more suited to his nature. Always an avid hunter and fisherman, that coupled with his love of firearms led him naturally to the State Game and Fish Commission.

In August of 1927, he was hired as an "extra" Game Ranger under State Fish and Game Warden Ray O. Weems. The records of the current Oklahoma Wildlife Commission show that he received a special commission on an "expenses only" basis. Within three months, he became a regularly salaried Ranger drawing $150 a month. His listed address was Box 454, Cherokee, Oklahoma.

Now this presents another slight source of confusion. Since the Cherokee Indians are the largest tribe in Oklahoma and one of the largest in the nation, many settlements or geographical areas have their name incorporated in them. There have been, at various times, a Cherokee City, Cherokee County, Cherokee Agency and Cherokee Town, among others. Many are no longer in existence. Just plain Cherokee is in Alfalfa County in northwest Oklahoma, adjacent to the Great Salt Plains State Park and the attached federal wildlife refuge so that presents an attractive location for a State Game Ranger to be stationed. On the other hand, Cherokee Town was about thirty miles west of Ada in Garvin County. Later information seems to favor the latter location for Bryce's post.

His primary adventure during his short tenure as a State Game Ranger led to his first and only arrest—where he was the one arrested.

Just after Christmas of 1927, the Oklahoma Sheriff and Peace Officers Association (OSPOA) held one of their biannual conferences in Shawnee, headquartered at the Walcott Hotel. State Game Warden Ray Weems was one of the featured speakers and his topic turned out to be unintentionally ironic—"Cooperation between Peace Officers and the State Game and Fish Commission."

As usual, there was also a shooting competition held in conjunction with the conference. Many of the competing officers felt it was a foregone conclusion that the winner would be Tex Burdett. Burdett was then Chief of Police in Earlsboro, a small town seven miles southeast of Shawnee in Pottawatomie County. Apparently Burdett was known as one of the best marksmen in the state. Things didn't turn out as expected this year. The winner was a young Game Ranger named Delf A. Bryce and the first prize was a free pair of shoes from a store in Shawnee.

The small town Chief was evidently a sore loser. While Bryce was in the store picking out his shoes, his vanquished competitor came in and called him "a vile name" he didn't appreciate. Bryce punched Burdett once, knocking him down, picked out his shoes and left. Chief Burdett later swore out a warrant for Bryce for assault and battery and he was arrested. Bryce was released after friends posted a $15 bond for him. The charges were never formally filed, Bryce never went to court and never received a conviction. It is unknown whether this was because the petulant Chief merely wanted a symbolic victory or if some astute county attorney refused the charges on a legal basis.

Pyrrhic victory in hand, the Chief's character was at least consistent. He was later convicted of conspiracy to violate the Prohibition Act and sent to Leavenworth Penitentiary for a year.

That this incident actually occurred is documented in the background investigation in Bryce's FBI personnel file but, here again, there may be some variation of those facts.

Documentation from local newspapers show that the firearms competition at the Shawnee OSPOA conference took place on December 29, 1927. The Shawnee Morning News reported that the Shawnee PD team took first place in the team competitions with an overall score of 82 per cent. The OCPD team of Chief Ben Moore, Clarence Hurt, Bob Hurt and H.V. Wilder took second place with 73 per cent and the State Fish and Game Rangers took third place. In the individual matches, Shawnee officers took first and third places with a Waurika officer taking second place. After a shoot-off to resolve a tie, fourth place went to "D.A. Brice" (sic) who was stationed at Ada. The paper didn't report who Bryce's shoot-off was with to break the tie or who took fifth place.

Nevertheless, while the small town Chief's law enforcement career was nearing its ignominious end, Delf Bryce's was just beginning. After less than a year as a State Game Ranger, he was ready for something bigger and better but the choices were limited. In the middle of the Roaring Twenties in Oklahoma, there was no Highway patrol and the State Crime Bureau was a brand new agency which naturally drew its initial cadre from experienced law enforcement officers. The best and closest place to get such experience was the state's largest city.

IV
OCPD

In 1928, nearing the end of its fourth decade, the state capital of Oklahoma was a city of 175,000 people living in 19 incorporated square miles. The city government of Oklahoma City employed 571 of those people at an average annual salary of less than $1800. One of every five of those city employees, 115, worked for the Oklahoma City Police Department (OCPD). They were apportioned thusly:

1—Chief of Police
1—Secretary to the Chief
1—Assistant Chief
3—Captains
1—Traffic Captain
1—Bertillon Superintendent
3—Sergeants
12—Detectives
4—Auto Theft Bureau
4—Stolen Goods Department
50—Patrolmen
16—Traffic Officers
6—Motorcycle Officers
3—Jailers
3—Matrons
1—Gamewell Operator
1—Accident Report Clerk
1—Traffic Violation Clerk
1—Market Master
1—Welfare Board
1—Janitor

In 1911, Oklahoma City had adopted a commissioner form of government. It was intensely partisan and the administration of services was based largely upon political considerations. Many men were appointed or fired from the OCPD during this era solely because they were Democrats or Republicans, depending upon which party was in the majority at the time. In the ensuing 16-year period, the citizens gradually became aware of the inherent inefficiency and expensiveness of this form of municipal government.

In February of 1927, the city adopted a city manager form of government to replace the commissioner form that had been in place the previous 16 years. The theory was that the city would be run by a man who would be non-partisan because he was appointed and not elected. The fallacy of that theory was that the city manager was appointed by the City Council who were elected and each of whom had their own political agenda.

The form was a so-called "strong" city manager system which has persisted to the present day. The Mayor and eight Councilmen representing the city's four wards each had a single vote and had to confirm department head appointments. The Chief of Police, Fire Chief and other department heads were hired, appointed by and answerable to the City Manager.

Walter C. Dean was elected Mayor in 1927 and hired Edmond M. Fry as the city's first City Manager at a salary "not to exceed $1,000 a month." Fry was a civil engineer by training but had been Deputy Warden of the Oklahoma State Prison in McAlester for a decade before serving as City Manager of McAlester for four years. He had been in private business in investment banking in Tulsa and McAlester before taking the City Manager's job in the state capital.

It goes without saying that the OCPD of 1928 was very different from today. There were no police unions, no bargaining agents, no procedure or precedent for grievances, no impartial federal arbitrators who issued binding decisions upon city governments and police administrators. Men with no law enforcement experience at all could be hired as Chief of Police. Others could be hired at any rank, bypassing any rank at a commander's whim as long as the Chief and City Manager didn't object. Similarly, summary firings, demotions, transfers and suspensions were frequent occurrences. There was no appeal to disciplinary action except to appeal to the mercy of the commander issuing it.

A man didn't have to get into trouble or be disciplined to be bounced between ranks. Officers occasionally went up and down the rank structure depending upon haphazard budgetary considerations.

The Chief of Police was Benjamin B. Moore, fifty-one years of age, eighteen of them in law enforcement. After farming into his mid-thirties, he had served eight years as an Oklahoma County Deputy Sheriff, two years as a Federal Prohibition Officer and seven years as a special officer for the Missouri, Kansas and Texas Railroad. Appointed as Assistant Chief under Chief Martin C. Binion in 1927, he served one year in that capacity before Binion retired to run for Oklahoma County Sheriff. Moore was appointed to succeed him as Chief on May 15, 1928.

On his first day as Chief, Moore selected Charles A. Becker as his Assistant Chief. A year younger than Moore, Becker had joined the force in 1921 as a clerk in the Stolen Goods Bureau after a career as a travelling salesman and hotel manager. The next year he was made head of the bureau. He was appointed Assistant Chief exactly two months before his seventh anniversary on the force. For the time being, he would continue running the Stolen Goods Bureau in addition to his new duties as Assistant Chief.

Among the innovations Chief Moore introduced were a "show-up" system where witnesses could view and identify suspects without being seen. Many other changes would be realized in the next few years that got their start under Chief Moore. In the planning stages were a police radio system, creating police substations at four fire stations in different quadrants of the city, more electric traffic signals, introducing sidewalk signals to replace ones in the center of the street that confused pedestrians and a police pension system. Two of his most recent innovations would have met with the approval of one of his newest officers.

The first was a three-way mirror installed in the officer's rest room. Insisting on neatness and presentability in his officers, Moore required each officer to inspect himself thoroughly before going on duty.

The second was a police pistol range. Himself an excellent shot and a member of the OCPD Pistol Team, Moore had won the railroad special agent's pistol contest in Kansas, Oklahoma and Texas. He required each of his officers to practice on the range twice a week.

One can almost imagine the smile on Delf Bryce's face when he heard these requirements. Bryce would eventually spend many hours in front of that mirror, not primping but practicing his fast draw. That was probably a source of amusement for some of the older officers. That amusement would soon turn into awe.

One of Chief Moore's first actions was an injection of new blood into the Department. Ten veteran officers were retired to the reserve list at half pay of $75 a month and would now work four hours daily, most in inspection duties. They ranged in rank from Patrolman to Captain, all were in their sixties and all had between 19 and 28 years of service. Twenty-one new men were hired to bring Department strength up to 131. One of them was a dapper young man named Delf Albert Bryce, not quite eight months past his twenty-first birthday.

Bryce's official OCPD personnel file shows two dates of entry. An obviously earlier, handwritten card gives it as June 16, 1928. A typewritten personnel sheet dated in 1931 gives the date he entered service as July 15, 1928. There is some evidence for both dates.

A verification for the earlier date is given on an application for vacation he filled out on August 15, 1929, in which he gave his date of last vacation as June 16, 1928. The handwritten card shows that he received no vacation days and had taken no sick days up to the August 1929 vacation request, thus indicating the June 16 date as his date of hire. This is also the date he gives in his later FBI application.

However, as we shall see shortly, there is evidence that Bryce was still a State Game Ranger as late as June 21, 1928, which gives credence to the later date.

Both personnel records show that he was hired as a Detective in the Auto Theft Bureau at a salary of $150 per month, skipping the Patrolman or "Scout Car" rank entirely. He was the youngest detective on the force. He was assigned Badge Number 012 and showed an address of 421 East Sixth Street in the near northeast quadrant of the city. In the City Directory for that year, he brazenly listed his occupation as "city detective." And a legend was born.

And on that subject, a slight digression is merited.

Throughout the history of the human race, men with superlative or extraordinary qualities, talents and adventures admired by others have spawned superlative tales. Some are true, some are false, and over time, many become a little bit of both. As time passes, it becomes harder to differentiate between the two but some judgements can be made by inference.

One of the favorite tales about Jelly Bryce is that of his initial recruitment as a police officer. The story goes that one day the OCPD Pistol Team was firing in a shooting competition when a young Delf Bryce approached one of the team members, Clarence Hurt, and asked if he could compete with them. Stories abound alleging Bryce joined the OCPD while still a teenager, some saying as young as 16, but we have seen that he was 21, albeit a baby-faced 21.

The veteran officers scoffed at the ancient .38 pistol the boy was carrying and Hurt allegedly said something to the young man to the effect that "You think you can shoot?" When Bryce replied he thought he could, Hurt decided to test him. He put a target in the crook of a tree and, pacing off the regulation shooting distance, told the young man to shoot at it. In one version of the story, the target was an old envelope. In another, it was a playing card. At any rate, the young Bryce allegedly asked if he could draw and fire instead of just standing still in the normal shooting stance. That agreed upon, Bryce drew with blinding speed and placed all six shots in an area the size of a silver dollar. At that point, Hurt, then the Night or Assistant Chief of the OCPD, immediately hired him on the OCPD.

What actually happened is probably some version of that tale but with some substantial differences.

That Clarence Hurt was himself an excellent shot and a member of the OCPD pistol team is demonstrably factual. That Delf Bryce was capable of that kind of shooting demonstration at a very early age is also factual. One point of confusion with the story is that when Bryce was hired on the OCPD, Hurt was not the Assistant Chief. He had the somewhat grandiose title of "Superintendent" of the Auto Theft Bureau but, in reality, he held the rank of Sergeant and was in charge of the four detectives in that unit. Even in 1928, Sergeants didn't hire police officers on the spot.

BUT Ben Moore was also on the Pistol Team at the time and he was the Chief of Police. The paperwork in OCPD personnel files and news reports of that day indicate that even the Chief couldn't hire officers immediately with nothing more than an imperious wave of his hand. He could with the prior written approval of the City Manager and the Mayor but the title, authority and pay that went with the job didn't start until that entire chain of command had literally signed off on it.

A smaller confusion is that law enforcement shooting competitions were and are not open to the public. Ordinary citizens, regardless of their firearms prowess, don't just wander in with daddy's rusty old gun and ask to try out. While law enforcement firearms training is certainly more sophisticated and comprehensive today than it was in the 1920's, I feel this factor is one of the constants.

In addition, these competitions are not merely target shooting, they are combat shooting, an extension of firearms training intended for shooting at human beings who are shooting back. As a result, they are timed, distances are specified, different shooting positions are specified and only certain calibers and types of firearms are allowed (usually large—you won't find anything smaller than a .38 in a law enforcement match). Other factors such as night matches with dim lighting, reloading within specified times, shooting with both strong and weak hands (in case the strong hand is disabled by a wound), using full combat loads instead of lesser powered target loads that reduce recoil, blast and muzzle flash, and other stress factors are occasionally interjected into them to increase realism and simulate combat conditions. They are restricted to law enforcement officers, whether local, county, state or federal, the only possible exception usually being some military teams. However, Bryce's status as a State Game Ranger would have gained him entrance into the competition and that is undoubtedly what happened.

Local news reports state that on June 21, 1928, the OSPOA held their firearms competition in conjunction with their conference in Pawhuska. First place was won by the team from Luther PD which included an officer named Lester Savage who was a second cousin of this author. They won with a score of 449. State Game Rangers won second place with a score of 443, OCPD was third with 422 and Shawnee PD was fourth with 409. Two Shawnee officers named Budd and Akin tied for first place in the individual scores with a 94. Officer Budd won the shoot-off between them. Clarence Hurt of OCPD tied for third place with a 92. Three men tied for ninth place with scores of 88. Of those three, the shoot-off was won by State Game Ranger Delf Bryce who scored 92 and won a billy club for his prize.

In all probability, Bryce became acquainted with the OCPD Pistol Team members during the December, 1927, pistol match in Shawnee. Those acquaintances were no doubt renewed during the match at Pawhuska in June of 1928. On both occasions, his shooting ability was evident and he undoubtedly let the OCPD officers know he would like to join them. It probably took a few weeks to accomplish but accomplished it was.

On August 29, 1928, news reports stated that the OCPD Pistol Team consisted of Chief Ben Moore, the Hurt brothers (Clarence and Bob), H.V. Wilder and Delf Bryce. They would be holding a pistol competition the first three days of September at Lake Overholser.

Another legend concerns how Bryce acquired his nickname. "Jellybean" was a common appellation in the Roaring Twenties for a dandy, foppish or sharp dresser.

No one who ever met Delf Bryce can remember him dressed "casually." Even his casual clothing was dressier than most people consider dressed up and when Bryce was dressed up, he was dressed up. No one ever recalls him as anything less than absolutely immaculate and his assignments as a detective and federal agent gave a new definition to "plainclothes."

Although known to wear straw hats and derbies, his favored head dress was usually a felt hat with the brim snapped down sharply and cocked at a jaunty angle. While others sported traditionally conservative suits in the normal browns, blacks and blues, Jelly Bryce would show up in perfectly tailored white Palm Beach suits and sport coats. A neatly folded and pressed handkerchief was always perfectly arranged in his breast pocket. Spotless white shirts, sometimes made of silk, were offset with precisely knotted patterned neckties. He favored shiny, patent leather "Spectator" shoes. His slacks always had a knife-edge crease.

One of the legends has it that he interrupted a bank robbery and killed the two bank robbers in a shoot-out. One of the dying robbers allegedly gave the well-dressed detective his nickname with his dying words by saying "You @#$%& jellybean. If you ever tell anybody a jellybean like you plugged me, I'll kill you."

Another version has the gunfight occurring in a theater in Ohio while Bryce was a FBI agent years later and the name coming from one of two dying federal fugitives.

All evidence points to Bryce having received his nickname while on the OCPD and prior to his FBI service. The most frequently repeated and seemingly the most credible version has Bryce arresting a drunk after some time on the force and being called a "jellybean" by the drunk. That always seemed much more likely to me than the statement of a man who knew he was dying. But we don't really know. Perhaps the nickname came from Johnny Robinson, Roy Gage or Jack Vaughan, whom we'll meet later.

Another popular legend has it that Bryce killed a car thief and two burglars during his first few days on the OCPD. The story about the car thief has some basis in fact, even if the timing and details are somewhat off, and we will address it later. As for the second story, some versions say it was a shoot-out with two burglars in a dark alley and Bryce killed both of them. Another version has it as a gunfight with three hijackers (armed robbers) in the downtown railroad station.

Bryce allegedly loaded the bodies in his police car and drove them to Police Headquarters. There he approached the Night Chief of Police, Clarence Hurt and, showing him the bodies, asked him what he wanted him to do with them. Hurt allegedly told him to "take 'em to the morgue, son." After that chore, Bryce then allegedly went home and "slept like a baby." Clarence Hurt himself used to tell this story to other FBI agents on visits to the Oklahoma City office in the mid-1950's.

I have some doubts. I have no problem believing Bryce capable of killing two (or more) men who were trying to kill him and "sleeping like a baby." I've known more than one police officer like that, know the intimate details of their encounters and see nothing wrong with it. Speaking from personal experience, there is no love lost for people who try to kill you in this job and I don't see that reaction as sociopathic, conscienceless or any other pseudo-psychological term that might be applied to it by someone who has never had such an experience.

BUT Clarence Hurt did not become Night Chief or Assistant Chief of the OCPD until May 15, 1929, ten months after Delf Bryce was hired, and held that position until June 1, 1931. Also, even though the two-way police radio was not in use in Oklahoma City in 1928, telephones were available as was a system of Gamewell call boxes for police use. Then or now, I have trouble envisioning a police officer putting two bleeding corpses in his police car and transporting them anywhere. Not out of concern for the corpses but out of concern for the police car.

I suspect police officers in that era viewed the police car much like the officers of my generation. In fact, since cars were so much rarer in those days and so many officers walked beats, the officers who had a car probably valued them even more. That car is their office and their home for at least eight hours a day and they will probably spend as much (or more) time in it as they do their homes. They don't like it when temporary occupants like prisoners urinate, defecate, vomit or bleed in it or leave their body lice, crabs or body odor behind them. The prisoner goes somewhere else, the cop has to get back in the car. The officer has to clean up the mess himself and since he shares the car with officers on two other shifts, he's going to hear about it from them, too. If an officer comes upon a woman about to give birth, an injured citizen, an injured officer or someone else who doesn't have time to wait for an ambulance, those considerations naturally go out the window at once. But, if these men were beyond help, why load them up and transport them anywhere? There were ambulances and coroner's wagons available even in 1928 and that was their jobs. So if the story was meant to demonstrate Bryce's lack of sympathy with bad guys, I'll buy that. But that same lack of sympathy would prevent him from messing up his police car just to keep them from having to wait for other transportation to the morgue.

Another problem I have with some of these tales is The Oklahoma City Times and The Daily Oklahoman of this era. The Times was an afternoon edition and the Oklahoman was the morning edition of a paper by the same owner, The Oklahoma Publishing Company. The Times was particularly assiduous in their attention to police reporting. Then as now, the police department was always a good source of headlines. Reporters who specialized in police reporting hung around headquarters around the clock and sometimes even had their own offices in the station.

Just from 1931 through 1934, the Times contains no less than 52 stories listing D.A. Bryce's name and exploits, both notorious and mundane. There are literally hundreds of other stories that seemingly report on every murder, robbery, burglary, car theft, liquor raid and shooting (especially where police are involved), not to mention hirings, firings, demotions, suspensions, reassignments and promotions within the OCPD. Many issues carry a daily listing of every car stolen in the city the previous day including the tag number and motor number. Suffice it to say that, as media coverage goes, the OCPD was covered like a blanket in the late 1920's and early 1930's. To think that Bryce or any other officer could kill a single criminal, much less multiples of them, without it being extensively covered in one or both of these newspapers is beyond the reach of imagination.

That it could have been covered up and kept quiet is possible but one has to wonder why they would bother? This was a different era. People didn't often sue police officers, police departments or city governments successfully. Violence and lawlessness were rampant. Cops and gangsters were shooting each other every day in this country. Innocent bystanders got hit more than once. This happened in the captures of Wilber Underhill and John Dillinger, among many others. It also happened to an Oklahoma City businessman named W.L. Johnson as we will examine later. When cops shot down felons and fugitives in the line of duty, there was no public outcry or flood of protests and lawsuits. There was no reason to hide it, quite the contrary, in fact. The headlines sent a dual message. One to the citizens that their police were out there doing their jobs and one to the crooks, advertising that they could expect no quarter. The Oklahoma City Times reported officer-involved shootings in both August and September of 1928, both stories boldly placed on the front page with banner headlines. The September shooting involved Detective Mickey Ryan and a man wanted for bank robbery. Neither was any more or less justifiable than the previous ones attributed to Jelly Bryce.

Many other legends grew up around Bryce after he joined the FBI. At one time or another, he was credited by some with being involved in the arrest and/or killing of virtually every notorious gangster of the era. Some of these turned out to be false and some didn't. As much as possible with the existing evidence, they will be dealt with later in a chronological fashion.

The point of all this is to eliminate any misunderstanding. I am not a debunker. That is not my intent. The job of debunker, in my opinion, should come into play when legend is created as a fictional replacement for fact. When falsehood is necessary to elevate the truth to levels that fact could not.

For instance, to describe John Edgar Hoover as the consummate law enforcement officer (his "arrest" of Alvin Karpis aside) would be absurd. Although it is not possible in his case, try describing him, personally and professionally, to any experienced, operations-minded law enforcement officer and ask him the pertinent questions—Would you want to ride with him?—Would you go through a door with him?—Would you entrust your life to him?—Would you want him watching your back? He probably wouldn't be your first choice. But to describe him as the consummate bureaucrat, the master organizer and political manipulator I think is a title well deserved. His personal motive aside, his professional accomplishments must speak for themselves if not colored by your political prejudices.

My point is that legends grow up around extraordinary men, many times without their knowledge, encouragement or participation. Many of those legends, perhaps exaggerated or even false, are created to illustrate the representative traits of those men to those who did not know them. Jelly Bryce doesn't need the legends. There is plenty of documented truth to sustain the legend without them.

As 1928 began, the OCPD had no promotional tests, no assessment centers, no Police Academy and no official training program. Jack Vaughn, another officer who started his 34-year police career in 1928, attended a Retired Officer's Association meeting almost half a century later and reminisced about his "training." He was hired with nine other young men and their training consisted of a of a very short speech from a Captain—"I hope to hell you can handle yourselves." End of training.

Formal OCPD Training was born barely three weeks after Bryce was hired. On July 9, 1928, City Manager Fry inaugurated the Oklahoma City Police School. Inspector Timothy J. "Jack" Tellegen was placed in charge of it. A Police Manual was created from other manuals written by criminologists. The course of study included legal training, study of the city charter and the managerial form of government, the state penal code, criminal procedure, city ordinances, evidence procedures and criminology.

Two classes were held every week for each shift. During the three summer months, the Police School was discontinued and a training school for recruits was conducted. The classes for the shifts were to resume on October 1.

The timing is inescapable. Although there is no written record of it, Jelly Bryce may have been in the first formal OCPD recruit training class.

Auto theft was taken more seriously in the decades of the 1920's and '30's than today. Henry Ford had taken the automobile from a luxurious curiosity for the wealthy and made it available to the common man. Accordingly, it was becoming more of a necessity in an increasingly mobile society moving from rural areas and becoming more concentrated in large urban cities. In the Depression era, the common man was becoming less a member of the middle class and descending into the burgeoning lower class. Oklahoma had no laws requiring auto insurance or driver's licenses as there are today. Besides, in times when many were barely putting food on the table and many others in bread lines or soup kitchens weren't, who had money for insurance premiums? If a car was wrecked or stolen, the owner just absorbed the loss, which could be considerable in times when the price of a car could be half as much or equal to the cost of a home. The average car cost between six and eight hundred dollars at that time.

Property crimes had the public's attention. Many people were existing with the mere necessities of life. If and when a man might be able to provide a few extra comforts for his loved ones—a radio, a water-fed air cooler, a Victrola—they could ill afford to be lost to the predations of sneak thieves and burglars. Whether a man had his car or not might determine whether his family slept in beds at home and ate at a dining room table or slept in alleys and ate in soup kitchens. A lot of people might not have had very much but they definitely wanted to try to hold onto what they did have.

How seriously it was taken in Oklahoma City might be evidenced by the fact that the OCPD had no specialized squads assigned to investigate homicides, robberies or sex crimes but they did for investigating Auto Thefts and Stolen Goods. Four detectives were assigned to each of those squads while a dozen others handled all the other crimes.

Stealing cars was about to become a damned dangerous business in Oklahoma City.

Bryce's new boss was the Auto Theft Bureau Superintendent, Sergeant Clarence O. Hurt. Almost from Bryce's first day on the job, their careers would closely parallel each other for the next three decades. Like Bryce, many legends grew around Hurt that proved to be false. Also like Bryce, he wouldn't need the false legends. The true ones would be plenty.

Some published accounts have said that Hurt joined the OCPD at the tender age of 14 and was the first to drive an OCPD police car. Very impressive but not true. The OCPD acquired its first vehicles, both cars and motorcycles, in 1911. In 1911, at the age of 16, Hurt was still in high school in Frederick in southwestern Oklahoma. In those days, underage boys could occasionally slip into the military and go to war but they couldn't police a large city on a daily basis.

Born March 14, 1895, in Springfield, Illinois, Hurt came to Oklahoma as an infant with his parents. Graduating from high school in Frederick in 1912, he moved to Oklahoma City. He was in the taxicab business for several years there until 1917 when he joined the Army to serve in The Great War. Discharged after the armistice, he joined the OCPD on September 25, 1919. During his first two years, he worked as a patrolman, jailer, motorcycle officer and as a secretary to the Chief. During that era, men filled the secretarial and clerical positions. The only place for women in the PD were the matrons who functioned as jailers for female prisoners.

In 1921, Hurt moved into plainclothes work and not uneventfully. Around 2:00 A.M. on December 1, 1922, Hurt and his partner, Jess Sosbee, were fired on from ambush while patrolling the near northeast section of the city. Sosbee was hit and died from his wounds. Three black men were arrested and one was convicted of the murder.

From 1923 until 1927 Hurt was assigned as a "special investigator" out of the Chief's office, spending much of his time working on the notorious Indian murders in Osage County with U.S. Marshals. In 1927 he was promoted to Sergeant in the Auto Theft Bureau.

Maintaining an old police tradition for breaking in rookies, Hurt decided Bryce's first partner should be the Auto Theft unit's "old hand." B.D. "Chick" Faris was that man. Faris immediately had something in common with his rookie partner—unusual Christian names that inevitably fostered a simpler nickname. It should be no surprise that he had picked up a nickname since his given names were Burnel DeBost.

Three months short of his fiftieth birthday in the summer of

1928, Faris had first joined the OCPD in 1914. His personnel file lists him as five feet, eight and one quarter inches tall and one hundred seventy-eight pounds at that time. Fourteen years later, he wasn't any taller but he wasn't 178 pounds anymore and he had gained a set of false teeth. His photo in the 1928 OCPD Annual shows a handsome but jowly man with a still-dark widow's peak which he kept covered in subsequent photos with a fashionable dark fedora.

Another thing Faris had in common with his new partner was that he was a fairly snappy dresser, wearing a three-piece, vested suit with a bow tie in his group photo. A native of Kansas City, Kansas, he had brought two years of business college with him to the police force. After two years as a Stolen Goods Detective, he had served eight years in Auto Theft. Leaving the department for three years to serve as a special officer for the Myer-Kiser Corporation, he had been rehired in Auto Theft on May 1, 1927, and showing the new guys the ropes usually fell to him. His new rookie partner would prove to be a quick learner.

On the afternoon of November 7, 1928, Mrs. Don H. Anderson parked her car at First and North Walker and went on a shopping spree in downtown Oklahoma City. Johnny D. Robinson was also shopping. New in town from Chicago, Robinson and a friend from New Orleans, Johnny Walker, had no intention of paying for their shopping spree. They were shopping for a car to steal. About 3:30 they found Mrs. Anderson's car and considered it a good candidate. Walker acted as lookout while Robinson got in the car and began manipulating the ignition wires under the dashboard. Walker evidently wasn't doing his job very well because Robinson was startled when he looked up and saw a young man standing next to the car looking down at him. A fancy dresser, but still just a kid.

Robinson was partly right. Jelly Bryce was a fancy dresser, was still a month away from his twenty-second birthday and had been on the police force for less than five months but he wasn't a kid.

Bryce very briefly explained to Robinson that he was a police officer and was arresting him for trying to steal the car. Bryce and Chick Faris had been following the suspicious pair for several hours. Then Robinson made his second and worst misjudgment of the day. He reached for the gun he had concealed on him. Before Robinson got his gun into action, Bryce put a bullet through his arm. Faris dragged Walker up and they arranged for Robinson to be taken to Oklahoma City General Hospital at Twelfth and North Walker. A little over a week later, the two very active detectives made the front pages again when they arrested a man who tried to sell Bryce a stolen car for $100.

Although popular legend would consider Johnny D. Robinson as the first man killed by Jelly Bryce, the Oklahoma City Times reported that he survived and the Oklahoma State Health Department records no death certificate for anyone of that name in Oklahoma City during the decade of the Twenties.

Another popular story that has been printed and repeated concerning these events says that when police responded to the call, Bryce was so new on the force that he was not known to the Captain who had responded to the shooting scene. Bryce allegedly hadn't been issued a badge yet so the Captain had him arrested for murder and jailed. Fel Bryce allegedly was notified in Mountain View and came to Oklahoma City with a lawyer to represent his son but Bryce was released without his father's help when Clarence Hurt found out he was in jail and vouched for his status as a police officer.

Unfortunately we can't ask Clarence Hurt, Fel Bryce or any of the other involved parties about this tale. We have learned that it didn't happen in Bryce's first few days on the job but almost four months later. Bryce's OCPD personnel file shows that he was issued Badge Number 012. It doesn't say when it was issued but one would like to think they got around to it in the first four months, even with 1928 efficiency standards. I suppose it is possible that the responding Captain wouldn't have known Bryce although the force had barely 100 field personnel, only 20 of them detectives. Even so, Chick Faris had been an officer for quite some time and it is highly improbable that he was unknown to any of the four Captains. One would think that Chick Faris's vouching for his partner would have been enough to prevent his arrest without waiting for Clarence Hurt. No record of any such arrest has been found.

The Sunday evening of March 10, 1929, was one of those peculiar weather days the old timers called "bass-ackwards." The temperature had barely dipped to the freezing mark early in the morning and by the evening hours, it has risen into the mid-50's, positively balmy for the end of an Oklahoma winter. Many Oklahoma City residents were relaxing and taking in some entertainment before having to start another work week. Some were at home, listening to Amos 'n Andy or Major Bowes or Guy Lombardo's orchestra on the radio. Others were being entertained in the bustling downtown area and, with admission prices ranging from a dime to a quarter, the movie theaters were doing a land office business.

Lillian Gish was showing at The Majestic, Tom Mix at The Folly, Dolores Del Rio at the Criterion and John Gilbert at the Capitol. Making The Grade starring Edmund Lowe and Lois Moran was showing at the Liberty Theater at 19 North Robinson along with an Our Gang comedy short and Movietone News. The Orpheum at 217 West Grand offered both a movie and vaudeville acts. Patrons could take their choice of seeing Blockade with Anna Q. Nilsson or a selection of five vaudeville acts including Jerry and Her Baby Grands, four attractive young women performing on pianos in concert. In the future, both theaters would be modernized into two of downtown's premier theaters. The Liberty would later become the Harber and the Orpheum would become the Warner.

As the patrons relaxed to the fantasies on the silver screens, harsh reality intruded and their evening entertainment was interrupted by the sounds of gunshots echoing off of the concrete buildings. Real gunshots.

The incident had started a little earlier in the evening when Auto Theft Detectives Bryce and Faris were looking for the car of Harold Haisell which had been stolen from his home at 1525 Northwest 35th. Finding it parked in front of a rooming house at Northwest 5th and Hudson, the officers parked a short distance away and watched the car. Shortly, three men came out of the rooming house and got in the car. Bryce and Faris approached them and arrested all three.

The three men were M.M. "Roy" Gage, 35, of Garber, H.G. "Jack" Vaughan and Earl Johnston. The last two men were both 25 years old and from the small town of Maud in Seminole County. The officers found a gun on Gage when they searched him.

In those days before officers were issued all their equipment, officers bought their own guns and ammunition. Hardly overpaid, many didn't bother with the extra expense of handcuffs. The detectives decided the best way to get the car and the men back to the jail was for Faris to ride in the stolen car covering the three prisoners while Bryce followed them in the police car. Ordering Gage to drive and Vaughan to ride in the front seat, Faris sat on the passenger's side in the rear seat with Johnston to his left. With his three prisoners unfettered, Faris kept his gun out as they started for the Police Station.

The City Jail and OCPD Headquarters was then located in a station house at the intersection of Maiden Lane and Wall Street. Maiden Lane was actually not much more than an east-west alleyway that bisected the first block north of Grand Boulevard (now Sheridan) between Broadway and Robinson. Wall Street was another alley that ran north from Grand in mid-block, the two forming a "T" intersection in the center of the block. The Jail was on the southwest corner of the "T". It was less than nine blocks from the scene of the arrests.

The officers started to the station with the stolen car leading and Bryce following. Most of the trip was uneventful but as the southbound convoy crossed the intersection of Main and Robinson, Faris told Gage to turn left into Maiden Lane. At that moment, Gage told Vaughan "Take the wheel." As Vaughan grabbed the steering wheel, Gage vaulted over the seat back and tried to grab Faris's gun.

With Gage's foot off of the pedals and Vaughan steering the car unsteadily from the passenger's side, the car slowed but continued rolling south on Robinson under its own momentum. The combination of seeing the car missing the turn into Maiden Lane, slowing down and the men struggling over the seat alerted Bryce to the trouble.

Quickly guiding the police car to the curb north of the alley next to the Liberty Theatre, Bryce jumped out and ran over to the other car, drawing his gun as he ran. Just as he jumped on the passenger's side running board of the rolling car, Faris regained enough control of his gun to fire twice, hitting Gage in one shoulder and the abdomen. Unable to tell who was shooting whom from his vantage point, Bryce fired a round into Gage's back. He then ordered Vaughan to "Stop this car!"

As they reached the intersection of Robinson and Grand, Vaughan ignored the order and turned the wheel to the right, turning the car west onto Grand. Bryce fired twice, both bullets entering Vaughan's chest under his right arm.

The car finally coasted to a stop in front of the Orpheum Theater. Crowds from both theaters abandoned their movies and started pouring out into the street to watch the real-life drama in progress.

Gage was taken to Oklahoma General Hospital but died from his wounds soon afterwards. Auto Larceny charges were filed against both survivors the next day but Vaughan also died from his wounds.

Two weeks earlier, Faris had been in another gun battle. When he caught 19-year-old Lee Montgomery in a stolen car, Montgomery shot once at Faris, missing, and Faris fired back twice, hitting him both times. Montgomery survived his wounds and explained his resistance by confessing to several recent armed robberies.

Jack Vaughan is the first man that can be verified as having been killed by Jelly Bryce and his bullet undoubtedly contributed to Roy Gage's demise even though Gage had already been shot twice by

Chick Faris. The next week, Chief Moore put out an order for all plainclothes officers to call the Police Patrol Wagon to transport their prisoners for them.

After less than a year, Chief Ben Moore was under a different kind of fire from several different quarters. In an old Oklahoma City tradition, the primary complaint was vice enforcement. The County Attorney was vocally critical of the Chief and his Department, saying the city was "wide open" to vice. In April of 1929, the City Council interviewed the County Attorney and the Federal Prohibition agent in charge of Oklahoma. The County Attorney charged the OCPD with "indifference" to vice enforcement and said his "wide open city" statements meant the city was overrun with slot machines and punch-boards, a variation of the numbers racket. Neither witness had any information on payoffs or protection involving the police.

The investigation closed with no conclusive results but rumors persisted that Moore was being ushered out to be replaced by Assistant Chief Charles A. Becker. The Women's Christian Temperance Union initially objected to Becker's appointment because he used to be a salesman for a distillery. When it was determined that Becker's time as a whiskey salesman had been before Prohibition became the law, they withdrew their objections.

Chief Ben Moore resigned in May, saying that after "going fishing for a few days," he intended to return to his former job as a special officer for the railroad. After exactly one year as Assistant Chief, Charles Becker was appointed Chief of the OCPD on May 15, 1929.

Born in Chicago on January 24, 1878, Becker had been a salesman traveling between Chicago and San Francisco until he moved to Oklahoma City in 1898. He continued his sales career and was manager of the Bristol Hotel for four years before he joined the OCPD on July 15, 1921, as a clerk in the Stolen Goods Bureau. He became the head of that bureau the following year and held that position until he was made Assistant Chief in 1928.

Becker appointed Clarence Hurt, Bryce's boss in the Auto Theft Bureau, to the position of Assistant (or Night) Chief of Police. The appointment was made with the understanding that Hurt would continue his duties in Auto Theft as well as his additional duties, perhaps a recognition of the old axiom "If it ain't broke, don't fix it."

The 1929 OCPD Annual bragged on the Auto Theft Bureau for having recovered a record 81.26 per cent of the 961 cars that had been stolen in the city that fiscal year. Sergeant G.A. Burnhame was in charge of the office as a reward for his record. Operating without a partner, Burnhame had recovered 41 stolen cars in one month including seven in one night.

Several of the car theft rings successfully broken up by the Auto Theft Bureau that year were described in the annual. The only team mentioned twice for their efforts were B.D. "Chick" Faris and his partner, identified as "J.A. Bryce." The two rings mentioned were the Gage/Vaughan bunch from the previous March's shooting and another headed by a man named John Hughes. Bryce had been hired too late the previous year to be included in the 1928 annual but was pictured in the 1929 edition. His photo with a dozen other detectives shows a serious young man wearing his "game face" and nattily attired in a dark suit, vest, white shirt, tie and a snap-brim hat jauntily cocked at an angle. A handkerchief neatly arranged in his breast pocket, both his youth and sartorial splendor stands out among this group shot of "old hands."

This and future photos starkly point out the close resemblance between Bryce and movie tough-guy George Raft. Eleven years older than Bryce, Raft grew up in the mob-ruled area of New York City known as Hell's Kitchen which no doubt brought authenticity to his later movie roles as gangsters. Raft made his debut in Hollywood in 1929 and studios originally tried to make him a romantic leading man with his dark, brooding good looks. His role in Scarface in 1932 made his reputation as a movie tough guy and set his course for future roles as gangsters, convicts and cops. Since the "Bryce-look" predated the "Raft-look," it is doubtful if Bryce actually patterned his dress or manner after the movie star but he undoubtedly benefited from future comparisons as the real-life version of what Raft portrayed in the movies.

Since vice enforcement had been the Achilles heel of the previous Chief, it stood to reason that it would be a priority of the new Chief.

On January 4, 1930, Bryce was transferred to the Liquor Raiding Squad under the command of Lt. Robert Hurt, Clarence's younger brother. Actually, as a specialized unit it was more probably a promotion in fact if not in rank because it also entailed a pay raise to $165 a month. One of the first, closest and, in some ways, most unlikely friends he immediately made was a 41-year-old Yankee.

Charles Thomas Ryan was a native of Portland, Maine, and a five-year veteran of the OCPD. His Christian names were all but forgotten in the presence of his universal nickname "Mickey", probably in reference to his Irish heritage. After less than two years in a scout car, Ryan had been promoted to Detective in the Liquor Raiding Squad and had almost three years in that assignment before Bryce came into the unit. Prohibition was still in effect but, while it was their primary assignment, the Liquor Raiding Squad was not expected to turn a blind eye to other crimes. Therefore, as long as they maintained a curb on the illegal liquor traffic, the detectives were allowed to seek out other malefactors as their penchants indicated. Mickey Ryan seemed to have a knack for tracking down the more violent criminals and had several commendations in his file for the arrest of murderers and armed robbers.

The new decade began with the coldest month in Oklahoma City's history. Thermometers dipped nine degrees below zero on several days and a week passed without the temperature rising out of the teens. In the eastern part of the state, they recorded the coldest temperature ever recorded in Oklahoma, 27 degrees below zero.

An old cop's saying is that the weather makes a good policeman. Criminal activity usually drops dramatically during bad weather. Many of those long winter nights also produced boredom among the policemen. Almost all men who handle deadly weapons on a routine basis occasionally get careless with them. Firearms safety was an individual responsibility and occasionally there were accidents, sometimes with tragic consequences.

One friend of Bryce remembers hearing a story about the detectives sitting around the station one slow night when an officer brought in some stolen hubcaps. To this day, objects like these that can never be identified or returned to the owners litter police property rooms. Bryce started rolling the hubcaps down the hallway of the police station and shooting at them to pass the time. If there were typical policemen around, there was probably some wagering going on about the marksmanship.

Just because you worked on the Liquor Raiding Squad didn't mean that was all you were expected to do. As was later noted in his personnel file, Bryce's proven reputation still got him assigned to look for especially dangerous men. Two weeks after Bryce was transferred to the squad, one of those unfortunate incidents occurred that happens around men who work with deadly weapons all the time and Jelly Bryce almost got shot for the second time.

Shortly before midnight on January 18, 1930, Bryce got a phone call from an informant telling him where a man named Leon Lemons was located. Lemons was wanted for armed robbery and was supposedly at a house in the Capitol Hill district. It had been snowing and the streets and sidewalks were very slick.

Bryce and Sgt. G.A. Burnhame went to the residence of the owners of the house where Lemons was staying. Burnhame called Assistant Chief Clarence Hurt at the police station and asked him to send two more men to meet them at the suspect's house with a search warrant. Hurt sent Patrol Officers N.V. McCollum and Kenneth E. Treadwell.

In Hurt's words, the department was "very short on riot guns so I allowed Officer Treadwell to borrow my personal twelve-gauge shotgun loaded with double-ought buckshot, warning him to be careful with it because it was very easy on the trigger." Due to the Department's shortage, Hurt frequently loaned the gun to officers on dangerous calls at night.

When the officers met the detectives at the house, Treadwell covered the rear of the house with the shotgun, Burnhame and Mc-Collum covered the sides and Bryce went to the front door alone with the warrant. After finding that Lemons was not in the house, the detectives went across the street to the landlords house to talk with them.

Police patrol cars of that era were not purchased with any super-fluous comforts like heaters. Veteran officers from those days tell of heating bricks on the iron potbelly stove in the station during the winter, wrapping them in blankets and putting them on the floor of their patrol cars to keep their feet from freezing.

Bryce and Burnhame had gone to the scene in Burnhame's private car, a Packard coupe. When the detectives returned to the car, the two patrolmen had gotten in the Packard to stay warm. McCollum was in the driver's seat and Treadwell was sitting in the front passenger's seat with the shotgun lying across his lap. Bryce placed one foot up on the passenger's side running board and said that they might as well go back to the station since their fugitive wasn't there. Burnhame opened the driver's door while McCollum got out. Burnhame started to get in while Bryce stepped back and Treadwell started to get out of the other side of the car.

When Treadwell opened the passenger side door, the shotgun slid out and the hammer caught on the running board. Bryce jumped back as the gun fired, the charge of buckshot passing in front of him "going past my belt buckle, missing me by some two inches, going back into the Packard coupe where Officer Treadwell was just getting out."

The charge of buckshot struck Treadwell in the lower right leg, blowing part of the calf and ankle away. When the officers tried to start the Packard to take him to the hospital, they found that the buckshot had also torn the wiring loose under the dashboard. They then carried him over to the police car and took him to Oklahoma General Hospital, letting Bryce off at the police station to make a report to Hurt.

Treadwell survived but was discharged from the Department in June of 1931, unable to return to duty. Six months later, he sued the City for $20,000, alleging that the accident was caused by Bryce opening the car door. The statements and reports made by all the officers who were witnesses refute that charge. Current City records give no information on whether a settlement was reached or not.

The year would end with another tragic accident. On the night of October 25, 1930, Bryce, Mickey Ryan and Lt. Robert Hurt were patrolling the near northeast side of the city when they passed a small grocery store at 715 North Stiles.

As they passed, they saw a man backing out of the front door carrying a canvas moneybag and stuffing a revolver in his coat. Stopping the car and jumping out, they identified themselves as police officers and drew their guns. Hurt yelled at the man "Stay where you are." The man turned and walked toward the center of the street when he drew his gun and fired at them, missing all three officers.

1931 OCPD Pistol Team. Left to right: Det. H.V. Wilder, Det. D.A. Bryce, Lt. Robert S. Worthy, Lt. Robert Hurt, Capt. Clarence Hurt. (photo courtesy of R.V. Wilder)

They returned fire and the man collapsed in the street, wounded in the left leg.

The officers had thought the man was a robber and he had thought they were robbers. They were all wrong. After taking him to the hospital, it was discovered that he was W.L. Johnson, the owner of the store. He had just been locking up for the night and leaving with the daily receipts. Two days later, all three officers were suspended by City Manager E.M. Fry pending an investigation.

Mr. Johnson's attorney, Charles Ruth, started an offensive in the newspaper. He said he was going to call for a grand jury to investigate the shooting and intended to present charges against the officers as soon as Mr. Johnson had improved.

The officers were reinstated six days later and City Attorney George M. Callahan made a press release stating that no charges would be filed against anyone unless Mr. Johnson made a specific complaint. He noted that the only complaint so far had been from Johnson's lawyer.

Although Mr. Johnson is probably counted as one of the men killed by Jelly Bryce, the Oklahoma City Times reported that he survived and the State Health Department does not record a death certificate for a man of that name during the decade of the Thirties.

On January 12, 1931, the Oklahoma Sheriff and Peace Officers Association held their annual state pistol championship. Six teams competted but, for the fourth time in a row, the OCPD team won first place. Consisting of Clarence Hurt, Jelly Bryce, Robert Hurt, Robert S. Worthy and Houston V. Wilder, they scored an average of 94.3 points out of 100. Shawnee PD placed second and Bryce's former collegues in the State Game Rangers placed third.

In early 1931, Bryce was making only $15 a month more than the salary he had been hired at almost three years earlier. During the year he moved from the house at 421 East Sixth to an apartment, perhaps as a cost-cutting measure. If it wasn't, it would need to be before the year was half over.

His new address of 315 1/2 North Walnut, Apartment F, is now covered by a parking lot across the street from the First Cavalry Baptist Church. Although only about five blocks from his previous address, it was within a block of the "Deep Deuce" area of Northeast Second Street, the downtown of the black population in a rigidly segregated city. A teenaged Charlie Christian was creating legendary styles in jazz guitar then but that could hardly have lent any prestige to the address in the early 1930s.

Another Bryce story comes from this period. As printed in a history of Kiowa County, it relates:

"One Sunday night while Bryce was with the Oklahoma City Police Department he was returning on the train from Chicago with Arthur Coots, a suspect in the $900 robbery of the King's Laundry in Oklahoma City. In front of him sat a woman with a crying baby. For an hour the baby cried.

Finally Bryce could stand it no longer. 'Listen, lady,' he said, 'I've got to stay awake anyway. There is no use in both of us losing sleep. Let me have the baby.'

For three hours, Bryce walked the train with the baby in his arms, as he kept one eye on his prisoner. The baby slept peacefully. So did the mother. On Monday, Bryce's pistol arm was slightly stiff."

On January 7, 1931, The Daily Oklahoman printed a story stating that the Kings Laundry at 428 West Washington (later Southwest First Street) had been robbed that morning by two men. One of the men had concealed his gun behind an armful of dirty laundry. The men had escaped with $750.

Two weeks later, the paper printed another story saying that Lt. Robert Hurt and Detective D.A. Bryce had arrested two men in the Kings Laundry robbery. The men were identified as Cody Stout and Vernon Stacey.

Perhaps the Kings Laundry had another robbery on which I haven't been able to find a report. But the Oklahoma State Corrections Department shows no record for anyone in their prison system by the name of Arthur Coots during the 1930's.

On more than one occasion, it had been noted that City Council meetings should take place at the Stockyards Coliseum because sometimes they came closer to resembling boxing or wrestling matches than political proceedings. Even so, they were tamer now than in territorial days when everyone carried guns.

The spring elections of 1931 brought another flurry of sparks to City Hall. Most of the sparks centered around the newly elected councilman from Ward Two, J.E. Taylor. Taylor was a contentious, unabashedly partisan, blatantly self-serving individual, perfectly suited to Oklahoma City politics of the day. He would provide the Council and citizens with more entertainment or fireworks, depending upon your point of view, since the early territorial days of Council.

Taylor immediately went to war with Ward One Councilman John Frank Martin. Martin nominated John McClelland for City

Manager and Taylor supported Louis Abney. In another of the Council's heated 5-4 decisions, Abney won. Martin called Taylor "Oklahoma City's Judas" and Taylor started after him. This time, Taylor was escorted from the Council chambers before he could extract any pieces of silver or anything else from Martin's hide.

Since the beginning of the City Manager system, it had become almost automatic that new City Managers got to pick their own police chief when they chose to use that option. On April 20, 1931, Louis Abney was sworn in as City Manager. Anticlimactically, he resigned two days later and Councilman Martin's former candidate, John McClelland, was appointed to the post. Chief of Police Becker retired the same day and McClelland immediately appointed John Johnston Watt to take his place.

Watt, 31 years old, had no previous law enforcement experience and was appointed to the Chief's job directly from being a branch manager for the Miller Rubber Company. His primary qualification seemed to be that he was a close personal friend and previous associate of the City Manager, a man McClelland said he could trust. Evidently the City Manager had an unpopular agenda for the new Chief, one that called for a man with no ties, no friendships and no debts within the OCPD.

Watt's first problem was to confront the budget. First, he tried a "reorganization" on May 1, radical cost-cutting measures that brought bold headlines in the newspaper. Clarence Hurt was demoted from Assistant Chief to shift Captain, Jack Tellegen was demoted from Captain to Desk Sergeant and a number of other transfers were announced. The Raiding Squad was abolished with Lt. Robert Hurt, Mickey Ryan and D.A. Bryce transferred to Scout Car. After three years on the force, Jelly Bryce was in a marked police car in uniform for the first time. Then it got worse.

Two weeks before the end of the fiscal year on July 1, the police budget ran dry. On June 15, Watt fired 25 men to try to make ends meet. Ten of the men were rookies who had been hired the previous February but 15 were veterans. Among the discharged veterans were Jack Tellegen, Jelly Bryce, Mickey Ryan and Lee Mullenix along with several scout car and motorcycle officers. Watt said that a few of the firings were for "the good of the service" but most were an economy move. Watt said he expected the move to save $1,900 since the average officer's salary was $150 a month. The dismissal of the 25 men dropped Department strength to 185 but Watt said when the new fiscal year's budget began, he hoped to be able to add 45 men to bring it up to 230.

Fourteen of the discharged officers, including Tellegen, Ryan and Bryce, filed a protest alleging that under provisions of the City Charter they could only be discharged for specific and proven charges.

Their protest evidently having fallen on deaf ears, the officers filed a lawsuit against the Chief, City Manager and City Council on September 17. They asked for reinstatement and back pay to the date of their discharge. A hearing was scheduled for the morning of September 25 before a District Judge.

The officers must have had a good case because the day before the scheduled court hearing, six of them were reinstated effective September 26. Hearings before the City Manager were scheduled for five more officers that afternoon and the rest would be scheduled the next week. Among the first six reinstated were Mickey Ryan, Lee Mullenix and Jelly Bryce, back as a Detective at his salary of $160 a month, five dollars less than the salary he had been making when he was discharged three months earlier. Two of the scout car officers reinstated, Ray Clark and Douglas Gates, would lose their lives in the line of duty before the decade was over.

A week later, the Raiding Squad was back, in fact if not in name. Lt. Robert Hurt, Mickey Ryan, Bryce and another officer raided a garage in the 1100 block of North Eastern just after midnight. Although everything appeared normal at first, Bryce and Ryan noticed a hole cut in the floor under the water heater tank. Draining and removing the tank, they pulled up the floorboards and found a large room excavated under the floor. Four men were arrested and 180 gallons of whiskey were confiscated.

Even in the midst of the labor-management dispute during the summer of 1931, there was evidence that it was a temporary fiscal matter.

On July 13/14, 1931, the Oklahoma Sheriff and Peace Officers Association held their semi-annual convention at McAlester. Part of the festivities was the pistol competition. The OCPD team won the First Place prize of $100 in gold. The team consisted of Delf Bryce, Robert S. "Bob" Worthy, Houston V. Wilder, Robert Hurt and Clarence Hurt. They scored 469 out of a possible 500 points to beat the next two teams from Tulsa and Shawnee PD's.

In the individual shooting matches, D.A. Bryce scored first with 97 points, Bob Worthy was second with 96 and H.V. Wilder third with 95. Interestingly, they also had a Ladies Pistol match and Mrs. Wilder came in third.

Most of the lifelong friendships Bryce formed were with his colleagues from the days with the OCPD. One of these was Lee Mullenix.

Mullenix had joined the OCPD in 1915 and four years later had been placed in charge of the Bertillon Department, the forerunner of the modern Records Bureau and Crime Laboratory. His son Jack joined the department the same year Lee retired, in 1946. After retiring from his own career as Chief of Detectives, Jack Mullenix went on to another career as Undersheriff with the Oklahoma County Sheriff's Office. Jack recalled that Bryce and Lee used to go dove hunting when he was a boy. As they were driving down the road one day, they saw a dove flying by. Bryce quickly pointed his shotgun out of the car without aiming, snapped off a shot and hit the dove. Jack remembered it so well because he had to run out in the field and fetch the dove.

Jack's first childhood memories of Bryce were of how fastidious he was, dressed in a derby hat and a luxurious overcoat with satin lapels. In warmer seasons, Bryce was known to favor immaculate, perfectly tailored palm beach suits, two-tone brown shoes and a natty straw hat. Jack said that his whole family called Bryce "Delf" and he never heard any of his really close friends ever call him "Jelly."

Another lifelong friendship was formed with Lawrence James "Smokey" Hilbert. One point of common ground was their Indian heritage. From a union that could probably only happen in Oklahoma, Hilbert was one of 13 children from a German father and a full-blood Choctaw mother. Hired on September 17, 1929, a little more than a year after Bryce, Hilbert was three years his senior in age. A graduate of a two-year course in embalming in Missouri, Hilbert worked as a funeral director, embalmer and ambulance driver for Capitol Hill Funeral Home for seven years before joining the OCPD. He got his nickname from (depending upon who you asked) his chain-smoking habit, the way his gun smoked on the pistol range, his "road-burning" driving habits as an ambulance driver or his fastball delivery as a baseball pitcher during his days as a student athlete at Capitol Hill High School.

After a short time in a Scout Car, Hilbert was promoted to Detective in the Auto Theft Department in May of 1930.

Bryce took his first recorded sick leave on Halloween of 1931. He was off for six days recovering from a tonsillectomy but then it was back to the job, only a small percentage of which was recorded in the local newspaper. He and Robert Hurt arrested two armed robbers. He and Mickey Ryan arrested the man who had robbed the safe at the Steffens Dairy, recovering a portion of the illicit proceeds. He and Ryan also arrested a man for three armed robberies and a car theft in the city and, finding him wanted in Texas, transported him to Dallas.

Sometime during this time period, Bryce made a more intimate contact through the OCPD. One of his fellow officers was Walter Clyde Elliott. Nicknamed "Red", at half an inch under 5'10" and 222 pounds, Elliott was a red-headed, blue-eyed fireplug of a man. With three more years on the department than Bryce, Elliott was also a hot-tempered Irishman. His OCPD personnel file contains one 15-day suspension for slapping a Negro who failed to call him "Sir." He was later to gain a modicum of fame for being a longtime member of The Flatfoot Four, the OCPD barbershop quartet. The group started out singing hymns at officer's funerals but soon entered national competition and, in 1940, became the National Champion Barbershop Quartet.

Nine years older than Bryce, Elliott was a native of Georgetown, Texas. He had a niece named Frances Maxine Wilson who preferred to be known by her middle name. Maxine is described as a beautiful, blonde former cheerleader for Georgetown High School. She is also described as strong-willed, iconoclastic and exceedingly independent for a young woman of her era. In an era when it was extremely unusual, she would eventually be married five times during her lifetime.

Still a teenager at this time, she met Jelly Bryce and they shortly entered into their first marriage together. Exactly when and where they were married is uncertain, unable to be verified even by their son. No record of the marriage during this period can be located in Bryce's home in Kiowa County, Oklahoma, in Maxine's home in Williamson County, Texas, or in Oklahoma County, Oklahoma. The union was destined to be short and stormy almost from the outset. What is verifiable is that she became pregnant with what would be their only child in late 1931.

On January 20, 1932, Bryce took a 30-day leave of absence from the OCPD. Considering later circumstances, it may have been to go to Georgetown, Texas, and try to patch up his failing relationship with the two-months-pregnant Maxine. Regardless of the reasons, he didn't take the entire leave he requested.

Another of the legends about Jelly Bryce that has found its way into print has him involved in the killing of New York gangster Vincent "Mad Dog" Coll. A life-long New Yorker (he died at age 23),

Coll was an ambitious member of "Dutch" Schultz's gang. Following an attempted coup of Schultz's organized crime empire, Coll was machine-gunned to death in a phone booth on West Twenty-Third Street in New York City on February 8, 1932. The suspects were four of Dutch Schultz's gunmen.

Based upon information supplied by Chief John Watt, on the morning of February 9, 1932, OCPD Detective D.A. Bryce and Lt. Walter Acord busted a dice game on the sixth floor of the Oklahoma Savings and Loan Building in downtown Oklahoma City. Eleven men were arrested.

I suppose Jelly Bryce could have flown back from New York after killing Coll in time to assist in the misdemeanor gambling arrests but I doubt it. Plus assassination never seemed to be his style.

During 1932, Bryce moved again, this time to a more fashionable, respectable area, possibly in an attempt to bolster his troubled union with Maxine. Perhaps he talked her into returning to Oklahoma City with him, at least temporarily.

Their new address was 3400 North Robinson, Apartment 1. Directly north of the fashionable Heritage Hills district, the new address was in the Jefferson Park edition about three miles due north of the downtown area. Robinson Street is an extension of one of the primary north-south arteries of the downtown area. The west side of the street in Jefferson Park consists mostly of small but ornate brick homes, built before the era when neighborhoods were mass-produced and today telegraphing their age by the fact that each one is slightly different from its neighbors. The east side of the street consists primarily of two-story apartment buildings with steeply gabled roofs, many of red Spanish tiles.

The one the Bryce's moved into was typical of the area, a yellow brick exterior interspersed with and surrounded by a wainscot of darker bricks. The whole building is barely thirty yards long and half that distance wide. Bisected by a hallway, it contains eight apartments, four on each floor. Apartment One is the first one on the north side of the building after entering the main entrance through a small foyer flanked by plaster stucco walls. What was once a sedate neighborhood a few blocks from the Santa Fe railroad tracks now backs up to a busy Interstate highway.

D.A. and Maxine Bryce are listed at that address in the 1933 R.L. Polk Directory for Oklahoma City. The information for these directories was routinely researched during the late summer and early autumn months of the year prior to their publication. It was the only

OCPD Detectives H.V. Wilder and D.A. Bryce. The early '30's George Raft "tough-guy" look, only these guys weren't acting. (photo courtesy of R.V. Wilder)

year they would be listed in the directory together.

During this time of upheaval in his personal life, Bryce's troubled partnership with Maxine was balanced by more stability in his professional life when he got a new partner, an old friend from the pistol team. It was to become his longest partnership with anyone in the OCPD and one of the most active. It would also become the basis for another lifelong friendship and one that would extend into the next generation. He and his new partner must have commented on their parents' tendency toward unusual names.

Houston Vard Wilder joined the OCPD on June 11, 1919, after serving in the Army in World War I. Before that, he had been a rodeo rider and had a job breaking wild horses at the Oklahoma City Stockyards for five dollars a day. Fittingly, one of his first OCPD assignments was with the newly-formed Mounted Patrol. After serving as a mounted officer, motorcycle officer, jailer and desk Sergeant, on March 31, 1932, he transferred to the Detective Bureau. Thirteen years older than his new partner, Wilder wasn't quite as good a shot as Bryce but the difference was, as they used to say, "just a tad," as their pistol team scores testified.

On August 4, 1932, Bryce and Wilder investigated a home invasion robbery at 2201 North Jordan in which some jewelry, a watch and a car were stolen. Three days later, Jelly Bryce became a father for the first time when Maxine gave birth to William Delf Bryce in Georgetown, Texas. Like the marriage, it was not destined to be a happy relationship.

Bryce and Wilder were an unusually active pair of detectives, covering a wide range of crimes and apparently jumping into whatever illegal activity they could find. For the next year, hardly a week went by without one or more of their adventures being printed in the local newspapers. They arrested three men for robbing a grocery store at 2311 West Main. They arrested a black man who was "walking gingerly" because he had a half gallon of illegal liquor in a bulging pocket. Five days later, they arrested a burglar and a week after that, investigated the shooting of a man by a butcher in the grocery store he was trying to rob. Then they testified in the trial of a man they had arrested in a hit and run fatality accident. They went to a house after a man with a warrant for stealing an overcoat. The man wasn't there but another man was—cooking illegal booze in a twenty-gallon still. Bad timing.

Someone once described police work as months of boredom and routine punctuated by moments of stark terror. Then and now, it is all that but also much more. Police work isn't all alternating bouts of tragedy, boredom, danger, thrills and paperwork. Many officers, particularly in the patrolman and detective ranks, would tell you that the best feature of the job is not knowing what each day will bring. A constant variety of people, experiences and adventures cross your path every day in the course of doing your job. Many of those people, experiences and adventures are not available to most other professions. Some of the same are mundane but many are also highly humorous, especially in light of the broad and somewhat cynical sense of humor one usually develops when they get to know more about people and their proclivities than is good for anyone. Detectives Bryce and Wilder seemed to have more than their share of these situations. Some of these humorous tales were used to lighten up the daily news.

On June 2, 1932, they investigated the burglary of a store at 1400 West First. All that was missing were 52 bottles of soda pop. Do you suppose they were looking for kids as suspects?

On September 20, the detectives were called to break up an unusual "free for all" fight in the unit block of South Harvey, a notorious "skid row" section of the city. The combatants were three blind men, a one-legged man, a woman with ginger paralysis (probably caused by drinking "Ginger Jake", homemade spirits made with wood alcohol not intended for human consumption), a narcotics addict and an 87-year-old man. The weapons involved were a pair of crutches, a brick, a pair of false teeth and an empty whiskey bottle. The battle was over a half-pint of whiskey that wasn't empty. Although it took two more officers to separate the melee, the event was resolved with only minor injuries.

In a flashback to the soda pop theft, the next year they investigated the burglary of the Owl Cafe at Grand and Dewey. All that was missing was $17 worth of cigars and cigarettes. Later that night they heard a report of some boys passing out cigars and cigarettes to people in front of an expensive downtown hotel. Checking the hotel, they found three 11-year-old boys registered in one of the more expensive rooms. They left the boys sleeping in the matron's office at the police station since they were too young to be booked in jail.

As previously stated, cops get used to diversity. It's one of the primary attractions of the job. A new radio call, a new bad guy to chase, a new crime to investigate. After a while on the job, they develop a low boredom quotient. When the citizens don't provide enough humor for them, they provided it for one another. It is a long-standing tradition to mess with your partner's mind occasionally. The closer partners are, the more often it happens. Bryce in particular developed a love of harmless practical jokes.

One night Bryce and Wilder were checking the area around the Santa Fe Railroad Station for activity. Wilder spotted a coyote running down the tracks and snapped off a shot at it. Thinking no more about it, Wilder went on about his business without realizing the wheels were turning in his partner's head.

The next day, Bryce approached his partner very secretively and told him other officers had found a black man dead near the downtown railroad tracks. One bullet wound. Probably shot with a .38 sometime the previous night. Not robbed or beaten. No apparent motive. No suspects. The unspoken implication was that the man had been a hobo lurking in the darkness around the tracks and Wilder's shot at the coyote had killed him accidentally. Bryce kept his partner sweating for most of the shift before exposing the joke. There was no dead man.

We don't know Wilder's reaction but I suspect it was amused relief. I also suspect he repaid Bryce sooner or later. I wish I knew that story.

The fall of 1932 saw more shooting on the streets of Oklahoma City. This time it didn't involve Jelly Bryce for a change but it did have eerie parallels to Bryce's Gage/Vaughan shooting three years earlier. It also set a future colleague on a similar career path.

Shortly before 2:30 P.M. on October 17, 1932, the police dispatcher broadcast a call for OCPD units to respond to a "shooting scrape" at the corner of Frisco (later Southwest Fifth Street) and Robinson Streets. Car Seven, Officers Roy Bergman and J.B. McGuffin, started in that direction. So did Clarence Hurt, back on the streets as a working detective after two years as Assistant Chief under Chief Becker. Hurt had missed his chance at the top job when City Manager McClelland had appointed his friend John Watt.

When the officers arrived, they saw that a 1932 Chevrolet coupe with Kansas license plates had run up over the curb on the north side of Frisco just east of Robinson and crashed into a parked car in a used car lot. Detective George Baker was sitting in his car in the street with E.A. Peery in custody. Baker's partner, Detective Charles Gerald "Jerry" Campbell was standing next to the wrecked car with a gun in each hand and blood all over his shirt. The blood wasn't his, however. It came from the dead man slumped in the driver's seat of the wrecked Chevy, his head and body pierced by several of Campbell's bullets.

The incident had begun a block further south, at Choctaw and Robinson. Campbell and Baker, assigned to the Stolen Car Department, were scouting the south part of town when they noticed the Chevy coupe with two men sitting in it. Their suspicions aroused, perhaps by the Kansas plates, the officers circled the block and parked behind the car. Approaching the car and identifying themselves as officers, they began questioning the men and examining the car. Their suspicions were justified when they discovered that the motor number had been altered. After arresting both men, Baker took Peery back to the police car while Campbell got in the stolen Chevy with the driver. The two cars then started toward the police station, one suspect driving the stolen Chevy with Detective Campbell on the passenger's side followed by Baker and Peery in the police car.

The convoy had gone less than a block when Campbell noticed a lump under the rear seat floor mat. Turning sideways in the seat, he lifted the floor mat and saw a sawed off shotgun. The driver had seen his movements and took his left hand off of the steering wheel, dropping it back out of Campbell's view. Just as Campbell told the man to keep both hands on the steering wheel, the man drew a .45 pistol and shoved it into the officer's chest. Campbell batted the gun away just as it fired, scorching his right arm with a powder burn. Campbell then drew his own weapon and, before the man could fire again, fired five shots at him. In the arms-length gun battle in the front seat of the moving car, four of the bullets struck the man in the jaw, neck, shoulder and chest.

The car veered and came to a halt as it jumped the curb into a car lot, crashing into one of the used cars. Campbell grabbed the driver's .45 and jumped out of the car, still covering him with his own weapon in case the man had survived and still had some fight left in him. He hadn't and he didn't.

Later found in the car was a Remington twelve gauge automatic shotgun fully loaded with five rounds of buckshot, a .25 automatic pistol and plenty of extra shotgun ammunition. The car had been stolen out of Shawnee. Peery also had a car that proved to be stolen out of Texas. The dead man was identified as Elbert "Cole" Oglesby. After the newspapers printed the story, Oglesby's background began coming to light.

Oglesby came from a Texas family of outlaws and this wasn't their first contact with the OCPD. Two years earlier, one of Cole's brothers, John, had been shot by OCPD Detectives J.M. Mabe and Jack Roberts while they were chasing him through one of the city's oil fields. The Oglesbys were first cousins of the infamous Newton brothers who had masterminded a $2 million train robbery in Illinois in 1924. Cole had been involved in that enterprise and also had an auto theft conviction in Texas. He had been very busy for a young man of 28 years.

Cole was wanted for a murder that had occurred in 1928 in Abilene, Texas. He was also wanted for bank robberies in Lumberton and Columbia, Mississippi, that had occurred during the first two months of 1932. His brother Jerry had been killed in a gun battle with pursuing officers following the Lumberton job. He was also wanted for bank robberies in Moline, Kansas, as well as Decatur, Paradise and Canton, Texas, where he was "considered a bad man and a killer." The books were closed on a lot of crimes when Jerry Campbell closed Cole Oglesby's book permanently.

Unfortunately there were to be more deadly twists of fate between the Oglesby and OCPD families, all of them on Robinson Street. Fourteen months later, OCPD Officer Douglas Gates was killed by another Oglesby brother, Ernest, in another shoot-out over a stolen car, this time at Northwest Twenty-Third and Robinson. Gates' younger brother, Jack, had been killed in 1930 in a gunfight with armed robbers at Fourteenth and Robinson.

Jerry Campbell's reputation as a man who could handle himself in a gunfight was made that day in the fall of 1932.

During this tumult of professional activity, Bryce's personal life was no more placid. The records of the Oklahoma County Clerk, Docket Number 13396-D, Book 23, Page 196, reflect that on November 9, 1932, Maxine Bryce filed a petition for divorce from Delf A. Bryce. The alleged grounds were neglect and adultery, although no co-respondents were listed. Three days later, District Judge Sam Hooker issued a restraining order against Bryce and ordered him to pay alimony in the amount of $75 a month until the case was resolved. A hearing was scheduled for the morning of Saturday, November 19.

Bryce evidently either didn't want to face the inevitable or was busy elsewhere. He didn't appear for the hearing and Maxine was back in court the following Monday morning with her lawyer "—praying the court for an order of arrest of the defendant requiring him to be held in custody by the Sheriff of Oklahoma County and brought before the court." On November 26, District Judge R.P. Hill issued an order to the Sheriff to arrest Bryce and produce him in court two days later. The order was served on Bryce that day and a copy is in his OCPD personnel file.

Apparently Bryce wasn't actually arrested but he did relent to the inevitable. The Oklahoma County Sheriff's Office shows no record of such an arrest nor does his later FBI background investigation. The uncontested divorce was granted to Maxine Bryce on December 9, 1932, allowing her alimony of $40 a month for the support of a minor child, four-month-old William Delf Bryce.

The year 1933 was to be the blackest in OCPD's history. Starting in February, three officers would die in the line of duty during the year, the first year the Department had lost more than one in the same year. It almost started earlier and it could have been worse.

During the early morning hours of January 4, scores of telephone calls began coming into the OCPD from citizens to report a cacophony of explosions and gunshots all the way down Northeast Twenty-Third Street. Police radios were only one-way at that time. Officers could receive calls from headquarters but couldn't transmit back to them. The police could only dispatch cars toward that area to try to catch up with the chaos. They should have known that Jelly Bryce and H.V. Wilder would be right in the middle of it.

About 2:30 A.M., Bryce and Wilder were prowling near Northwest Twenty-Third and Walker when they spotted two men in a car

OCPD Detectives H.V. Wilder (left) and D.A. Bryce following their running gun battle on January 19, 1933. (photo courtesy of Oklahoma City Times)

with Texas license plates. The car drew the Raiding Squad officers' interest by circling the block three times. When the officers ordered the suspects to stop the car, the car started speeding east on Twenty-Third with the cops in close pursuit.

The officers saw what looked like fireworks sparklers being tossed out of the car and landing in the road in front of them. When one of the "sparklers" exploded, they figured it out. During the first mile of the chase, the suspects threw six sticks of dynamite back at the police car but, luckily, only the blasting caps exploded. They apparently ran out of explosives in front of the Governor's Mansion and started firing at the officers. Bryce, hampered by having to drive the car, and Wilder both returned fire—vigorously.

The hell-bent chase continued for almost fifteen miles through the suburban towns of Spencer, Nicoma Park and Choctaw with more than sixty shots exchanged. About three miles west of Harrah, Oklahoma, one of the suspects' bullets hit one of the rear tires on the police car, putting the frustrated officers out of the chase.

After changing the flat tire, the officers went to Harrah and telephoned the Shawnee PD to alert them. They then continued through Harrah to Shawnee and Meeker. A night watchman in Harrah told of seeing a car speeding through town on a flat tire, the rim scraping the ground but only one man in it. Because the second man wasn't seen in the car, officers theorized that one of the suspects might have been hit but they were never found.

Bryce and Wilder didn't stop looking, though. On January 14, they checked three men at a gas station at Northeast Twenty-Third and Lottie, along the same route as the chase. All three men were armed. They were arrested for carrying concealed weapons and were scheduled to be questioned about holdups and whiskey running.

Shortly after 5:00 A.M. on January 19, Bryce and Wilder were hanging around Northeast Twenty-Third and Lottie again when they tried to stop another car with two men in it. This one also had Texas tags. When Wilder blew his police whistle at them, the men opened fire and, once again, the chase was on and, once again, east on Twenty-Third. It was beginning to look like Texans had it in for the Raiding Squad pair.

The officers held their fire for six blocks until they passed a filling station with people standing around outside but then, with no more innocent bystanders in the line of fire, they made up for lost time. As a result, this chase was much shorter than the previous one. After slightly more than a mile, the officers managed to shoot a tire out and the suspects careened into a driveway at 2219 Northeast Twenty-Third. As they jumped out and ran off into the night, the empty car rolled into an orchard.

Unable to find the scampering suspects in the pitch blackness, the officers returned to the suspects' disabled car and examined it. It contained a police radio, still turned on and squawking with the voices of their own dispatchers. They also discovered it was a good thing they hit the tire because they'd have never caught up with the car. It had a supercharged engine. It also had 37 of their bullet holes in it. Pretty impressive firepower for two guys in a little over a mile and one of them driving at that. Although the fugitives weren't located, it was considered possible that they were suspects in the six armed robberies that had occurred the night before. Two of the victims had been pistol-whipped. The suspects escaped justice this night but not because Detectives Wilder and Bryce didn't try. How hard they tried might best be expressed by the fact that they had to buy their own ammunition.

It's a small world, they say. On February 24, 1933, Bryce and Wilder were looking for a pair of men named Clarence Stone and Hugh Smith wanted for questioning in the theft of a car in Shawnee the day before. The fairly common names didn't ring a bell with either officer.

Later that day, the officers had successfully traced the men and located them on an Oklahoma City street. Bryce stealthily approached Stone from the rear and stuck his gun in his back, greeting him with a menacing "Hands up!" The man cautiously looked back over his shoulder and said "Why, Bryce, you don't want to shoot me. Don't you recognize me?"

Stone had been one of Bryce's grade school classmates in Mountain View. Nevertheless, he was under arrest.

Bryce and Wilder continued to scourge the streets. They confiscated a load of spiked beer and a week later, got 375 pints of real beer out of a roadster with Kansas tags. Bob South and Charlie Montgomery had been transporting the load from St. Joseph, Missouri, to Capitol Hill. The paper noted that it was the first real beer found here as opposed to the homemade concoctions drinkers had been subsisting on since the advent of Prohibition.

They also started hunting for Brady Koontz after his escape from the OSP. In spite of the fact that Koontz had only been serving a one-year sentence for larceny of fowls and hardly seemed to merit their efforts these days, he was an escapee. Koontz made the mistake of coming to Oklahoma City and borrowing a friend's car. He then made the second mistake of returning the car. Bryce and Wilder were waiting for him and found him hiding under a bed.

Mid-summer of 1933 saw the two biggest criminal events in the Midwest. Future years would see much speculation as to whether Jelly Bryce was involved in the cases.

On June 17, three gunmen mowed down half a dozen lawmen at the Union Station in Kansas City. The investigation fanned out across the country but Jelly Bryce and H.V. Wilder continued to patrol the streets of Oklahoma City.

On July 22, George "Machine Gun" Kelly and Albert Bates kidnapped oilman Charles Urschel from his mansion at 327 Northwest 18th in Oklahoma City. Urschel was ransomed and released a few days later. A number of printed accounts have stated that Jelly Bryce had a part in the Urschel investigation, usually prematurely alluding to his later FBI career. His exact contributions to the investigation are uncertain but it is probably safe to say that he had some hand in it, at least on the local level. Given the size of the detective force in the OCPD at the time and the magnitude of the case, it is probably safe to say that virtually every OCPD detective at that time had something to do with the Urschel investigation. The investigation spread to 17 states with arrests made in 5 of them, all by FBI agents and local officers in those jurisdictions. If any OCPD detectives, Jelly Bryce included, contributed anything especially significant to the Urschel investigation, it doesn't exist in any report I have been able to locate in the files of the OCPD or FBI.

In 1933, the Depression was getting deeper. The economy was so bad that even bank robberies were in a slump, only 30 bank robberies in the state as opposed to 59 in 1932. Times were harder for Jelly Bryce, too.

After more "cost-cutting" pay cuts, his $40 monthly alimony payments to Maxine accounted for more than a fourth of his salary. On July 1, he got a raise to $146 a month but that helped only marginally. His personnel file is filled with duns from creditors, large and small. He owed $150 to former OCPD officer, former Oklahoma City Mayor and current attorney O.A. Cargill, probably for his divorce. He owed L.B. Price Mercantile $13.45, $6.67 to the Jefferson Park Grocery, $106.32 to the Lee Thagard Music Company for a radio bought in 1931, and $30.50 was still owed to the doctor who performed his tonsillectomy the same year. He was also being dunned for a dollar here and there for making personal long distance telephone calls from the police station. Although the reason for these calls is unknown, they could logically have been attempts at reconciliation with his ex-wife in Georgetown, Texas. Each of these complaints brought forth a letter from the Chief of Police, threatening suspension or worse, if they were not immediately handled. This was not exclusive to Bryce.

The OCPD has long been sensitive to any criticism of its officers taking undue advantage of their positions for financial gain. While individual instances of police corruption have occasionally surfaced over the years, those instances have been rare and the Department has long taken stringent measures to maintain its reputation for honesty. During the Depression era, many if not most OCPD officers got letters in their files for past due bills. It didn't take creditors long to realize that a complaint to the Chief's office got fast results, no matter how petty the amount involved. During his tenure as Chief, John Watt seemed to be especially sensitive and responsive to those criticisms, perhaps as a result of his background as a businessman. He was also very Draconian in his measures, issuing strongly worded letters and frequent suspensions from duty for these infractions.

On September 26, 1933, George "Machine Gun" Kelly was arrested in Memphis, Tennessee, for the Charles Urschel kidnapping. It was allegedly during this arrest that the federal agents (arguably) received their future nickname of "G-Men." Jelly Bryce wasn't there. He was getting himself in trouble in Oklahoma City.

Police officers handle stress differently from most people, perhaps because they deal with so much of it. Sometimes they handle it in positive ways like exercise, hobbies like hunting and fishing or escaping to lakes and mountains on their time off. Sometimes they handle it in more negative ways like drinking, smoking, gambling, cursing, chasing women and others. Many find financial stress worse than any caused by investigating murders, car chases, fights, hostage situations or their other professional stresses.

On September 26, 1933, the City Manager received a letter from Mrs. Adeline Caldwell of Shawnee. The previous Sunday night she had gone to the annual Oklahoma State Fair in Oklahoma City. While leaving, she had been involved in a minor traffic accident, hitting the rear bumper and fender of another car. According to her, the other car's driver had lost his temper, cursed considerably and demanded she give him $5 to fix his fender. She gave him $3 and they exchanged information so she could be billed for the rest by the Pontiac dealership who would do the repairs. The man gave her a card reading "D.A. Bryce-Police Department."

Bryce was suspended the next day, the main complaint being that he had used his position as an officer to collect a personal debt, i.e. the money to fix his personal car in an off-duty accident.

The complaint was investigated, the gatekeeper at the Fair was interviewed and the Fair Association said the witnesses said Bryce was not at fault and the lady's complaint was "absolutely unfounded." Chief Watt sent a memo to the City Manager, saying he thought "the lady has been a little unfair to the officer." Bryce was returned to duty three days later without loss of pay. It was just as well. Everything he had didn't seem to be enough. On October 1, he got a pay cut to $129.70 a month.

He wasn't demoted or transferred or reprimanded. He just had his pay cut $16.30 a month. We don't know if he was the only one or if it was another of the Department's periodic "cost-cutting" measures. In those days they didn't have to give any reason and they didn't. He was still a Detective but he was making $35.30 a month less than when he'd been transferred to the Raiding Squad two and a half years earlier.

In October of 1933, H.V. Wilder was transferred to another assignment in the Detective Bureau and Bryce got a new partner. Although they would develop neither the tenure nor the lifelong bond that Bryce and Wilder had, they still had points in common.

Philip M. Isenhour was two years older than Bryce but they had graduated from high school in the same year, probably as a result of the fact that Isenhour came from a town even smaller than Mountain View. His hometown of Hastings, some 65 miles southeast of Mountain View near the Texas border, had fewer residents than the police department where he now worked. Although older than Bryce, Isenhour was less experienced in law enforcement. He had spent his first four years out of high school as a salesman, first in Chickasha and later with the Union Carbide Company.

Hired by the OCPD on February 20, 1931, Isenhour spent two years as a scout car officer before being promoted to Detective in July of 1932. During his first year as a Detective, Isenhour had not developed a reputation as a dangerous man like Jelly Bryce but he had tried to rival his future partner's reputation in another area. Evidently a handsome man, Isenhour took pride in his appearance and was such a fancy dresser that his sense of fashion drew comments from the local newspapers.

The Bryce-Isenhour partnership would be much more mundane than the Bryce-Wilder union. Although their adventures on the city streets would be heralded twice in their first month together, it would be for investigations as pedestrian as the theft of a car's gas cap and a scam artist defrauding citizens. It was quite a change from car chases and shootouts that had punctuated the Bryce-Wilder partnership.

Another gangster Bryce has occasionally been mistakenly credited with bringing down violently was Verne Miller. The most often repeated story is that Bryce had cornered the wanted Miller and he made a run for it in his car. Bryce, armed with a Thompson submachine gun with a circular fifty-round drum magazine, allegedly hit the fleeing car with 49 of the 50 rounds. Later confronted with this statistic, Bryce supposedly said he thought he had been shorted one round. A shaken Miller supposedly surrendered in the next town he came to, saying "a wild Indian from Oklahoma was trying to kill (him)." Great story but it doesn't stand up under much scrutiny.

Vernon C. Miller was born in 1896 in South Dakota. He served honorably in World War I after being trained as a machine gunner. Back home, he parlayed his war record into two terms as a Sheriff in his home state. Unfortunately his integrity didn't hold up and one of the people he sent to jail was himself. On April 4, 1923, he was sentenced to serve two-to-ten years in the state prison for embezzlement of public funds in Beadle County, South Dakota. Serving barely the low end of his sentence, he began moving up in his new profession, bootlegging and eventually becoming a gunner for Al Capone in Chicago. He first came to the attention of federal law enforcement in October of 1925 when he was indicted for violation of the Federal Prohibition Act. Moving on to Kansas City, he continued his activities in vice in that wide-open town.

His greatest fame was to come there in June of 1933. Although Adam Richetti's and Pretty Boy Floyd's involvement as two of the gunmen in the Kansas City Massacre has been disputed and doubted by many historians, almost everyone accepts that Verne Miller was the third. Frank Smith, the lone unscathed lawman in the debacle, said that Verne Miller was the only gunman he saw and could identify. On July 11, 1933, the FBI issued a wanted notice for Miller.

Although Miller's escape routes cannot be conclusively proven, it is believed that he went to New York, then New Jersey and then Detroit. Unwelcome at every stop because of the heat he had brought down on all of organized crime, he had much worse enemies than the FBI. On November 29, 1933, Miller's mutilated nude body was found in a drainage ditch outside of Detroit. Tied up like a Christmas turkey, his tongue and cheeks had been stabbed with an ice pick, flat irons had burned his body and his head had been beaten unrecognizable. Fingerprints had to be used to positively identify his body.

While I need hardly point out that this again doesn't appear to have been Jelly Bryce's style, it does appear to have many of the earmarks of vengeance wreaked by the gangsters Miller had alienated nationwide. Besides, Bryce was on duty in Oklahoma City, having returned from a 15-day vacation three days earlier.

With the number "13" and a black cat engraved on his pistol grips, Jelly Bryce's attitudes toward superstition were fairly evident. Bryce made his own luck. His opinions must have been somewhat reinforced by a case he and Phil Isenhour investigated on December 14, 1933.

An old man reported that he had been robbed in the 600 block of North Western, barely half a mile from the police station. The robber had taken the old man's suitcase and $500 in cash. The victim lamented his bad luck, saying that he had purposely delayed leaving on a trip to California on the previous day because he "always had bad luck on the 13th."

V

The Tri-State Terror

On Memorial Day, May 30, 1933, eleven convicts took the warden and two guards hostage and escaped from the Kansas State Penitentiary in Lansing. One of them had a date with destiny in the form of some Oklahoma lawmen including Jelly Bryce.

Thirty-two years old, Wilber Underhill had a record for robbery, burglary, auto theft and murder in Oklahoma, Kansas and Missouri stretching back to his teens. Feared and reviled even among other hardened outlaws for his viciousness and penchant for violence, Underhill had acquired the nickname "The Tri-State Terror." In later years, Bryce would call Underhill one of the most cold-blooded killers who ever lived, quite a statement considering the source. One of Underhill's associates told officers about them coming back from a bank robbery in Kansas. Passing through Perry, Oklahoma, they saw Chief of Police Howard Cress standing on a street corner. Although the officer was oblivious to their presence, Underhill wanted to shoot him "just for fun" but the others talked him out of it. This is how Underhill got the reputation that he'd "kill an officer just to see him kick."

This also wasn't the first time Underhill had proven to be hard to hold in custody. He had escaped from the Okmulgee, Oklahoma, jail while being held for a murder in January of 1927. Eventually recaptured and sentenced to life to prison, he had escaped from the OSP in McAlester in July of 1931. After another string of robberies, he had killed a police officer in Wichita, Kansas, a month later. Recaptured, he was sent to the Kansas State Pen with another life sentence for the officer's murder.

Within a week, Underhill was hatching another escape plan. He recruited some accomplices but they all wanted to escape by stealth, not wanting to risk violence or a murder rap. Underhill was scornful, saying "I wouldn't miss a chance to kill a bunch of lousy screws." Underhill may have even exceeded the blood lust of Baby Face Nelson when it came to scaring his colleagues in crime. One of his accomplices snitched the plot off to the warden and Wilber went to solitary confinement. The only apparent effect this had was to give him time to think. When he got out, he immediately began hatching another plan and recruiting more reliable cohorts.

That plan came together on Memorial Day of 1933. Using guns smuggled in to them and shotguns fashioned from iron gas pipe, they forced their way out of the prison with their hostages in tow. With uncharacteristic benevolence, Underhill released his hostages unharmed and even gave them a dollar to get some food and cigarettes. His good mood didn't last long.

The next night, a policeman was killed in Chetopa, Kansas, only 15 miles from where Underhill had last been seen. He was never positively identified in the crime but the coincidence is overwhelming. The rest of his behavior speaks for his rehabilitation.

On June 1, he robbed a filling station in Miami, Oklahoma. On June 17, he was listed as a suspect in the Kansas City Massacre although a number of historians have since debunked that allegation. Not that Wilber wasn't capable, he was just probably busy with other crimes elsewhere. On July 3, he robbed a bank in Clinton, Oklahoma. Two days later, another bank in Canton, Kansas. Then banks in Kingfisher, Oklahoma, and Stuttgart, Arkansas. Evidently deciding he liked Oklahoma, he robbed a couple of people in Purcell and followed up with banks in Tryon, Haskell, Okmulgee, Harrah and Coalgate. The attempt in Harrah failed when the safe fell through the floor.

The last two jobs occurred on December 12 and 13. The next day, Underhill eluded a posse near Konawa that succeeded in capturing two of Underhill's gang. Also snared was a farmer named George Nash who had been forced to harbor Underhill. Nash was released for cooperating after he told them Underhill was sick and running a high fever. The gangster had also recently been seen with a man named Ralph Roe.

Most wanted posters issued by the U.S. Bureau of Investigation have the charge in bold print across the top of the order. Although Wilber Underhill had a poster issued for him on June 22, 1933, it just read "WANTED." In spite of all the bank robberies, murders, burglaries, auto thefts and running back and forth across state lines, the Bureau had no jurisdiction over these crimes yet. In the fine print at the bottom of the poster, it said he was wanted in connection with the murder of four lawmen and their prisoner in the Kansas City Massacre. One of the lawmen had been a FBI agent and the prisoner was Frankie Nash.

In spite of these legal hampers, one man who was closely watching the Underhill situation was the agent in charge of the FBI's Okla-

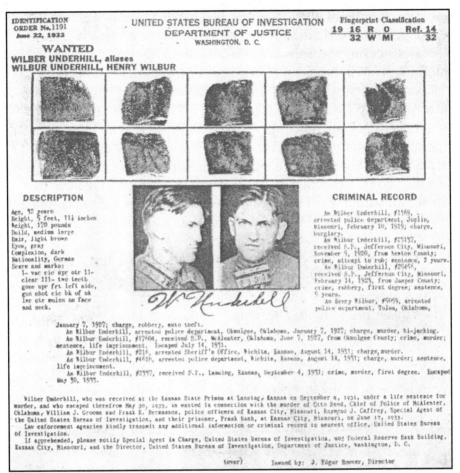

FBI wanted poster for Wilber Underhill

homa City office, R.H. Colvin. On December 29, he received information from an informant about the most wanted man in the region. It was very circumstantial but some of it fit recent developments.

A tall, thin man had been seen entering a beauty shop in Shawnee, Oklahoma, to call a doctor for medicine for a bad cold. A man had also recently rented a house in Shawnee under the name of Sullivan. This man fit the description of Ralph Roe.

Although Shawnee is in neighboring Pottawatomie County, Colvin contacted the Sheriff of Oklahoma County, Stanley Rogers, and called for a meeting in the FBI office in Oklahoma City. Rogers' presence is best explained by the fact that he was also the current president of the Oklahoma Sheriff and Peace Officers Association. Since the advent of the highly mobile, travelling criminal had presented such problems to smaller agencies, and in Oklahoma everything except Oklahoma and Tulsa Counties constituted smaller agencies, the sheriffs of all 77 counties had banded together in mutual cooperation to battle them. The OSPOA was the result.

Considering the crew who showed up in Shawnee the next morning, Colvin probably also asked for recommendations for some "shooters," men who didn't flinch at the prospect of having to take men who didn't want to be taken. Wilber Underhill fit that description better than any other man in the country at that moment. Wanted for at least eight murders, five of them lawmen, four escapes, two armed robberies and nine bank robberies or attempts, and considering his known temperament, there was every reason to believe that Underhill would resist as violently as possible. The men assembled in his office and Colvin briefed them. Then a convoy of cars started the 37-mile journey to Shawnee.

They arrived in the early morning hours, just before 3 A.M on a thoroughly miserable morning. The temperature was in the upper thirties, it was raining and foggy, and everything that wasn't paved was a quagmire of mud. The house at 606 West Dewey was a small five-room house. Inside were Underhill, his wife of six weeks, Beatrice, who went by the name Hazel, Ralph Roe and Eva Mae Nichols, the Shawnee beauty shop operator whose place Underhill used as a rendezvous. In the layers of fog and drizzling rain, a formidable force quietly surrounded the house.

Across the street in front of the house was FBI Agent T.M. Birch

Wilber Underhill's Waterloo. The house at 606 West Dewey in Shawnee, Oklahoma, as it appeared in September of 2000. The front of the house faces south. The two rear windows on the east side are where the gun battle began on the foggy morning of December 30, 1933.

with a shotgun. Behind separate trees to the east of the house were OCSO Deputy George Kerr, OCSO Deputy Don Stone and Frank Bryant, the Shawnee Night Chief of Police. On the porch of the house to the east were OCSO Deputies Bill Eads and John Adams. Also on the side perimeter was FBI Agent J.M. Edgar. At the rear of the house were FBI Agents Colvin, Frank Smith, K.D. Deaderick and Paul Hanson, OCPD Lt. Clarence Hurt, Sgt. Mickey Ryan and Detective Delf Bryce. Hurt was armed with a gas gun and a Thompson submachine gun, Ryan and Smith with shotguns, Bryce and Colvin with Thompsons. Agent Smith was a survivor of the Kansas City Massacre from six months earlier.

The Underhill Posse. Left to right: OCPD Det. D.A. Bryce, FBI Agent R.A. Colvin, OCPD Lt. Clarence Hurt (pointing to the window Underhill opened fire through), OCPD Det. Mickey Ryan (photo courtesy of D.A. Dawson)

Seeing a light in the bedroom on the northeast corner of the house, Clarence Hurt stepped up to it and looked in. The man inside was in his underwear. Recognizing their quarry, Hurt called him by name and yelled for him to surrender. Not unexpectedly, Underhill's response was to pick up a Luger pistol in each hand and empty them through the windows, so close that the screens were scorched with powder burns. Then everyone else raked the house with return fire.

Photos of the officers taken later show Bryce's and Hurt's machine guns with twenty-round clips while Colvin's has a fifty-round drum. Later estimates were that the officers fired at least a thousand rounds and Underhill sixty. Since the Lugers held eight-round clips, he would have had to reload both weapons at least three times, not an impossible feat considering the aftermath.

Ralph Roe was hit in the shoulder while lying in bed. His wife hit the floor and was not wounded. Eva Nichols was hit twice in the stomach. Although you couldn't tell it right away, Underhill was riddled.

Wilber burst out of the front door like a bloody apparition, still wearing only his underwear. The officers at the front and side immediately opened up on him with their shotguns. Taking heavy fire from the front and east, Wilber bolted to the west, falling three times and rising each time before he disappeared into the fog behind the second house to the west. Some officers tried to pursue while others entered the house to secure the other suspects. Colvin called for reinforcements to help expand the search.

Ralph Roe was jailed in Shawnee while other officers searched the house. In Underhill's clothing they found $5,300 in stolen bonds from the Franklin Title and Trust Company of Franklin, Kentucky, in denominations of $100, $500 and $1000.

Sheriff Stanley Rogers arrived about 6:45 A.M. With him were some police bloodhounds, his son Kendall, OCSO Deputy Everett Agee, OCPD Sgt. John Cassidy and OCPD Dispatchers Jack Roberts and Johnnie Whalen. As the search headed toward the area of downtown Shawnee, a citizen called the Shawnee Police headquarters. The citizen told motorcycle officer Bill McKenzie "Someone wearing nothing but his underwear is trying to break in the rear of the Owens furniture store." McKenzie saw five officers passing by in a car and ran out to meet them. Saying "I know where he is, let's go!," he jumped on the running board and they raced to the Owens Furniture Store at 509 East Main.

About 7 A.M., Cassidy, Roberts and Whalen covered the rear of the store while the two Rogers, McKenzie and Agee went in the front door after kicking it down. Underhill was lying on a cot at the rear of the store, conscious but silent. He didn't speak and didn't fight. He had two bullet wounds in his abdomen, one in his right arm, one in the left leg, several buckshot in his right arm, a bullet graze on the left side of his forehead, five machine gun wounds, a total of thirteen bullet wounds from the officers fusillade. The store was sixteen blocks from the scene of the shooting four hours earlier.

Underhill was taken to a Shawnee hospital and Dr. J.A. Walker operated on him for two hours with three officers on guard. His torso wounds were in the kidneys, stomach, spine and the head wound gashed to the bone. On New Years Eve, his wife was allowed out of jail to visit him for 15 minutes. Eva Nichols died from her wounds that day. After the visit, Hazel Underhill and Ralph Roe were taken to the Oklahoma County Jail.

Underhill confessed to seven bank robberies but emphatically denied any involvement in the Kansas City Massacre, saying he had been in Oklahoma City at the time with Harvey Bailey, another renowned bank robber.

After six days, Underhill actually seemed to be improving and getting stronger. He even asked a nurse "How far is it to the highway?" What a guy. When Colvin found out about his question and that the hospital had been getting some anonymous calls asking about Underhill's condition, he had him moved by ambulance to the OSP in McAlester on the morning of January 6, 1934. Ten FBI agents and prison guards armed with machine guns followed the ambulance in two cars. They arrived at the prison shortly before noon. Twelve hours later, Underhill died. The reign of the Tri-State Terror was over and Bryce and his cohorts returned to their more mundane duties.

An amusing incident in the new Bryce-Isenhour partnership was chronicled in the Oklahoma City Times on February 9, 1934. A teacher's convention was meeting in the city and the downtown area was flooded with even more personable young women than usual. The article began "Two dashing detectives from the city police department, both noted for their Adonis-like appearance and sartorial splendor, were a social failure (today)." It seems Detectives Bryce and Isenhour drove up in front of one of the hotels frequented by the out-of-town teachers with a sign in the window reading "Teachers Ride Free," offering to transport the ladies to their convention headquarters. Several of the ladies were standing in front of the hotel and, seeing the sign, approached the new sedan.

What both officers had failed to consider were the facts that, while snappily dressed, they were wearing nothing to identify themselves as police officers, the police car was unmarked and this was the gangster era in a large city. When Isenhour opened the car's rear door with a flourish, the first teacher stepped forward, saw a pair of sawed-off shotguns on the back seat, immediately stepped back and somewhat nervously said "Oh, I guess we'll take the next car."

Sometimes its hard to tell the good guys from the bad guys.

The Bryce-Isenhour partnership would continue for another few months but both men's careers with the OCPD were winding down. In March of 1935, Isenhour would resign to become an agent with the State Crime Bureau.

In March of 1934, they helped the Secret Service arrest seven men in three downtown hotels and confiscate several hundred dollars in counterfeit twenty-dollar bills. On the first of April, Bryce received a raise back to the $146-a-month level he had been at six months earlier but it wasn't enough to alleviate his financial problems. Twelve days later, Chief Watt got a letter from Dr. Harper Wright, dunning Bryce again for the remaining $30.50 he owed on his tonsillectomy in October of 1931.

In spite of his continuing financial woes, Bryce had moved to a better address. The small, modest duplex at 2512 Northwest Twenty-First was a one-story bungalow-type dwelling and offered its residents their own driveways with detached one-car garages in the rear. Of buff-colored brick with a small, enclosed front porch, it was in the Cleveland addition off of Peach Street (later Villa Street) at what was then the far western edge of the city. This was the 1930's version of the suburbs. Originally platted the year before statehood, the addition had been built in spite of the cancellation of plans to extend the streetcar lines out Northwest Nineteenth Street, with most of the construction taking place between 1924 and 1930. Although it is not known if he considered this aspect, Bryce's new address would probably have been more acceptable to any conservative inquisitor—such as a federal agent checking his background.

On May 8, Bryce filled out an application for appointment as a Special Agent with the Justice Department's Division of Investigation. The starting pay was $2,900 a year. It would be a raise of almost a hundred dollars a month if he got the job. The application was filled out in longhand with a broad-tipped fountain pen. His handwriting is easily read and even resembles calligraphy with its alternating bold and fine strokes with occasional ornate flourishes. He lists himself as five feet, eight and one-half inches tall and weighing 168 pounds. His Mountain View education is listed but the "College or Technical" section was left blank. In a fine bit of understatement, under the "Miscellaneous" section he lists "Instructions in use of firearms including pistol, rifle, auto rifle and machine gun." Under "Memberships", he listed only the Masonic Lodge.

Jelly Bryce was still doing his job in Oklahoma City while Justice Department agents were investigating his background and considering his application. Not only would he continue doing his job and earning his $146 a month, he wasn't through adding to his resume.

Gangsters and the law were still having it out tooth and nail in the summer of 1934. Barely a year had passed since the Kansas City Massacre, Machine Gun Kelly's arrest following the Charles Urschel kidnapping in Oklahoma City and Buck Barrow's death in a gunfight with officers in Iowa. Less than seven months earlier, Wilber

Underhill had met his demise, in which Jelly Bryce had assisted. In May, without Bryce's assistance, Bonnie Parker and Clyde Barrow were machine-gunned into oblivion by Texas Rangers and other officers on a lonely road outside of Gibsland, Louisiana. Dillinger gang members Tommy Carroll and Eddie Green died in gunfights and Homer Van Meter would follow in another month. Within the next six months, John Dillinger, Baby Face Nelson, Pretty Boy Floyd and Ma Barker would perish along with her malignant son Freddie. Four Oklahoma City Police officers had been killed in the line of duty in the last four years, all by gunshot wounds, and five more would die before the decade was over. It was going to be a long, hot summer, in more ways than one.

In 1905, the Smith & Wesson Arms Company had begun development of a new handgun and a new cartridge. The S&W .44 Hand Ejector Model was the first of what were designated the "N-Frame" handguns. This was the frame that would later be used for their more powerful handguns of .45 caliber as well as their famous line of Magnums, the .357, .41 and .44. Heavier and more solidly constructed than their previous "K" frame models, they were so named because they featured a thick metal shroud covering the rod that was pushed to eject spent shells from the cylinder. This shroud was to become an especially attractive feature for law enforcement officers. If they occasionally found it necessary to use their guns to hit suspects over the head or dropped the gun, the exposed extractor rod could become bent, making it impossible to use it to eject spent shells or possibly locking the cylinder closed and making reloading impossible. The thick metal shroud very much decreased the chances of this type of malfunction.

The gun was also attractive because of the new cartridge being developed for it. The S&W .44 Special cartridge was a 246 grain bullet backed by 26 grains of black powder. The company advertised that this bullet would penetrate nine pine boards, each seven-eighths of an inch in thickness, almost eight inches of solid wood.

The new gun went into production in 1908. Even though they were priced at a very reasonable $27, the company viewed sales as disappointing. Slightly over 15,000 were produced before production stopped. The modified Hand Ejector Second Model was produced starting in 1915. The primary feature of the Second Model was the deletion of the steel shroud under the barrel, again exposing the extractor rod.

Even though sales of the Second Model topped those of the

1908 Model, Smith & Wesson got a large number of inquiries about the production of a new model again featuring the shrouded extractor rod. The inquiries indicated a large interest especially from law enforcement agencies in the Southwest.

The inquiries took on more meaning when Wolf and Klar, a company in Fort Worth, Texas, that did a large business with lawmen, placed an order for 3,500 of the guns with the shrouded extractor rod. Wolf and Klar specialized in selling pistols that were ornately engraved and frequently featured ivory handle grips with a steer's head scrimshawed on one side. In October of 1926, Smith and Wesson ordered production of a S&W .44 Hand Ejector Third Model with the shrouded extractor rod. S&W made it available in either blue or nickel finish with barrels of four, five and six and one-half inches. It could also be had with either fixed or adjustable sights.

The first production run of 1,500 guns were ready on Christmas Eve of 1926. The first 1,000 were shipped to Wolf and Klar. In keeping with its popularity with law enforcement officers, the gun was not featured in the S&W catalogs but was a special order weapon. Up until the beginning of World War II, 4,976 of the Third Model or Model of 1926 were manufactured with N-frame serial numbers ranging between 28,358 and 62,488.

On the appropriate date of April 13, 1932, the Oklahoma City Times had printed a picture of a gun and a small story behind it. It was a nickel-plated, ornately engraved Smith & Wesson .44 Special revolver with ivory handle grips and a four-inch barrel. It wasn't particularly streamlined or beautiful except to one who fancies guns. Words like blunt, thick and heavy come to mind. A heavy metal shroud below the barrel protected the spring-loaded extractor rod. One feature it didn't have was adjustable rear sights, a sharp, notched blade sight that might get caught in a suit coat during a fast draw. Besides, sights aren't needed when you aim by instinct instead of by sight. A steer's head was engraved on the right side of the ivory handle grips, a black cat and the number "13" on the left side. The short accompanying article stated that D.A. Bryce had carried his "lucky gun" since his days as a State Game Ranger and it was valued at $125, almost a month's pay. Bryce said he had "carried (the gun) for five years and had not been shot during that time." It then states that "Bryce was wounded shortly before that in a gun battle."

Maybe Bryce gave the reporter this false information to emphasize his trust in the weapon. Maybe the reporter asked him if he'd ever been shot and he answered "Once" without explanation or elaboration on the circumstances. At any rate, the article began with the statement "Bandits who are superstitious should not engage D.A. Bryce, city detective, in a gun battle." But not everybody read the Times. Bryce would need both the revolver and the luck on the morning of July 18, 1934.

Wednesday, July 18, 1934, dawned like most other Oklahoma summer mornings. It was going to be another clear, hot, sunny day. By 8 A.M. in those days before Daylight Saving Time, the sun had already been up for almost two and one-half hours. The temperature was already in the mid-80's, rising at the rate of a degree every ten minutes and nearly twelve hours of daylight remained. By afternoon it would be over one hundred again and no relief in sight.

Even at that early hour, the rising sun was already thirty degrees above the eastern horizon but most of the concrete canyons of downtown Oklahoma City were still shielded from its scorching rays by the tall buildings and the fact that it rose somewhat to the south of the east-west axis of those streets. The 400 block of West Main Street was no exception. The two blocks to the east had Halliburton's and Kerr's Department Stores, the Hightower, Hales, Majestic and Security office buildings, all ranging from eight to twelve stories. Even taller buildings, thirty stories or more, stood further east and south.

By the mid-morning hours, only a sliver of sunlight would begin illuminating the north side of the four-lane street while the building fronts and broad sidewalks on the south side of the artery remained in cooler shadows.

The north side of that block was occupied by a hodgepodge of businesses marketing ladies wear, jewelry, furniture and pianos as well as a barber, an electric company, two auto parks, a hotel, two restaurants and several vacant spaces.

The south side of the street was similar. The Davis Brothers General Merchandise Store occupied the addresses of 404, 406 and 408. The far west end of the south side of the block was dominated by the eleven-story Harbour-Longmire Furniture Company at 420 West Main.

This ornate monolith was the latest success of a handshake partnership in 1910 between James F. Harbour and William M. Longmire. Opened in 1925, the building enclosed a complete two-story model home and offered separate departments for custom-made cabinets, upholstering, flooring and drapery. Besides its opulent sales rooms, the company acted as its own manufacturer, distributor and wholesaler. By 1934, it was the second-largest furniture store in the country, surpassed only by one in Los Angeles. Six decades later, the business would have passed into history and the building would be remodeled for the offices of an expanding city government.

At 408 1/2 West Main, sandwiched in between the Davis Brothers store and the Singer Sewing Machine Company at 410, was The Wren Hotel.

In stark contrast to the more opulent surrounding buildings, The Wren was the type of place the words "flophouse" and "seedy" were invented for and was in its first year of business under that name. Not surprisingly, the location changed names and owners frequently but it continued to survive in one guise or another because those places had a very definite place in Depression era society.

The Wren Hotel (then The Hotel Ramsey), early 1930's. (photo courtesy of Gary Pryor)

From Main Street, it consisted of a narrow doorway barely wide enough to admit a single person at a time. It opened into a tiny vestibule and another door led to a dark, claustrophobic stairway just slightly wider. Two dozen steps separated by a narrow landing formed the steep stairwell that led to the hotel on the second floor.

There a thinly carpeted but broad central hallway lit by perpetually dim ceiling globes extended all the way south to the alley at the rear of the building. A dozen of the hotel's 25 rooms faced out on the hallway with the remainder clustered at the front and back of the building. Two communal bathrooms branched off at the rear of the hall. Some of the rooms had connecting kitchens but most were about twenty feet square, sparsely furnished with the only common fixtures being a wash basin with a mirrored medicine cabinet above it, a floor heater and a bed.

The previous afternoon, OCPD Detective C.D. Pierce had

conducted a routine check of The Wren. As he was leaving, a man bumped into him in the narrow entrance. Pierce thought he recognized the man. The next morning, he mentioned to Bryce and Mickey Ryan that he had bumped into Harvey Pugh. Ryan had been promoted to Sergeant of Detectives two weeks earlier and both officers were immediately interested.

Harvey Pugh was an old associate of the recently deceased and unlamented Bonnie Parker and Clyde Barrow. Before meeting their demise, the murderous pair had murdered at least thirteen people, at least eight of them law enforcement officers and several of those in Oklahoma. Cops take a very dim view of that. That is as personal is it gets in that profession.

Pugh was temporarily free on a $10,000 bond, awaiting trial for the murder of McPherson, Kansas, police officer Charles Bruce on May 14, 1933. The three officers decided they wanted to know what Pugh was doing in town. It was prudent to assume he had some associates of like mind with him.

A modern police department might send a SWAT Team on a mission like that. There were no SWAT teams in 1934 but these three officers presented a formidable force nevertheless.

Most of his fellow officers would have been surprised to learn

The old Wren Hotel building, 408 1/2 West Main Street, Oklahoma City, as it appeared in September 1999. The hotel entrance is the narrow black doorway to the right of the street light.

Detective Clyde D. Pierce's true first name. Almost all written references to him are as C.D. Pierce but he was almost universally known as "Charlie", probably based upon a general (and erroneous) assumption of what the "C" stood for. Although he had only been with the OCPD for three years, the 51-year-old officer had over 20 years experience as a federal, city and railroad detective including four years with Tulsa PD. Evidently seeking adventure had been a lifelong enterprise for Pierce. He was a veteran of the Spanish-American War when he was only 16. If there was going to be any trouble, he was in good company with Mickey Ryan and Jelly Bryce.

The officers arrived at The Wren Hotel shortly after 8 A.M. Since you never knew when one of these situations might go bad, they stationed a uniformed officer named Cox on guard outside the front door. His multifaceted job was to divert innocent citizens from wandering into a potentially dangerous situation, keep other bad guys from coming in behind the detectives and stop any that might get past them. They approached the clerk on duty, Mrs. Nora Bingaman, and asked to see the owner. She said she was from out of town and had been in town for three weeks visiting her daughter, Mrs. Myrtle Bowen, who was the owner. Mrs. Bingaman offered to take the officers to her daughter's room. She led them down the hallway and knocked on a door on the west side of the hall.

The rooms along the central hallway were laid out like the addresses on the city's streets, odd numbers on the west, even numbers on the east. Rooms 9, 11, 15, 17, 19 and 21 progressed from north to south. In keeping with some of the superstitions of the time, there was no Room 13. On this particular day, it wouldn't matter. Somebody's luck had already run out, he just didn't know it yet.

When Mrs. Bingaman knocked on the door, Bryce was standing next to her with Ryan to one side and Pierce behind them. Mrs. Bingaman opened the door and started to step inside but immediately stepped back, trying to close the door.

What had startled her was not the sight of her daughter sitting on the bed but the man lying across it on his stomach facing the door. The man was holding an automatic pistol in both hands, aimed at the door.

Before she could close the door, a foot stopped it. Jelly Bryce's foot. Opening the door, Bryce saw what Mrs. Bingaman had seen but reacted much faster. He later told a newspaper reporter "He had the gun pointed at me so I jumped back and let him have it." Doubtlessly it took much longer to tell it than it did to do it. Faster than the eye could follow, the hand swept back the suit coat and the .44 came out as Bryce automatically went into a slight forward-leaning crouch.

Standing outside the front door, Officer Cox later told other officers that he heard a shot come from inside the hotel. What he had actually heard was five shots, fired so fast that the sounds melded together into a single report, faster than the ear could distinguish between them.

Before the man could squeeze the trigger a single time, Bryce drew and fired five times. One newspaper account said that all five shots hit the man in the head. Another said only four of the shots hit the man in the head, the first one probably directly in the chin, and one went into the mattress. Either way, he was dead before his gun hit the floor. Mrs. Bolen, no slouch at reflexes herself, leapt off the bed and took cover. She was unhurt.

The dead man was J. Ray O'Donnell, 28, a gangster friend of Pugh. Both women were arrested and led the officers to another associate in another room, Tom Walton. Harvey Pugh was arrested soon afterwards when he came back to get his car. His brother, B.J. Pugh, was also caught up in the net. All three were charged with Vagrancy and held for investigation. Mrs. Bolen was released that afternoon after posting a $20 bond for disorderly conduct. The next day, Carl Traub, police justice, gave the coroner a verdict of justifiable homicide in the death of O'Donnell. Later in the day, the Pugh brothers and Walton were released on $20 bonds on the vagrancy charges when victims of recent robberies failed to identify them in showups.

Apparently the notoriety of the shooting was the last straw for The Wren Hotel's owner. The next year, it became The Alva Hotel under different ownership.

VI
The Bureau

The federal government is replete with bureaus, many of which are agencies of federal law enforcement. The Bureau of Internal Revenue evolved into the Internal Revenue Service. The Alcohol Tax Unit of that bureau evolved into the Bureau of Alcohol, Tobacco and Firearms. The Treasury Department's Federal Bureau of Narcotics evolved into the Justice Department's Bureau of Narcotics and Dangerous Drugs which has since evolved into the Drug Enforcement Administration. The Customs Bureau has evolved into our present Customs Service.

The U.S. Bureau of Investigation had evolved into the U.S. Division of Investigation in the summer of 1933. On July 1, 1935, it was renamed the Federal Bureau of Investigation. Since the arrest of Machine Gun Kelly in August of 1933, the public had come to know them by the highly publicized nickname "G-Men" although many prior histories have alleged that the catchy moniker was more attributable to the public relations instincts of the agency's ambitious Director than the invention of the bumbling hoodlum George Kelly.

Like many other things, that particular lingo never caught on with the rest of the law enforcement community. Even today, if you ever hear a professional law enforcement officer use the phrase "G-Men", they're probably being sarcastic. Those people are much more likely to use the generic term "Feds" or occasionally "Feebs," a contraction of FBI. But the most frequent nickname among them is "The Bureau," meaning THE Bureau because that was the status they had been elevated to by the gangster era of the 1930s. When a cop says "The Bureau," another cop never needs to ask which bureau he means.

It is ironic that it was a failure of the U.S. Treasury Department's Secret Service that ultimately resulted in the creation of the FBI. In 1901, the death of our third President to die by an assassin's bullet, William McKinley, vaulted the youngest man to ever occupy the office into the leadership of the nation.

Along with his youth, vigor and independence, Teddy Roosevelt brought with him a unique view of the Presidency of the United States. Never one to accept many limitations, he approached the office from the standpoint that he could do almost anything he wanted as long as the Constitution, law and common decency didn't forbid it. Once he fulfilled McKinley's term and was elected to another in his own right, he accepted even fewer limitations. Thus he began "borrowing" Secret Service agents as investigators in his campaigns to battle big business trusts in the east and land thievery in the west. In the Spring of 1908, a miffed Congress forbade the Justice Department and all other executive branch agencies outside of the Treasury Department to use Secret Service agents for their investigations.

Hardly deterred, Teddy ordered his Attorney General, a grand-nephew of Napoleon Bonaparte, to create an investigative agency within the Justice Department. The President wanted federal investigators under his control and, by God, he'd have them.

Two months after Congress forestalled his use of the Secret Service, on July 26, 1908, an unnamed agency called only the "Special Agent Force" was established. On March 16, 1909, it finally got a title—the Bureau of Investigation.

Teddy got his investigators but he must have been dismayed at the reputation they fostered during their first decade and a half. Descriptions like inept, ineffective, highly political, nepotistic, incompetent and corrupt predominated. One former agent called it "a dumping ground for political hacks, ex-convicts, alcoholics and, in one instance, an expert furnishing friendly chorus girls to a top government official." Agents without training or discipline were hired and retained primarily through political connections. American-based German saboteurs and espionage rings ran rampant throughout World War I with little to fear from the agency. The agency's involvement in President Harding's Teapot Dome scandal was the last straw.

President Calvin Coolidge gave his Attorney General (and future Chief Justice of the U.S. Supreme Court) Harlan Fiske Stone a mandate to clean up the agency. On May 10, 1924, Stone gave the job to the Bureau's Assistant Director, a young lawyer named John Edgar Hoover.

A stern disciplinarian and a masterful organizer, Hoover did just what he was told and then some. The political hacks and somebody's brothers-in-law resigned or were fired. He began giving hiring preference to men with college degrees in law and accounting. The organization, their competence and their public image improved apace but their jurisdictional responsibilities remained relatively narrow.

For Hoover's first eight years, the Bureau had minimal criminal law enforcement responsibilities. Their primary duty was as investigators, not law enforcement officers, and a very definite line was drawn between the two distinctions. They started out investigating bankruptcy frauds, antitrust crime and neutrality violations. World War I had given them jurisdiction over espionage, sedition, sabotage and draft violations. The Mann Act, a white slavery act that outlawed taking women across state lines for immoral purposes and the Dyer Act, making interstate transportation of a stolen vehicle a federal crime, later fell within their purview.

When Prohibition became the law of the land in 1920, business picked up for the Prohibition Bureau but it was part of the Treasury Department at the time, not Justice. Most of the Justice Department's agents time was spent investigating civil crimes for the Attorney General's Office. In fact, Hoover's early agents acquired the nickname of "briefcase agents" because that was about the only equipment they were allowed to carry. They were forbidden to carry firearms except under extraordinary circumstances and then only with prior authorization. With a mentality of "it's better to be judged by twelve than buried by six," some agents did arm themselves on hazardous assignments but knew they did so at the risk of their jobs. They were also unable to make arrests without a local police officer present or the assistance of a fully empowered federal officer like Secret Service agents or Deputy U.S. Marshals. J. Edgar Hoover didn't like it any more than his agents did. He didn't want the federal equivalent of a private investigation agency, he wanted an American Scotland Yard. The hoodlums and gangsters would give him enough ammunition to enforce the change in the coming decade of lawlessness.

The changes began in March of 1932 with the kidnapping of the infant son of national hero Charles Lindbergh. Three months later, Congress passed the "Lindbergh Law," the Federal Kidnapping Statute. It gave jurisdiction to the Bureau of Investigation when any kidnapped person was taken across state lines for the purpose of ransom, reward "or otherwise". On July 1 of that year, the agency's title was officially changed to the United States Bureau of Investigation.

The new law would have to wait more than two years to get its first test but it would come in Oklahoma. On November 26, 1934, a man named Arthur Gooch and an accomplice got in a gunfight with two policemen in Paradise, Texas, wounding one and taking both hostage. Taking both officers across the border into Oklahoma, they got in another gunfight with officers but lost this one. Gooch's accomplice was killed and Gooch captured. Tried and sentenced to death under the Lindbergh Law, Gooch was executed in the Oklahoma State Penitentiary in McAlester on June 19, 1936. Since he was a federal prisoner, Gooch was hanged instead of electrocuted, the state's official method of execution at that time.

Hard on the heels of the Lindbergh Law came the Kansas City Massacre at that city's Union Station. On the morning of June 17, 1933, three men ambushed a force of lawmen transporting escaped bank robber Frank Nash back to Leavenworth Prison. The ambush killed Nash, Kansas City Police detectives William J. "Red" Grooms and Frank Hermanson, McAlester, Oklahoma Chief of Police Otto Reed, and U.S. Bureau of Investigation Special Agent Raymond J. Caffrey. Two other Bureau agents, Reed Vetterli and Frank J. "Joe" Lackey, were wounded. Only Agent Frank S. Smith survived unscathed.

Two days before the Kansas City carnage, the Barker-Karpis gang had kidnapped St. Paul, Minnesota, brewing millionaire William A. Hamm Jr. for a then-record $100,000 ransom. The record didn't stand long. Barely five weeks later, on July 22, George "Machine Gun" Kelly (whose nickname proved to be considerably tougher than he was) and Albert Bates kidnapped oil millionaire Charles Urschel from his opulent Heritage Hills mansion in Oklahoma City. The ransom demand, $200,000, was paid.

The Urschel case was a godsend for Hoover's ambitions for himself and his Bureau. The record ransom demand and the interstate nature of the case made all of Hoover's points for him forcefully; kidnapped in Oklahoma, hidden out in Texas, ransom note mailed from Missouri, ransom money recovered in Minnesota and Oregon, the investigation covered 17 states with arrests made in 5 of them.

On August 10, 1933, the Bureau of Prohibition was incorporated into Hoover's agency. To put it on an equal level with the Justice Department's other agencies, it was renamed the Division of Investigation but the national melee continued into 1934.

On April 23, 1934, a force of Bureau agents confronted the Dillinger gang at a hunting lodge in Rhinelander, Wisconsin. George "Baby Face" Nelson, whose nickname proved to be just as misleading as George Kelly's but in the opposite direction, machine-gunned Special Agent W. Carter Baum to death before making his escape in a Ford belonging to the Bureau.

Enough was enough. Attorney General Homer Cummings and Hoover had been pressing for new laws. On May 18, 1934, they got them. The U.S. Congress passed half a dozen of the requested laws and three more the next month that gave the Bureau a broad range of federal jurisdiction. A Fugitive Felon Act forbade fleeing across state lines to avoid prosecution, harsh penalties were enacted for killing or assaulting federal officers and agents were given the authority to makes arrests and carry firearms. The laws also allowed them to enforce statutes against the robbery of any federally insured institution, interstate extortion including those using telephones or any other means subject to interstate regulation, interstate transportation of stolen property worth more than $5,000 and a host of others.

However, Mr. Hoover was having to deal with the old axiom "Be careful what you ask for—you just might get it." Raising the hiring and training standards for an organization will raise the integrity level and sending newly graduated lawyers and accountants through some comprehensive training for a few months might make them more efficient investigators but giving them a badge, a gun and having them shoot a few holes in paper targets made them law enforcement officers in name only. When it comes to getting a college degree in survival instincts, little can compete with policing the streets of a large city a minimum of eight hours a day—or night—for a few years. Graduate school comes when the targets are no longer made out of paper and start shooting back.

The U.S. Bureau of Investigation had two agents slain in the line of duty during its first 23 years, before they had the authority to carry firearms. Virtually every other federal law enforcement agency had long since surpassed that casualty figure. Some, like the U.S. Marshal's Service and Treasury's Prohibition Bureau (later ATF), had surpassed it hugely.

But now, in the Spring of 1934, Hoover had lost two armed agents in the last ten months, Raymond Caffrey in Kansas City and W. Carter Baum to "Baby Face" Nelson in Wisconsin, and several more had been wounded. The malevolent Nelson would kill two more, Samuel P. Cowley and Herman E. Hollis, before the year was out. If someone had gazed into a crystal ball in 1930 and told Hoover that he would have nine agents slain in the line of duty in the coming decade (the same number the OCPD would lose), he'd have thought them mad. But now it was really happening. These kinds of casualties among his agents were totally unacceptable. Even worse, given the proprietary and paternalistic attitude that Hoover had toward "his" Bureau (and not without much justification), it can be seen where he would have considered these losses as a personal affront and a public embarrassment. Even before the new laws, agents had been arming themselves for self-defense on certain assignments but now they were going up against the worst bad guys the nation had to offer. The Bureau needed some men with special capabilities they weren't going to find in business or on college campuses and they needed them now.

All of a sudden, the college degree requirements for new agents disappeared occasionally. Experienced police officers who had survived one or more shootouts with the opposition started showing up in Bureau training next to the lawyers and accountants. English Composition wasn't their strong suit and they didn't have a broad knowledge of sociology but they exuded a quiet, solid sense of self-confidence. They were hard-looking men with a certain look in their eyes and many of them seemed to have Southwestern accents. Men like former Texas deputy sheriff Charles B. Winstead, former Texas Rangers Gus T. "Buster" Jones and James "Doc" White, former Dallas PD Chief of Detectives Bob Jones, former Waco Chief of Detectives William "Buck" Buchanan, Leo Uselding from Amarillo and Jim Durrett from Santa Fe PD, New Mexico. Between June and October of 1934, the OCPD would supply three men to this effort and more later. The normal six-month training period somehow got accelerated as well.

A month after the Dillinger gang escaped from the Bureau in Wisconsin, Bonnie Parker and Clyde Barrow were tracked down in Louisiana but not by the FBI. On the morning of May 23, 1934, they were ambushed outside of Gibsland, Louisiana, by a posse of six men. Frank Hamer and Manny Gault were both former Texas Rangers and had been employed by the Texas Prison system specifically to hunt down Bonnie and Clyde. With them were Dallas [Texas] County Deputy Sheriffs Bob Alcorn and Ted Hinton, and Sheriff Henderson Jordan and Deputy Prentiss Oakley of Bienville Parish, in whose jurisdiction they were operating.

Years later, Jelly Bryce would show his longtime friend, Leon Cleary, a pair of eyeglasses he said Bonnie Parker was wearing when she was killed. They still had dried blood on them. Bryce never actually said that he was involved in the killings but Cleary inferred that. The inference was wrong.

Several pictures of the posse exist showing the six men involved. If Jelly Bryce was there, why wasn't he in the picture? He'd never been camera-shy before. The fact that he was an OCPD officer would have caused no problems since four of the men were already operating far outside of their legal jurisdiction. It isn't that much farther from Gibsland to Oklahoma City than it is to Dallas. Jurisdictional problems in those days were viewed pretty much with a "the end justifies the means" attitude, especially in big cases and Bonnie and Clyde were about as big as they got in the Southwest at that time. Besides, two local officers were present so that legalized all of them as much as necessary.

If those glasses really belonged to Bonnie Parker, Jelly Bryce didn't take them off of her body.

On June 5, 1934, OCPD Chief John Watt and City Manager O.M. Mosier granted Clarence Hurt a one-year leave of absence from the OCPD. A similar leave was granted to Jerry Campbell. The 30-year-old Campbell had just under four years on the force while Hurt, a 15-year veteran, had been promoted to Lieutenant of Detectives a little over six months earlier. In spite of the fact that this was the man who had probably cost him the Chief's job, Hurt had become good friends with Chief Watt. He promised to stay in touch and he did.

Hurt wrote to Watt from Washington, D.C., on June 18 while attending the Bureau's school. He noted that they had completed the last test of the school that day and he and Campbell were the only ones in the school that weren't lawyers. He mentioned that the rainy capital weather was a nice change from a typical Oklahoma June and it was fortunate that there was plenty of cheap seafood available because "steak is worth forty cents a pound and a one-room apartment rents for $60 a month." He also mentioned that crime in Oklahoma City was mild compared to the nation's capital. As an example he told Watt of a recent case where three hijackers had robbed a policeman, stolen his car, robbed everyone they came across for the next ten days and killed a filling station operator, listening to broadcasts about themselves on the stolen police car's radio all the way. Watt's reply on June 26 was encouraging, telling Hurt that he and Campbell would get through the Bureau school just fine because they already had what the lawyers would need years to acquire, "practical experience." He also said he had "heard from Mickey (Ryan) that you and Jerry have been transferred to Chicago. You are probably due for some excitement." Chief Watt always was good at understatement.

On July 21, 1934, an East Chicago, Indiana, police sergeant named Martin Zarkovich was told by an informant that she had recently seen John Dillinger. Zarkovich told his Captain, Timothy O'Neill, who informed Melvin Purvis, SAC of the Chicago FBI office. An interview with the informant, Anna Sage, disclosed that Dillinger was taking Sage and another girl to a movie the next night.

Sage would wear a red dress to make it easier to identify her.

On the afternoon of July 22, Sage told agents they would be going to either the Marbro or Biograph theaters. Agents staked out both theaters until Purvis saw Dillinger enter the Biograph with the two women about 8:30 P.M. Then all agents were called to the Biograph at 2433 North Lincoln Avenue.

While the patrons were inside watching Manhattan Melodrama, a force of 20 FBI agents and four East Chicago police officers surrounded the theater. Five agents and two officers were stationed across the street on both sides of the theater. One of the agents to the north of the theater entrance was Jerry Campbell. Two agents and the other two officers were stationed on the same side of the street as the theater to the north. Five agents were stationed to the south of the entrance including one in a car and SAC Purvis in the doorway nearest the entrance. The next two agents were Herman Hollis, standing beside the car, and Charles B. Winstead in the next doorway. Eight agents were stationed in an alley south of the theater. The one nearest the alley entrance was Clarence Hurt. All the officers were armed with pistols, no shotguns or machine guns, partly because of concealability but primarily because Purvis forbade the more destructive weapons to prevent indiscriminate firing in a crowded street situation. In the next two hours, the electricity generated by those 24 men could probably have lit up the theater's neon marquee.

About 10:30 P.M., people began coming out of the theater. As Dillinger and the two women passed Purvis, he gave a signal that confirmed the identification and as a sign for his men to move in. As agents started walking toward Dillinger, his instincts were triggered and he ran for the alley, trying to draw a gun from his pocket. Three agents, Winstead, Hollis and Hurt, chased him into the alley and fired at him. Winstead fired three rounds from his .45 automatic while Hollis and Hurt fired one round each, believed to be from .38 caliber pistols. Dillinger fell, hit once in the chest and once in the head. A Bureau legend says that Dillinger died while Clarence Hurt was holding him in his arms. Although ballistics tests were not run, it has always been Bureau lore that Winstead had fired the fatal rounds.

Hoover wanted the FBI as an organization to get the credit for Dillinger's demise, not individual agents. He privately commended all three agents who had fired but the Bureau did not make their names public for more than half a century, after they and Hoover were all dead. Two days after Dillinger was killed, Ivan "Buck" Barrow, Clyde's brother, was killed near Dexter, Iowa, by local police officers.

Three months later, on October 22, Charles Arthur "Pretty Boy" Floyd was killed by a force of local officers and FBI agents led by Melvin Purvis near East Liverpool, Ohio. Jelly Bryce wasn't with the FBI that day either but he was being investigated by them.

On May 8, 1934, Jelly Bryce had filled out an Application for Appointment as a Special Agent for the FBI. The next day, Oklahoma City SAC Dwight Brantley sent a letter of recommendation to headquarters. He said he was personally acquainted with Bryce and that he had "rendered splendid cooperation to the Oklahoma City office." To balance the praise, he included that Bryce was "considered a bit wild, which perhaps can be contributed to his youth—some consider him unpolished, even to the extent of being uncouth" but Bryce "didn't impress him as being (that) way" and his "lack of polish and uncouthness could be overcome." His overall recommendation was positive, stating that Bryce "...is qualified to handle certain types of investigations..."

An interview with another SAC, R.B. Nathan, said Bryce "appears to be resourceful but not to have executive ability...is self-confident without being in any way boastful...would be amenable to discipline...good possibilities of development...would make a better than average agent if appointed."

On May 21, a thorough background investigation report was forwarded to Washington under the signature of E.M. Black, Acting SAC of the Oklahoma City office. Included were statements that Bryce was "...of good character...honest and reliable...an efficient officer...neat in appearance...one of the best detectives in the Bureau—good reputation...comes from one of the finest families in Mountain View...recommended for any position sought."

Also quoted verbatim was a penciled notation, handwritten and unsigned, in his OCPD personnel file; "This officer has worked in Auto Theft Department, Raiding and Vice Department, Detective Bureau, on general and special cases. Always selected when rounding up badly wanted men. Is a crack pistol shot. Has been instrumental in assisting state and federal officers in apprehending notorious characters, including Wilbur Underhill."

It also included details of several of the shootings he had been involved in and, objectively, recounted his previous arrest, divorce action, alimony payments and said his credit rating was "fair."

On August 7, the San Antonio office sent a report on the records of his attendance at the Civilian Military Training Camps in his boyhood. A summary of the investigation was forwarded on August 23 and on September 4, Bryce was given a physical examination by a doctor of the Veterans Administration in Oklahoma City. The physician certified that his only problem was a "slight infection of gums in region of one of lower incisors" and that he was "well able" to perform the duties of the position. A form from the Division of Investigation's Chief Clerk's Office dated October 15 optimistically and somewhat presumptuously scheduled Bryce for the October school and noted that he was "an exception," i.e. not a college graduate. On October 18, Mr. Hoover sent a letter to Bryce's home at 2512 Northwest 21st in Oklahoma City. A form letter written in the format of a telegram with no punctuation, it offered him an appointment as a Special Agent at a salary of $2,900 annually. After some bureaucratese about per diems ($5 a day) and retaining his travel receipts, he was told to proceed at his own expense to Washington, D.C., if he accepted and report to Headquarters at 9 A.M. on November 5, 1934.

Bryce applied for and received a six-month leave of absence from the OCPD to run from November 1 through April 30, 1935. Obviously not wanting the vagaries of travel to make him late for his appointment, he left a week early. Duly noted by the Oklahoma City Times, he left Oklahoma City on October 29. On November 2, Smokey Hilbert was transferred from the Auto Theft Department to fill Jelly Bryce's slot in the Detective Bureau. Bryce reported to FBI Headquarters as ordered on November 5 and signed his oath of office on that date.

The Division of Investigation that Bryce joined in 1934 consisted of 391 Special Agents, 451 civilian support staff and an annual budget of slightly more than $2.5 million. The agency was making an impact on crime nationwide far out of proportion to their numbers.

Three weeks and a day after Jelly Bryce signed his oath of office as an FBI agent, part of the Dillinger Squad cornered Lester J. Gillis, better known as "Baby Face" Nelson. They wanted Nelson badly and it was personal. During the gunfight with the Dillinger gang at the Little Bohemia Lodge in Wisconsin seven months earlier, Nelson had killed FBI Special Agent W. Carter Baum and escaped in the agent's government car. On November 27, 1934, Special Agents Sam Cowley and Herman Hollis spotted Nelson, his wife and an accomplice in their car north of Chicago, Illinois. In a horrendous gun battle, both agents were killed and Nelson fatally wounded. Hollis had been one of the agents who shot at Dillinger.

Much of Delf Bryce's FBI personnel file from this period has been destroyed but we can try to reconstruct it to some degree by examining the file of his friend and colleague Clarence Hurt.

Hurt began his leave of absence from the OCPD to join the FBI on June 5, 1934, and wrote a letter to OCPD Chief John Watt on June 18 from Washington, D.C. In it, he said that they had their last examination on that day and he was due "to leave here in about a week." He also mentioned that he and Jerry Campbell were the only ones in the class who were not lawyers so this might give a glimpse of the FBI training period of the time. If it was abbreviated or specially accelerated, it was apparently done for all agents and not just the former police officers.

Chief Watt replied to Hurt on June 28, telling him that he had just heard that Hurt and Campbell were being transferred to Chicago. On July 22, they got Dillinger. Hurt wrote to Watt again on September 17, this time from San Francisco, California. He said he had been "going a lot and have seen a lot of the country." He said he had been "on special assignment ever since I started" and had been with his wife only "one week since I arrived at Chicago in June." He said he planned to return to Chicago the following week.

If he went through the same two to three week training period, Bryce could have been assigned to the same squad as Cowley and Hollis but he didn't shoot "Baby Face" Nelson. Cowley and Hollis did that alone, at the cost of their lives.

In later years, Bryce would tell friends that he had been assigned to a "special squad" that specialized in the tracking and arrest of what would later become known as Top Ten Fugitives or Public Enemies. He told them that while he might work out of a particular field office, it was primarily because it was centrally located in the area he was working, he had no real home office and "just went where the case took him." Others say he worked with a "killer squad," a group of agents of proven experience in gun fights. They tracked fugitives reputed to be the most likely to fight it out and approached them from the standpoint that they "surrendered or died." Whatever gun battles he might have been involved in during this period would have to be recorded in the individual files of these gangsters.

On January 16, 1935, the FBI tracked Ma Barker and her son Freddie to a bungalow near Lake Weir, Florida. A four-hour gun battle with them killed both with no FBI casualties. The FBI has never released the names of the agents involved in that battle as they have the Dillinger case. Naturally, they weren't individually named in the press reports.

On February 19, Delf Bryce applied for credit to purchase a car through the General Motors Acceptance Corporation in Kansas City, Missouri.

During this period when the nation's newspapers were awash in headlines of gunfights between the law and the lawless with heavy casualties on both sides, the Smith & Wesson Arms Company developed a new caliber handgun. The .357 Magnum was a higher powered version of the .38 Special and its development was prompted by complaints from law enforcement that the .38 was not effective. The .357 cartridge was slightly longer than the .38, contained more powder and as a result, gave its bullet higher muzzle velocities and energy. A .357 cartridge could not be fired in a .38 caliber pistol but a .357 pistol could fire both cartridges.

Another legend has it that because of his firearms prowess, Bryce had one of the first .357 Magnum revolvers produced by Smith & Wesson. Some say he purchased it and some say it was presented to him. The company's records show that the first S&W .357 Magnum was produced on April 8, 1935, and the first one was presented to J. Edgar Hoover. If D.A. Bryce purchased or was given one, the records do not reflect it. A letter in Smokey Hilbert's OCPD personnel file shows that he and Lt. Newt Burns ordered two of the new guns for official duty purposes through the OCPD on February 10, 1936. One of the guns was blued and one was nickled, each costing $48.

If Bryce was an effective FBI agent, he wasn't perfect. He was

FBI Firearms Training Group, Quantico, VA, 1937. D.A. Bryce is on the far left. (photo courtesy of FBI)

promoted one grade and given a $300 annual raise on December 1, 1935. Five days later, he received a letter from Hoover addressed to the Chicago office. The letter took him to task for his participation in a surveillance of two suspects that had occurred in Bagley, Minnesota, on the previous October 25 and 26. Hoover wrote that "It is apparent that this surveillance was handled in an extremely unsatisfactory and inefficient manner" and "because of your negligence and lack of judgement," Bryce was being demoted one grade and his raise was being rescinded before he even got it.

On February 16, 1936, Bryce had his appendix removed. Presumably he could have been fit to return to full duty by May 1.

On that date, Alvin "Creepy" Karpis, the last survivor of the Barker gang, was arrested in New Orleans, Louisiana. The previous month, during a Congressional appropriations hearing, Hoover had been criticized by Tennessee Senator Kenneth McKellar for having never made an arrest personally. When Karpis was located in New Orleans, Hoover flew in for the arrest.

The commonly accepted story, also stated by Karpis in his autobiography four decades later, was that armed agents surrounded Karpis in his car. After he was well covered, Hoover approached him and told him he was under arrest. Clarence Hurt is credited with having actually had the gun on Karpis at the time and was definitely there at the time of the arrest. Recounting the story to agents in the Oklahoma City office years later when Bryce was SAC there, Hurt agreed with that version of the arrest. It is unknown if Bryce was present but, if he was, Hurt didn't mention it to any of the agents working for Bryce at the time which he probably would have if his friend had participated in the case.

Another portion of the story has it that Hoover ordered Karpis handcuffed and none of the agents had any cuffs on them. So one of them took his necktie off and tied Karpis's hands with it. A widely printed photo of the time shows J. Edgar Hoover leading Karpis into the New Orleans Federal Building with his hands tied in front of him. Walking at Karpis's right elbow is Clarence Hurt. Hurt is dressed in a fashionable light colored suit and hat, a white dress shirt buttoned at the collar but no necktie.

The Bureau had been expanding by leaps and bounds since Bryce had been hired. By 1937, the agency had 1,769 employees, 643 of them Special Agents. Now that they had the authority to carry firearms, someone had to teach them how to shoot.

From the beginning of his career, Bryce was periodically called back to Washington. Some of these occasions were to take his periodic physical examinations. Many others were to train new agents and give firearms demonstrations at the FBI's training facility at Quantico, Virginia.

A 1937 photo shows him with the FBI's Firearms Training Group. Another photo has been prominently displayed for years on the wall of his sister's room in her nursing home. Emblazoned with the official FBI seal, it shows Bryce drawing his gun, dressed in the range uniform of khakis with a short black tie. Old Movietone and Pathe newsreels of the day show FBI agent trainees dressed in exactly the same uniform. In one, several dozen of them in a line run up to the firing line, crouch with one leg and their upper bodies thrust forward, draw their pistols and hold it below eye level while they start firing at the targets in the likenesses of Dillinger, Nelson and Kelly. Their stances are a mirror image of every photo taken of Jelly Bryce drawing and firing.

As early as 1932, the Bureau's policy of frequently transferring agents was questioned during Congressional appropriations hearings. Agents were allowed to list their top three "offices of preference" (OP in Bureau parlance) but it rarely did any good for a number of years. Typically, a new agent's first office assignment was less than a year and a half. The second assignment was usually longer but it was usually quite a few years before he (there were no female agents throughout Hoover's 48-year tenure) had any hope of being assigned anywhere near one of his OP's.

Hoover defended his policy by referring to the previous politicization of the Bureau, saying his policy prevented agents from being influenced in their investigations by local politicians or other connections in their hometowns. He defended the frequency of transfers by saying he preferred new agents be supervised and trained by more than one SAC. The transfers were additional hardships on the agents because besides disrupting the family, the agent had to bear the cost of the move himself. Some agents never got to one of their OP's. For many, it took most of their careers. Some were more fortunate than others.

By February of 1938, after less than three and one-half years "on the road" assigned to other Bureau field offices and traveling squads, Bryce was assigned back to the Oklahoma City Field Office and had already received another commendation from Hoover for an investigation and apprehensions. In an era when it usually took agents the majority of their careers to gradually work their way back toward their OP, that fact couldn't help but be interpreted as a sign of the special relationship Bryce had developed with the Bureau's Director.

One common denominator among the agents who worked with and for Bryce over the years was the knowledge of his immense fondness and respect, even reverence, for The Director. Perhaps he even succumbed so completely to Hoover's paternalistic control of his Bureau that he came to view the man as a father figure even though there were only eleven years between their ages. Even though Bryce certainly had no need for a surrogate father figure, he wouldn't have been the first or only agent to view Hoover in that fashion.

There is little doubt that the respect and fondness were genuine. There is nothing in Bryce's life or background to indicate a propensity for sycophancy or hero worship. Quite the opposite, in fact. Although Bryce always accepted and was respectful of authority and supervision over him, he was never one to kneel before the throne and kiss the ring just because someone was the boss. Nor was he impressed or awed by titles, rank, seniority or position alone. His fight with the Chief of Police while a Game Ranger was not the act of a hotheaded youth, it was part of the man's character. When he knew he was wrong, he admitted it like a man, took his discipline and made amends. When he thought he was right, by God, he was right. And when he was right, it is doubtful if anybody pushed Delf Bryce very far.

Yet Bryce even began to model his attire after Hoover's choice of fashionable double-breasted suits and snap-brim hats. For a man as fastidious as Jelly Bryce, what greater compliment was there? Carl Tyler, later head of the Oklahoma State Bureau of Investigation, said that Bryce's friendship with Hoover was such that "he could have called him John if he'd wanted to but didn't, out of respect." While the respect lasted to the end of his life, over time it transcended the employer/employee relationship and relaxed more into the familiarity of personal friends. Bryce often sent pheasant and other game birds from his hunting trips to Hoover for the Director's table. It became common knowledge among his agents that Bryce could pick up the phone at any time of the day or night and reach Hoover immediately, completely bypassing the Bureau's upper chain of command hierarchy with impunity whenever he desired. From the end of World War II forward, many agents witnessed him make one of these calls, often beginning the conversation with an unprecedented "Hey, Hoover."

Sometimes people enjoy being around others who possess qualities they do not but wish they did. Another possibility is that the usually staid, prim and priggish Director was amused and entertained by Bryce's directness and the unpolished, rough edges that had been alluded to in his original background investigation. For a man as naturally restrained as Hoover, keeping company with a man like Jelly Bryce could definitely be a short "walk on the wild side."

Another possibly apocryphal story made the rounds within the Bureau. Supposedly Hoover and Bryce were on a trip together and went to a fancy hotel for dinner one evening. Seated in the dining room, they were kept waiting an exceedingly long time for service. Bryce reputedly drew his gun and fired a round into the ceiling whereupon the service immediately improved.

Another story shows another dimension of their relationship. By October of 1937, Bryce had been transferred to the resident agency in Aberdeen in north central South Dakota. It was at the agency's local office in the Alonzo Ward Hotel there that Hoover sent Bryce a letter of commendation on October 12 for the firearms demonstration he had given to the 23rd annual convention of the International Association of Identification at Quantico, Virginia. One version of the story has Bryce returning to Washington during a typical South Dakota winter and going straight to the Director's Office. Another version says Bryce telephoned the Director at home one night, waking him up. Either way, Bryce told Hoover he was having a little problem in Aberdeen. When Hoover asked what his problem was, Bryce told him "Well, I've got to wear underwear three inches thick to keep from freezing to death and I've got a two-inch dick." Reportedly, Hoover laughed and immediately transferred him farther south to Oklahoma City.

Most agents would have quailed at the very thought of that kind of familiarity, not to mention language, with the all-powerful Hoover. Maybe the story is apocryphal, maybe not. But there are some undeniable facts to lend it some credence.

During that era, FBI agents accepted as a fact of employment that they were facing a transfer every few years under the best of circumstances and even sooner if it was disciplinary in nature. Most counted themselves fortunate to get posted to a field office near their original homes or their OP toward the end of their careers. Jelly Bryce made it back to Oklahoma City, 100 miles from his hometown, in slightly over three years. He was never moved out of it until he was promoted to a Special Agent In Charge post. Even then, he was back in Oklahoma City again four years later. In fact, in his 24-year FBI career, he spent almost 14 years of it in Oklahoma City. And during the remaining two decades of his career after 1938, Bryce was never assigned any farther north than Oklahoma City.

Back in Oklahoma City but with a better job and making better money, Bryce moved up a little in the world. If he had to be concerned about his image before while a police officer, that may have intensified along with the scrutiny on his personal life as a FBI agent. In his previous years in Oklahoma City, his occupation had been listed in Polk's City Directory as "police officer" or "city detective." In the 1938 volume, he is listed as "salesman."

He had moved into Apartment 506 of The Aberdeen at 125 Northwest 15th. The appellation "Apartments" was usually ostentatiously ignored, at least by the residents. It was on the fringes of the fashionable Heritage Hills edition, the first upscale residential area built just north of the downtown area. Residents had names like Colcord, Skirvin, Overholser and Hefner, names that would later be on streets, luxurious hotels, skyscrapers, city water reservoirs and highways.

Built in 1927 as the city's first high-rise apartment building, it was a stately seven-stories of sculpted, patterned gold ochre brickwork with limestone-accented bay windows. "The Aberdeen" was boldly chiseled into the limestone facade over the awning-covered portico of the 15th Street entrance.

During this period, Bryce entered into his second marriage. She is a very anonymous person and not much is known about her. Her first name was Sandra and she was English, described as "very attractive" and "typically English", whatever that means. She was very petite and short, shorter than Bryce even when she was wearing high heels. Bryce allegedly met her in Chicago but their marriage is not recorded in South Dakota, Oklahoma County, Oklahoma, or Cook County, Illinois.

They are first listed together in the 1939 Oklahoma City Directory, living in a house at 2521 Northwest 24th, three blocks north of the old duplex apartment Bryce had lived in when he was hired by the FBI in 1934. The couple would continue to be listed together at that address into the 1941 Directory. The house was quite a departure for the usually ultra-conservative Bryce, perhaps reflecting his new wife's influence.

The house was in the Cleveland edition one block west of Shepherd's Lake which would be paved over and become the city's first large shopping mall two decades later. The south side of the block is mostly traditional one-story homes like those in Bryce's old neighborhood. The north side of the block, however, was different. Some were semi-traditional but some looked like Frank Lloyd Wright had come through town, showing a streamlined, art deco influence.

All of those were two-story homes, no two exactly alike, featuring very futuristic architecture for the 1930's. Rounded corners, second-story patios and balconies surrounded with curved metal pipe banisters and attached garages. The latter feature was a novelty for the time, signaling an admission that the automobile was now a permanent fixture of American life since we were making a place in our homes for them. While his wife may have liked the modern appearance of the house, Bryce probably had a more tactical appreciation for the narrow glass portal beside the front door, the upper story windows and the patio atop the garage looking out over the street, giving him "the high ground."

When John Watt retired as Chief of the OCPD in April of 1937, he was replaced by a politically ambitious 40-year-old lawyer with no previous law enforcement experience. Granville Scanland was a World War I Marine veteran and a graduate of the University of Kansas law school who had been a practicing attorney in the city for the previous 16 years. Making no bones about using the job as a stepping stone to political office, he took the Chief's job at less than half the salary he had been making as a lawyer. After two and one-half years as Chief, Scanland achieved his goal on October 1, 1939, retiring as Chief of the OCPD to become an Assistant District Attorney for Oklahoma County. Nine years later he would become the District Attorney and serve four two-year terms in that office. Scanland was replaced with 59-year-old Frank S. Smith. He was one of the first Chiefs to come from outside the Department not as a purely political appointee and certainly no one could dispute his credentials as a lawman. A native of Houston, Texas, as a young man he had served on both the Houston and Dallas Police forces. In 1915, Smith had been wounded five times in a shootout with a man named Red Kelly in Dallas. Leaving local law enforcement to join the FBI, Smith had been credited with solving the Osage Hills murder cases in the mid-1920s and had been in on the capture of Barker gang member Alvin Karpis. Smith was best known for having survived the famous Kansas City Massacre in June of 1933. Less well known was the fact that Smith was the man who had started the whole chain of events that led up to it.

On June 16, 1933, Smith and another Oklahoma City FBI agent, Frank J. "Joe" Lackey, drove to Hot Springs, Arkansas, to try to locate and arrest the fugitive mobster Frank Nash. Coincidentally, Nash was a native of Hobart, the county seat of Kiowa County, only 20 miles from Jelly Bryce's hometown of Mountain View, and he also went by the nickname "Jelly." Nash was a former member of the Al Spencer gang and a veteran burglar, bank robber and murderer. He had served two stretches in the OSP at McAlester and was currently an escapee from the federal pen in Leavenworth, Kansas.

Hot Springs was widely known as a "mob town" in the early Thirties, a good place for wanted men to hide out while the local police turned a blind eye. The two FBI agents brought with them a man who could positively identify Nash if they found him, McAlester Chief of Police Otto Reed.

Once in Hot Springs, the officers rapidly located Nash in a mob-owned cigar store. Smith arrested him while Reed and Lackey covered their exit from the store and they rapidly headed out of town with their catch. They stopped in Russellville, Arkansas, and Smith called his boss, Oklahoma City FBI SAC R.H. Colvin, the same man who would organize the demise of Wilber Underhill later that year. Colvin ordered them to proceed to Fort Smith and then take the train to Kansas City where he would have other officers meet them to return Nash to the penitentiary in Leavenworth. Unbeknownst to the lawmen, the mob grapevine was putting the word out and they were being tracked. If Colvin had chosen to have Smith bring Nash back to the home office first, what was to go down in history as the Kansas City Massacre could well have been the Oklahoma City Massacre. Frank Smith was the only man present at the debacle to come away unwounded.

One of Smith's first acts as Chief of the OCPD was to promote Smokey Hilbert to Lieutenant. Placed in charge of the Intelligence Unit, in the summer of 1940 Hilbert attended the Fifteenth Session of the FBI National Police Academy.

During his period as an agent in Oklahoma City, Bryce formed another life-long friendship. Weldon C. "Spot" Gentry was a contemporary of Bryce's in many ways. Another rural Oklahoma boy born in the same year as Bryce, he had taken a different career route by going to college. After playing varsity football at the state universities of Arkansas and Oklahoma, Gentry graduated in 1929. He then played professional football for the Philadelphia Eagles and the Providence (Rhode Island) Steam Rollers, a team that would later evolve into the Washington Redskins.

Coming back home from his athletic travels, Gentry decided on a career in law enforcement. In 1937, he was a member of the first graduating class of the newly-formed Oklahoma Highway Patrol. In this capacity, he became acquainted with Special Agent Jelly Bryce. They became friends and Bryce recruited him to join the FBI.

Like Bryce, Gentry had no birth certificate due to the territorial status of Oklahoma at the time of his birth but evidently the requirement was no longer being waived. He had to request one be filed at the Oklahoma State Health Department before the Bureau would approve his final background investigation. That led to a humorous situation when a FBI clerk noted the "I.T." in the "Place Of Birth" line on the document and told Gentry he "had to be an American citizen to join the FBI." When Gentry explained it meant "Indian Territory", the last roadblock was cleared and he became an agent in 1941.

In fact, on the day that "Spot" Gentry reported to Mr. Hoover's office to receive his badge and gun, Bryce was waiting in Hoover's outer reception area. After being sworn in by Hoover, Gentry remarked that he had seen his friend waiting outside to see the Director. Hoover said "I've just promoted him to SAC in El Paso but he doesn't know it yet."

Gentry would complete a twenty-year career with the Bureau, much of it in Oklahoma City with Jelly Bryce as his boss.

VII
Boss

In every FBI field office, the overall commander is the Special Agent in Charge. In his informative and refreshingly objective book about the FBI published the year after Jelly Bryce's death, author Sanford J. Ungar gave some interesting insights into the SAC position after interviewing hundreds of agents;

"The best job in the FBI, in the view of most veterans, is that of the special-agent-in-charge. Many aspire to it and spend twenty or twenty-five years of their Bureau career trying to reach that point; once they have attained it, they may hold on doggedly and resist all pressures and temptations to return to headquarters even as an assistant director. The SAC is ruler in his own realm. Even within the context of the countless rules and regulations prevailing at any given time, he can shape a field office according to his own style and his perceptions of how its workload can best be organized and handled. He may choose to be a tyrant or a teacher, frightening his agents into submission and efficiency or training them to perform intelligently, or some of each, but the choice is largely his. He can leave his door open or closed, encouraging agents and clerks to bring their ideas and gripes directly to him for discussion or requiring them to work through their supervisor at all times. The SAC may also encourage individuality among his agents, or he may supplement the Bureau-wide regulations with his own. He may establish an atmosphere of joviality and looseness in the office, or he may insist on sobriety and seriousness; he may know all the agents well, especially in a small office, or hardly at all. But he is very much in charge, and except in a few cases there is little ambiguity about his authority over day-to-day operations. At the same time, the special-agent-in-charge is a symbol, the supercop, the official embodiment of an organization that is widely considered to be the elite of law enforcement. To this day he is required, whenever possible, to lead all raids in search of someone on the Ten Most Wanted list and to be present during any other highly dangerous situation (a rule designed by Hoover to prevent SACs from arbitrarily sending their men into circumstances where they would not themselves be willing to venture). He should also be a public relations man and a promoter."

After only six and one-half years as an agent, Jelly Bryce was promoted to the coveted position of Special Agent in Charge and reassigned to the El Paso, Texas, field office on April 29, 1941. The prestige of the promotion was further enhanced by the fact that it was in a Bureau that was much smaller than it is today and with considerably fewer field offices, and thus fewer SAC positions, to go around.

This is not to say that the promotion was undeserved. Some former civilian Bureau employees had a much higher opinion of the former police officers working in the FBI than they did of other agents. One even said that when it came to catching bad guys, as investigators and lawmen, the former cops "usually ran circles around the lawyers and accountants." In spite of their relative lack of formal education and perhaps because of it, "they just worked harder." Their prior experience and street instincts probably helped also. More than one felt that the FBI owed a great debt to this small corps of non-college educated agents, particularly at that point in the agency's history. "They, as a group, and Jelly Bryce in particular, built a reputation for the FBI among the criminals as being tough guys and great shots."

Jelly Bryce would prove to embody the best qualities of a SAC in each of the four field offices he would serve at in that position. More than half a century later, agents who had served under him were still praising him as "the finest boss I ever worked for."

That description is indicative. Bryce became a boss but not an administrator. His talents did not lie in that area and he knew it. He had no interest in paper, files or columns of figures. When you think about it, those things had nothing to do with why he was originally hired by the FBI. His skills were with people and his talents in those areas, rooted in the small town Oklahoma values he was raised with, would prove to work just as well with good people as his capacity for violence had with bad people.

Besides, the Bureau had plenty of lawyers and accountants who did have the talents Bryce lacked. In every office he was to serve as SAC, one or two agents would be assigned to handle the routine administrative matters while Bryce was away from the office doing his public relations firearms demonstrations or bonding with local lawmen.

Several former employees of his talked about some of the differences between Bryce and other supervisors they had, the differences they appreciated. Most supervisors routinely summoned subordinates to their office to talk, some rather imperiously. Bryce usually would only do that when the conversation needed to be confidential or when it was an ass-chewing. He seemed to instinctively understand the basic supervisory principle of praising in public and punishing in private. Usually, however, when Bryce had something to say to someone, whether it was an agent, clerk or stenographer, he would seek them out.

Other supervisors had the annoying habit of communicating with their people almost exclusively by memorandums. As any former employee of a bureaucracy can attest, praising large groups for a good job done by a small portion of that group is only slightly less annoying than criticizing large groups for the misconduct of one or two individuals. As one former employee put it, "When Bryce had something to say to you, he talked to you, directly."

Bryce's speech was typically direct, blunt and to the point. His speech mannerisms often spilled over into his reports to FBI Headquarters and even those sent directly to Hoover. In one of those, he referred to an agent as having "constipation of the brain and diarrhea of the mouth." Many thought that kind of brash candor may have been one of the linchpins of Hoover's special relationship with Bryce. The Director, who doubtlessly had to deal with even more sycophants and toadies than most, probably enjoyed the rare individual like Bryce who would tell him the truth, regardless of the consequences.

Most law enforcement officers put a high value on truth in their personal and professional lives, perhaps because they get lied to so much by the people they deal with every day. Truth had a high priority in Bryce's relations with his subordinates and that raised their esteem for him also. When he gave his word to them, he kept it, even in the face of pressure.

It was a good thing that their new boss wasn't superstitious because the El Paso office had only 13 agents assigned to it when Bryce took charge. Two of them would later become much better known on the opposite coasts of the nation. The ASAC under Bryce was Daniel Sullivan. After leaving the Bureau, Sullivan would move to Florida and become the Director of the Miami Beach Crime Commission. Special Agent Peter J. Pitchess would become the Sheriff of the largest sheriff's department in the nation in Los Angeles County, California, serving until 1982 in that position.

Although one of the smaller field offices in manpower, the El Paso office covered one of the larger geographic areas. Since the Albuquerque field office would not be created until December of 1949, the El Paso office was responsible for investigations in 15 counties of west Texas as well as the entire state of New Mexico. Its proximity to the border with Mexico was about to give it even greater importance.

As previously noted, it was common knowledge that Bryce had an especially close relationship with Mr. Hoover. When he was in Washington, he was one of the few SAC's that was always invited to dinner at Mr. Hoover's home. It was also well known how outspoken Bryce was in his defense of the FBI and J. Edgar Hoover in particular. Sometimes his defense went beyond words and became actions.

At 10:27 P.M. on June 16, 1941, a man came into the El Paso FBI office and asked to see the SAC. That Bryce was there at that time on a Monday night shows how seriously he was taking his new duties. The man had been drinking but was by no means drunk. Upon being shown into Bryce's office, he introduced himself but his name has been excised from the official report. Evidently he had some past history with the Bureau because he then said "You can call the Los Angeles FBI Office and find out who I am, but before I start, I just want you to know what I think about your boss, J. Edgar Hoover. I think he is a half-nigger S.O.B."

Thus we can probably infer the man was white. After the incident, Bryce contacted Assistant Director W.R. Glavin and, at his direction, submitted a report to Headquarters. The third paragraph of the report states "It is exactly seven steps from where this remark was made to where the period was placed after it with (his) head in the plaster of a wall." Bryce ended the report by writing "I sincerely feel my action in this matter was justified."

The report was forwarded to Washington the next day and he received a reply from Hoover on June 28. Hoover's closing paragraph states "I want to communicate with you and express to you my sincere appreciation at the manner in which you handled this individual."

On Saturday, December 6, 1941, Delf Bryce celebrated his thirty-fifth birthday. The next day, he went across the border to Juarez, Mexico, and went to a bullfight. At 11 A.M., three time zones and 3,371 miles to the west, the whole world was changing and not for the better.

Over 2,300 American soldiers, sailors and Marines were dying during the Japanese Navy's sneak attack on Pearl Harbor in the American territory of Hawaii. America had just been dragged into the biggest, most destructive war in the history of mankind.

FBI agents were officially exempt from the draft during World War II but, even so, many took leaves of absence to join the military. Jelly Bryce contacted Director Hoover and told him he intended to join the Marines. Hoover talked him out of it by telling him that his post in El Paso was about to take on new importance due to its proximity to the Mexican border, Mexico being a hotbed of foreign agents and potential saboteurs, and El Paso being one of the more obvious points of entry into the United States. Hoover convinced him that he could serve the country better fighting Nazi spies on the Mexican border than slugging it out with Japs on some South Pacific island.

The rest of the world had already been choosing up sides since 1939 and men had been dying all over the world for more than two years before Pearl Harbor. In 1940, President Roosevelt had given the FBI jurisdiction over nonmilitary intelligence in the Western Hemisphere. There was already a large community of German expatriates in South America and a number of Latin American leaders were already allying their sympathies, if not their overt support, with Axis interests.

As a precursor of the Bureau's future Legat (legal attaché) program that would eventually station Bureau agents in American embassies all over the world, the first FBI agent officially assigned to duties outside the borders of the United States was Bryce's predecessor as Special Agent in Charge of the El Paso office. He had gone across the Rio Grande River on intelligence missions as early as 1939.

With his normal professional gregariousness, Bryce had cultivated friendships and professional liaisons in his new position. Two of the men he had established very cordial relations with were Bob Drennan, Chief of the El Paso Police and a FBI National Academy graduate, and General Jaeme Ciniones, who was in charge of the neighboring military garrison in Juarez, Mexico. General Ciniones had a ranch in Chihuahua, Mexico, and Bryce had visited the General at his ranch for hunting trips on several occasions.

Although Mexico did not declare war on the Axis powers until May of 1942 and then only after several Mexican oil tankers were sunk by German warships, they immediately took a pro-Allied stance after Pearl Harbor.

Soon after Pearl Harbor, General Ciniones contacted Bryce, advising him that there were a number of Japanese businessmen and residents in Juarez and asked Bryce what he wanted done with them.

112

Bryce told the General he had no instructions on that yet but he would try to find out how Washington wanted it handled.

Some time passed and no word came from Headquarters. General Cinione's called Bryce back, said he couldn't wait any longer and suggested he take the Japanese out on a mesa and shoot them. Bryce objected to this tactic and convinced Ciniones to wait a little longer.

When no direction from Washington came for a while longer, General Ciniones rounded up the Japanese, confiscated their property and had them transported into the interior of Mexico where they were interned, using the sale of their own property to finance the operation. It is a fair bet that the Mexican government has never appropriated reparations to these internees as America has done for the Nisei.

The war effort was reaching all the way back to the OCPD again. The day after Christmas in 1941, Smokey Hilbert, now the Lieutenant in charge of the OCPD's Intelligence Unit, requested an indefinite leave of absence after "having been recalled to duty with the FBI." Apparently the Bureau had liked what they saw when Smokey attended the FBI National Academy the previous summer.

When Smokey Hilbert took a leave of absence from the OCPD to join the FBI, during the next 18 months he and Jelly Bryce would have at least one more adventure together that Hilbert would tell his family.

Hilbert and Bryce were on the trail of two Italian organized crime mobsters and traced them to Cicero, Illinois, a notorious suburb of Chicago. One evening, they went to dinner. A neighboring table was occupied by several known mobsters and each group immediately recognized the other as an adversary.

As usual, Jelly was all decked out right down to his spats and as he and Hilbert walked by the gangsters' table, one of them made a comment to the effect of "Look at the jellybean", obviously meaning it derogatorily. His companions laughed, replying something about "the Feds (are) in town." Bryce and Hilbert took the next table.

As they were being seated, Bryce carefully removed his hat, overcoat, gloves and suit coat, blatantly exposing the revolver on his belt and leaving no one in the restaurant in doubt that the Feds were in town. Before he sat down, he leaned over to one of the mobsters at the next table and, in a low voice, said "Hey, greaseball, don't let these clothes get your fucking head blown off."

Another tale involving people underestimating Bryce because of his clothing occurred in California. Years later, Clarence Hurt would enjoy retelling the story on his visits to the Oklahoma City FBI office.

On an investigation that led them to the West Coast, Hurt and Bryce stopped in a small café for some hot cakes and coffee early one morning. When they entered, they noted that the cook was a large, beefy man with both arms heavily decorated in what law enforcement officers call "jailhouse tattoos."

In spite of the location, heat and time of day, both of the diminutive agents were well turned out in their Hoover-era uniforms of three-piece suits, white shirts, ties, shined shoes and snap-brim hats. With the same talent for misjudgment that probably got him the tattoos, the cook took them for a couple of dudes and decided to have some fun at their expense. Clearly he had no idea that the two "dudes" had traded bullets with the likes of Wilber Underhill and John Dillinger.

The cook started flipping the pancakes and about every other one landed on the floor. One landed near a cockroach which got scooped up with the pancake and tossed back on the griddle.

Bryce saw what was happening. When the plate was laid in front of him, he turned the pancake over, exposing the cockroach. He shoved it aside with the observation that it wasn't fit to eat. The intimidating cook leaned over and said "That'll be thirty-five cents for the hotcakes and coffee."

Bryce drew his pistol, laid it on the counter, fixed the cook with his patented stare and asked "What did you say?"

The cook replied "I said that would be five cents for a cup of coffee."

Later in the war, an American soldier named Dale Maples helped two German prisoners of war escape from an internment camp in Southern Colorado. Bryce received a call from a local lawman at Columbus, New Mexico, a small town barely a mile from the Mexican border some 60 miles west of El Paso. Officers had arrested Maples and the two Germans before they could cross the border.

All three prisoners were turned over to Bryce and taken to Albuquerque. Bryce and Howard F. Houk, the U.S. Attorney for that district, interviewed Maples who was a former student at Harvard. The young traitor was very arrogant and outspoken in his support for Hitler and the German war effort. At one point during the interview, Maples told Bryce they could settle the whole matter by going outside and having a duel with pistols, no doubt his idea of the Nazi code of chivalry. Bryce declined the offer by telling him the matter had to be settled in the courts but Mr. Houk was amused no end at the thought of someone suggesting a pistol duel with Jelly Bryce. Maples may have never known how close he came to committing suicide.

Maples was indicted for treason, aiding and abetting the enemy in wartime and other crimes. He was given a military trial in Washington, D.C., convicted and sentenced to death. President Roosevelt later commuted the sentence to life imprisonment. Maples was the only U.S. citizen convicted of treason during World War II.

When Bryce was assigned to El Paso, one of the agents working for him was a crusty old veteran who had been wounded in a gunfight with one of the Barker brothers. He had also been one of his new boss's training agents when Bryce was first hired.

The El Paso office received information that a German agent was going to cross the border from Mexico at a specified time and place. The old veteran and his younger partner were assigned to stake out the location and follow the German. They followed him into downtown El Paso and watched him enter a bank. The two agents stationed themselves across the street from the entrance and waited. When the German had not come out after some time, the senior agent called Bryce at the office and reported.

Returning to the surveillance, the two agents waited some more. After a while when the German had still not come out, the senior agent called Bryce again to report. Bryce told his men that the German agent was in his office, having somehow eluded them and made his way to the FBI office.

Naturally, the agents were required to write a memorandum explaining the incident and how they lost the surveillance. The junior agent wrote the report. He detailed what had happened as they followed the German to the bank, then said that "(the German agent) proceeded by underground tunnel to the Federal Building where the surveillance was continued by SAC Bryce." The imaginative young agent apparently judged his boss's sense of humor accurately because Bryce thought the explanation was so original that he didn't reprimand either agent.

Incidentally, I should caution uninitiated readers against judging this incident too harshly until they have tried to keep someone under surveillance themselves. If they'll try a brief random test of that on some unsuspecting stranger, they'll learn what law enforcement officers already know—it isn't as easy as it looks in the movies. I might also refer them to the movie The French Connection, which should educate them somewhat in how many men it takes to conduct a good, clandestine surveillance on one person and how many things can still go wrong with it under the best of circumstances.

Bryce had another crusty old veteran under his supervision but they didn't get along as well. The resident agent in Albuquerque, New Mexico, reported to the El Paso SAC and was under his supervision. When World War II began, that agent was Charles B. Winstead, the agent who had been involved in the killing of John Dillinger along with Agents Clarence Hurt and Herman Hollis in 1934.

By all accounts, Winstead and Bryce should have hit it off very well personally. Both were former cops, Winstead being a former deputy sheriff, and both were part of the non-college educated lawmen brought into the Bureau specifically because of their prowess as gunmen. Like Bryce, Winstead was known to be a man with a strong, individualistic personality, unpolished and unpretentious. Also like Bryce, Winstead was known to be "rough as a cob" in his language and manner, the kind of man who took no crap off of anyone. But those similarities didn't seem to be enough to provide a bond between the two men. Several agents have mentioned that there was some unknown source of antipathy between Winstead and his new boss. Since they were not known to have worked together in the past, it was assumed that it was some form of competitiveness of the "two roosters in the henhouse" variety.

Early in the war, Winstead gave his new boss some ammunition to use against him. He got in a verbal dispute with a woman in the artists colony in Santa Fe, the incident became public and some juicy quotes ended up in the local newspaper. Unwanted, unplanned, uncontrolled and unfavorable publicity was anathema in the Bureau. While other agents admit that Bryce probably had no choice other than to make an investigation and report to Headquarters on the incident, they also speculate that the outcome didn't cause Bryce to lose any sleep.

Based upon the investigation and report, Hoover sent out an order to give Winstead a disciplinary transfer to another office, effectively ending any hope of future promotion or favorable assignments. It didn't work. Winstead resigned. When interviewed by local reporters, Winstead provided them with some more quotes. He said "It's a free country. She had the right to say what she said about me. I had the right to tell her what I thought of her. Hoover had the right to transfer me. I had the right to quit. I quit."

Although generally popular and respected among his subordinates, Bryce could also be a stern taskmaster and Draconian in his discipline. Agents were required to be on call around the clock and respond to a callout within two hours. When Bryce found one resident agent unavailable for an entire weekend, Bryce had him fired.

He also believed that people should do a full days work for a full days pay. On one occasion, he walked into the stenographer pool while a clerk was entertaining the other girls with some "Kilroy stories." Asking her if she had his latest report finished, she replied that it was only ten pages and wouldn't take her very long. He then went back to his office and handed her a file he wanted included with the report as an enclosure. The enclosure was two hundred pages long. In the days before copy machines, that meant the entire two hundred pages would have to be retyped. He left her with an intimidating smile, saying "That should keep you busy."

He had a habit of suddenly appearing behind the stenographer's work stations. While at their desks typing, he would occasionally just stand behind them with his arms crossed, silently watching. Some thought that he just enjoyed surprising people and seeing how they handled what could be interpreted as silent intimidation under his steely gaze. That or to convey the impression that big brother was always watching, all-seeing, all-knowing, especially when you wanted the scrutiny the least.

Nevertheless, Bryce was equally popular and respected among the civilian employees who worked for him. Compared to the coarse, blunt language he habitually used around men, he was so soft-spoken with the women that they sometimes had trouble hearing him clearly. He was always polite, thoughtful and gentlemanly in the presence of females, never failing to personally thank them for putting in extra time or doing an especially good job.

It was during this period that his second marriage collapsed. Sandra was always thought of by Bryce's colleagues as an odd match for him and it was generally accepted that they were not suited for each other, with the possible exception that she was "just as feisty as he was." They had no children and one former acquaintance described her, apparently somewhat kindly, as a "social butterfly". She was determinedly undeterred from her social rounds and obligations just because her husband was always working. They always seemed to be going in different directions. They were divorced and she went out of Bryce's life as unknown a quantity as she had been when she entered it.

When one former associate ran into him a few years later and innocently asked him how Sandra was, Bryce answered with typical bluntness. He said "I divorced her. She was running around on me and I don't take that from anybody."

Bryce had other human failings. In an office full of college graduates, some of them attorneys, he appeared to be sensitive about his lack of higher education. One agent turned in a report with a section in it containing a lot of legal phraseology relating to the future legal prosecution of the case. Bryce criticized the agent for the report and ordered him to change it. He did and the report was forwarded to Washington. Bureau Headquarters sent it back and wanted the legal wording re-instituted in the report. Although Bryce took no action against the agent, their relationship was permanently strained and he never enjoyed the camaraderie with his boss some of the others did.

Other agents considered him "hard-headed" and "very set in his ways" but fair. He was known to be very firm with new agents, insisting that they call him "Mr. Bryce". On the other hand, he also insisted that the older, veteran agents call him Jelly.

One of those veteran agents was investigating the theft of some cattle from a Government reservation near Silver City, New Mexico. As he was being shown around the land by the man who leased it from the government, they saw a woodpecker drilling away at a tree. The leasor was apparently appalled, said that the woodpecker was ruining the tree and asked the agent if he could shoot it. The agent pulled his gun, snapped off a quick shot and clipped the bird's head off. Although he was a good shot, the agent later admitted "it was pure luck."

When the agent returned to El Paso, the man had already called Bryce, told him the story and was gushingly impressed with the shooting ability of all FBI men. Bryce called the agent in his office and told him of their conversation. Anticipating a reprimand for improperly using his weapon in the line of duty and not reporting it, the agent apologized profusely. Bryce dismissed the agent with the statement "Just as long as you didn't have to take a second shot." No reprimand was forthcoming.

One reason for Bryce's leniency in that case might be shown by another incident. Draft evasion was taken very seriously during the war. In October of 1943, 19-year-old Earl Ray Caudill was scheduled to report for induction into the military by his local draft board in Reserve, New Mexico. At their father's ranch near Quemado, Earl and his three brothers, Roy, 21, Walter, 28, and Jesse, 33, decided they would hide in the mountains of southwestern New Mexico to avoid going to the Army.

The Caudill posse, February 1944. Front row left to right: SA Eberle, SAC D.A. Bryce, SA Art Potter, SA Dudley Culp, Chief of NM State Police Frank Young, unknown NM state patrolman, SA Leo Uselding. Back row: unknown NM state patrolman, SA Don Johnson, 3 unknown NM state patrolmen. (photo courtesy of Don Eberle)

On October 7, 1943, the four brothers left Quemado in a pickup truck. After driving about 35 miles, the truck caught fire and they abandoned it, proceeding on foot into the rugged Escondido Mountains. Appropriately, in Spanish, Escondido means "hidden nest." Reaching an area known as Dark Canyon, they built a cleverly concealed dugout. Taking three days to build, the dugout was eight feet deep, eighteen feet long and twelve feet wide. It was covered with cedar poles which were then covered with dirt. A few days later, they built another dugout in Pretty Boy Floyd Canyon. The canyon, prophetically named as it turned out, had gotten its name because of a local legend that the late desperado once hid out there. This dugout was about 8 by 10 by 12 feet and similar in construction to the first. Both dugouts contained fireplaces and chimneys which were carefully concealed. They were comfortably stocked with bunks, bedding, clothing, home-canned foods, flour, salt, coffee, creamery butter, cooking and eating utensils, and guns and ammunition. They had still a third cave in Pretty Boy Floyd Canyon that was not roofed but consisted of a recess dug back into a cliff. This one was used when the weather was not severe because it gave them an excellent vantage point to see anyone who might try to enter the canyon.

Back home, many of the neighbors thought the boys had gone to the Army, that when Earl was called for induction, the other three had volunteered so they might all serve together.

Earl, Roy and Jesse were soon reported delinquent by their respective draft boards to the U.S. Attorney in Santa Fe for failure to appear for induction. A short time later, Walter was reported as delinquent for failing to report his change of address. The U.S. Attorney turned the matter over to the FBI's El Paso office which had jurisdiction for the area.

Agents looked into the matter and established information that the Caudills had fled to the mountains. All four brothers were well known for being excellent hunters, crack shots, expert woodsmen and knew those mountains like the back of their hands. The agents also got reports that the men were well armed, had no intention of being taken in and were well capable of covering their tracks with booby traps to discourage anyone pursuing them.

On February 3, 1944, two FBI agents and a New Mexico deputy sheriff went into the mountains with a guide who was a former peace officer. They had to go in by foot because the terrain was so rugged that horses couldn't make it. They proceeded through increasingly rugged terrain through areas known as Slaughter Canyon, Hell's Frying Pan, Leon Canyon and eventually into Pretty Boy Floyd Canyon. After climbing over three hours from an altitude of 7200 feet to 8700 feet in zero-degree weather and deep snow drifts, they found some human footprints. Following the prints for about half a mile, they found an area of well-trampled snow.

This area had a dozen antlered deer heads hanging in the pine trees and quarters of deer meat hanging from the branches. Cooking utensils were found hidden in the underbrush and a fireplace had been constructed of rocks nearby. They also found what they first thought was an old well but proved to be the cleverly concealed entrance to one of the dugouts.

The agents maintained a surveillance on the area while the deputy went back for food, clothing and to get additional help. On the afternoon of February 5, a posse of reinforcements arrived. The force now consisted of a dozen men, six FBI agents led by SAC Jelly Bryce and six New Mexico State Policemen led by their Chief, Frank Young.

A force conducting this type of search today might be expected to show up wearing denims, coveralls or military fatigues. Not Jelly Bryce. There he was in some of the roughest country in America's southwest, trimly turned out in dress slacks, a dark dress shirt with buttoned collar, a perfectly knotted fashionable necktie, snap-brim hat, waist-length leather jacket like General Eisenhower was making popular and carrying a clip-fed high-powered rifle.

Bryce contacted the boys' father and met him near the area with the other officers. Bryce pointed out the futility of his sons position and said that if he and his men had to hunt the boys down, they'd shoot first and ask questions later. The father said he'd bring the boys to his ranch if Bryce gave him some time. Bryce said he could have until the following morning.

Promptly at 9 A.M. on the morning of February 7, the father brought his four sons to the ranch where the officers were waiting. Bryce asked them if they had set any booby traps up the mountain and they admitted they had but said "they were only for wild game." Bryce told them they were all going back up the mountain and the boys were going to disarm all the traps. When the boys seemed hesitant, Bryce picked up a nearby tin can, threw it up in the air, drew with a blur and drilled it with one of his patented fast draw shots. As the boys sat there with their mouths hanging open, Bryce explained that he wanted them to make no unnecessary movements during the journey. They nodded mutely and started back up the mountain.

The Caudills pointed out several "trap guns" they had set up near their hideouts. They used .351 caliber cartridges and would have been deadly to unsuspecting travelers in the narrow trails and canyons. They also led the agents to a hidden fruit jar that acted as a post office where they left letters to communicate with their family.

The four boys pleaded guilty to violating the Selective Service Act and on March 13, 1944, were each sentenced to five years in prison. As Utopian as it sounds, one of the agents involved in this incident assures me that when the brothers were released after a year in jail, all four enlisted in the military and were later honorably discharged.

Don Eberle knew the FBI had a policy against interoffice fraternization that forbade agents dating female FBI employees in their offices. That didn't make much difference when he began to fall in love with one of the ladies in the El Paso office. He and Jean began dating as discreetly as they could but one night, they went in a restaurant in Juarez and guess who was sitting there? SAC Bryce and his date.

Bryce watched them for a few moments, then got up and came over to them, saying "Well, dammit, you're here so you might as well sit down." He was later the best man at their wedding.

One explanation for his leniency with Don Eberle would soon become apparent. He too was again becoming involved in affairs of the heart.

During the summer of 1944, Bryce himself was becoming infatuated with a lady. He met her while he was performing one of his shooting demonstrations in Roswell, New Mexico. Shirley Geraldine Bloodworth was originally from Chickasha, Oklahoma, barely fifty miles east of Mountain View. Her parents, John P. and Delona Owens Bloodworth, had relocated to Roswell. Born November 12, 1913, at 30 years of age she was almost seven years younger than her new beau. Strikingly beautiful, her dark complexion and long dark hair flowing straight down her back proudly proclaimed her American Indian heritage, offset by crystal blue eyes that showed the mixture of cultures. Word circulated around the FBI office that she was an Indian princess. Decades later, people who had met her only once remarked on her extraordinary beauty as their first overwhelming impression. Others described her as "an obviously high-class lady—glamorous—exotic-looking." She had the kind of beauty that turned men's heads everywhere she went but gave the impression of an innate shyness. One felt that she well knew the head's turned but was embarrassed by the attention.

On July 27, 1944, Delf and Shirley were married in the small town of Carrizozo, New Mexico, about a two-hour drive north of El

A family picnic around 1946 or 1947. Left to right: Shirley Bryce, Johnny Bryce, Jewell Hilbert (Smokey's wife), and Jelly Bryce. (photo courtesy of Tom Tate)

Paso on the edge of the Lincoln National Forest.

Bryce was popular and much appreciated by his men in El Paso. They remember him not only for his fairness and down-to-earth, occasionally self-deprecating sense of humor but his personality as a flamboyant showman, in and out of his shooting demonstrations. One of his agents said "He was a dapper and immaculate dresser when in the office, wore an eight-carat diamond ring on his left hand and drove a Cadillac automobile. He said he had the biggest diamond, the biggest automobile and the most tattered underwear of anyone in Oklahoma."

In late 1944, it was time for Bryce's career development to continue. In November, he was transferred to be in charge of the field office in San Antonio, Texas. Besides still being far enough south to have mild winters, it also had the advantage of being an hour's drive closer to his old home in Oklahoma. The primary event of his short time in San Antonio was that Shirley became pregnant.

As it turned out, the transfer was so short lived, it would hardly be worth unpacking his bags and the closer distance to home would be rendered inconsequential. After less than six months, in April of 1945, he was transferred back to Oklahoma City, this time as the FBI boss for the entire state. The title and position held considerably more prestige than it had when he had first joined the Bureau eleven years earlier or even in the four years he had been a SAC. In his short tenure with the Bureau, it had increased hugely in all respects. The FBI ended the war with 4,370 agents, 7,422 civilian support personnel and a $44 million annual budget, much more than a tenfold increase over the agency Bryce had joined barely a decade earlier.

With his penchant for the pleasantries of country living, at least as much as possible in the biggest city in the state, Bryce rented a house at 2500 Lake Shore Drive near Lake Overholser west of the city. That was where they were living when Shirley went into labor on the morning of August 22, 1945, two weeks overdue. Bryce drove her to Saint Anthony's Hospital and nine hours later, at 5:00 P.M. that afternoon, she gave birth to a healthy baby boy. In keeping with family tradition and in honor of Shirley and Delf's fathers, his two grandfathers, he was named John Fel Bryce.

On July 16, 1945, the world's first atomic bomb had been exploded only thirty miles due west of the small town of Carrizozo, New Mexico, where Delf and Shirley Bryce had been married. Within a few weeks the war was over, rationing of cars, gasoline, tires and other wartime essentials ended and the Bryce family soon followed the pattern of the rest of their generation. They moved to the suburbs and into a new house, almost literally this time. The street was even named for one of the heroes of the war.

Built in 1946 during the post-war building boom, it was located at 5308 North MacArthur Boulevard in the quiet little Oklahoma City suburb of Warr Acres. The attractive but modest exterior was a mottled gray and brown flagstone. The interior wasn't expansive, two bedrooms and two bathrooms, but it was large enough for them. A mile south was a major intersection with old Highway 66 where it turned into Northwest 39th Street and the Coronado Shopping Center provided easy access to shopping. The ten-mile trip to downtown wasn't prohibitive and it was an easy half-hour drive to the FBI office in the First National Building even in heavy traffic. The sale of the house was handled by an old bird-hunting buddy, Bob Graham.

Back in his home state, Bryce gradually introduced his new family to his old friends. In what was an obviously orchestrated move, Hilbert had returned to the OCPD from his FBI service on February 5, 1943. Skipping the rank of Captain, he was immediately promoted to Inspector (a title borrowed from the Bureau). It was the number two job in the Department, the old job of Night or Assistant Chief of Police having been abolished. Slightly over a month later, Frank Smith returned to the FBI and Hilbert was appointed Chief. Six months away from his fortieth birthday, Hilbert was the first OCPD Chief born in this century and the youngest man to occupy the office since statehood. Shirley Bryce would become extremely close to Smokey's wife, Jewell.

Bryce's old partner H.V. Wilder was now a Lieutenant in the Patrol Division and Mickey Ryan would soon be promoted to Lieutenant in charge of the OCPD's first specialized Robbery Squad.

These and many other friends would be frequent visitors to the house on North MacArthur. Predictably, most were professional law enforcement officers but there were a few others. One was Bob Graham, the realtor who had sold him the house and his young son. He recalled that Bryce had a miniature slot machine sitting on the coffee table in the living room and a toggle switch on the telephone that turned it into a direct line to the local FBI office. In the days before pagers and cellular phones, Bryce checked in with the office when he was going to be out of touch, telling them his destination and estimated time before he would return.

Another was Elmo Black, a dispatcher for the OHP whom Bryce had tried to recruit into the FBI. He remembered that the house was decorated in a western and American Indian motif, doubtlessly a touch applied by Shirley in deference to her heritage. Like most others, Black remarked about her beauty, her dark complexion and her long, dark hair. She was also renowned as a gracious host. On at least one social occasion, Bryce lovingly referred to her as "his squaw" but no one was fooled. Their devotion to each other showed and it was always obvious who was in charge of the house. When Shirley spoke, Delf jumped.

The marriage, like most others however, was not free of tensions. Other friends and relatives have described Shirley as "emotionally fragile—jealous—very possessive." Throughout the course of their lives together, she would allow no mention of Bryce's first two wives or his first son in her home. By all accounts, Bryce honored her wishes in this respect.

Many of Bryce's associates considered his feats of memory to equal those of his marksmanship. He developed a reputation for having an encyclopedic, if not photographic, memory. Several of his former agents said "he never forgot anything." Bob Gentry saw Bryce introduced to dozens of men at a law enforcement convention and afterwards recall all the names, putting the correct name with the correct face.

One new agent who served in the Oklahoma City office when Jelly was SAC got a rude introduction to his boss's memory as well as his direct, hands-on approach to law enforcement. While they were out one day, Bryce spotted a wanted bank robbery suspect sitting in a car. As Jelly prepared to arrest him,—the old "you take that side, I'll take this side" plan—the new agent, still thinking by the book, asked "Shouldn't we call for some backup?" Bryce looked at him with an expression of puzzlement and replied "Why? It's just one guy!" The guns were drawn and the arrest was made.

Like the agents in El Paso, Oklahoma City agents also became acquainted with Bryce's sometimes-mercurial temperament. Like most of us, sometimes his sense of humor worked and sometimes it didn't, probably depending upon the moment, the circumstances and the person.

At one point, the Oklahoma City office got some hand-me-down government cars from the Bureau's Chicago office. Bryce sent several agents on a train to Chicago to pick up the cars and drive them back to Oklahoma City. The other agents arrived but one agent did not. Several days later, the missing agent walked in Bryce's office and by way of explanation as to why he was late, dropped a broken crankshaft rod on his desk. That agent was destined for the lousiest assignments in the office for some time to come.

Another new agent got a little too familiar with his new boss. Bryce had an eight-ball mounted on a piece of marble on his desk. When he reported in for his first talk with the SAC, with Bryce looking across his desk at him with those unblinking eyes, the new agent joked "Who's behind the eight-ball, you or me?" The agent's answer was that he immediately went on a two-month road trip to "familiarize" himself with all areas of his new jurisdiction.

Sometimes the rules could be bent and sometimes they couldn't, depending upon which rule it was and who was doing the bending. The relative seriousness of the rule wasn't always the defining factor. Two instances will illustrate.

Oklahoma City usually has relatively mild winters with very few snowy days, therefore most residents aren't used to driving in snow. Even today, a few inches of snow that would hardly be noticed in Denver or Buffalo can easily paralyze Oklahoma City's traffic. One snowy winter morning, FBI Secretary Kathy Orr walked to work since she lived less than a mile away at the time. Typically, Bryce was already there.

That particular morning, she was in charge of the sign-in register where everyone had to record their comings and goings. At 8:15 A.M., Bryce came out of his office and checked the register. Ms. Orr told him that most of the agents hadn't gotten in yet because of the weather. Bryce drew a line across the register under the last name and said "By God, if I can get here on time, they should be able to." Everyone who reported for duty late that morning had to take an hour of annual leave to make up for their tardiness, some for being only a couple of minutes late.

Bryce was well known in all his assignments as an unrepentant stickler for punctuality, both coming and going. Anyone late for work was going to have to deal with Mr. Bryce and it was just as certain no one was going to leave early. As with the sign-in register, he would come out of his office when it approached 5:00 P.M. just to make sure the secretaries and stenographers didn't start putting the covers on their typewriters ten or fifteen minutes early. But Bryce adhered to his own standards in all respects. No one arrived earlier and no one stayed later than the boss.

On another occasion, Bryce had called a somewhat hot-tempered Tulsa agent down to his office to give a statement concerning a complaint that he had bodily thrown a man out of his office. The agent admitted that he had done that and said he felt justified in doing so. He told Bryce that the man was "a nut case", didn't have a legitimate complaint and wouldn't leave so he threw him out. Bryce regarded the agent with his cold, penetrating stare for a couple of minutes, silently judging either his truthfulness, the courage of his convictions or both. Then he spoke to his secretary, who was in the room to record the agent's statement, telling her to get the Director on the phone. She called Washington and got Hoover on the line. Bryce picked up the phone and briefly described the incident to Hoover, adding that he agreed with the justification. He then hung up and told the agent to report back to Tulsa. No reprimand, no censure, no ass-chewing, just "go back to work." Perhaps Bryce had a flashback to the man whose head he had driven into the wall of his El Paso office. If Bryce could be petty about things like tardiness, he could be understanding when the potential consequences were more important.

Besides his candor and sense of fairness, some of his employees experienced his dry sense of humor. Usually very formal and proper with his civilian employees, he would occasionally indulge in harmless practical jokes.

One junior Bureau secretary went to the wedding of another Bureau employee where a photographer was taking pictures. She had several pictures taken in various group shots. Not long afterwards, Bryce sternly called her into his office with no explanation. If this were not intimidating enough to the young girl, Bryce tossed several pictures on his desk and brusquely asked her for an explanation. They were the photos taken at the wedding but they showed her and several others holding drinks in their hands and bottles of liquor on the tables. Stammering, confused and scared, she tried to explain to her boss that there had been no drinking at the wedding party. Bryce then smiled wickedly and tossed another set of photos on the desk. These were the original photos. The photos had been delivered to Bryce and he had one set of them "doctored" by inserting the liquor bottles and drinks. The shaken secretary was then given her original, unretouched photos.

On another occasion, several of the secretaries were returning from their lunch hour when they met Bryce coming out of the First National Building. One spoke to him, saying "How are you, Mr. Bryce?" Bryce tersely replied "Worse." Without thinking, the girl immediately responded "Oh, Mr. Bryce, you couldn't possibly be worse." As they all caught their breath, he continued out of the building without comment.

Bryce occasionally had a penchant for using his employees for personal chores outside the scope of their employment. In Albuquerque, he prevailed upon an agent with a knowledge of electronics to fix his television once. In the Oklahoma City office, he had a secretary sew up a torn lining in a suit coat. Such was the unstated power of a SAC. Nevertheless, it is indicative that even among those who had some negative experiences with Bryce, they respected and liked him personally.

VIII
The Eyes of a Killer

Philosophers would have us believe that the eyes tell us who we are. The Sixteenth Century French poet Guillaume du Bartas called them "the windows of the soul." Three centuries later, Ralph Waldo Emerson modified it slightly by saying they showed "the antiquity of the soul." About the same time, the American writer Elbert Hubbard called them "the peepholes into the consciousness."

On the other hand, scientists would have us believe the eyes show us what we are or rather what we have become as a result of evolution and experience. The prey animals of this world—the rabbits, squirrels, horses, cattle, sheep—have eyes on the sides of their heads, giving them a wide field of vision so they can see potential danger in all directions without moving their heads much. The trade-off for this is some lack of depth perception and distance judgement. As a matter of basic survival, it is more important for the rabbit to see the hawk circling above him or the wolf moving up behind him than to be able to accurately judge how far it is away from him.

Predators, on the other hand, have their eyes closer together and facing directly forward. With fewer natural enemies than the prey animals, it is more important to their survival to be able to judge the distance between themselves and their intended prey. This is not only true of tigers and wolves but also domesticated animals that are still predators in their basic nature like dogs and cats.

Try staring at your dog or cat for a short period of time. The animal will quickly become unsettled, even though it might be perfectly comfortable and normally unafraid around you. Predators, by nature, use their eyes to scan their surroundings, taking in most of their visual information through their peripheral vision. They only look at something directly when it gains their interest, is perceived as a threat or a source of food. Animals interpret direct eye contact as a sign of hostility or aggression.

Anthropologists note that our eyes are close together and face forward in our heads. Man is, by nature, a predator, a hunter, a meat eater. Even though advances in our civilization have made that part of our nature largely unnecessary, it is still in our genes.

Police officers and criminals often use those traits to recognize

The eyes of Jelly Bryce through four decades
"...cold...hard...cut right through you...the eyes of a killer..."

one another. Professional criminals have said that is one way they can always spot a cop. Walk down a busy street in a large city and try to make direct eye contact with every person you pass. Among the furtive, nervous glances, some will avoid eye contact at almost any cost. Most will hold it for only a fraction of a second. A cop and a crook will react differently. They will look at the hands first, because they are what can hold the things that harm you. Then they will look you directly in the eye and hold the eye contact. They are assessing the threat to themselves. The crook is looking for signs he has been recognized and the cop is performing the additional function of running the face through his mental record bureau, trying to match the face to past arrests and wanted posters.

When you talk to people about someone they knew in the past and ask them to describe them, if they knew the person intimately, they start the description with statements about their personal qualities. If they knew them less intimately, they will start the description with statements about the person's most impressive physical attributes.

With Shirley Bryce, the first words are usually about her overwhelming physical beauty. With Delf Bryce, it is usually his eyes.

His eyes would seem to be the focus of most initial observations because anyone who ever saw him shoot couldn't help but realize that this man's vision was far better than average. Most people's vision begins to weaken near their fortieth year. In Jelly Bryce's annual FBI physicals from age 27 to age 50, his vision was always a perfect 20/20. In fact it may have been even better. Optometrists say that it is impossible to measure beyond 20/10.

Other writers have written stories concerning the purported extraordinary vision of some men, men whose success or survival depended upon their vision. It has been said that baseball legend Ted Williams could read the label of a phonograph record spun through the air and pilot Chuck Yeager could spot German fighter planes 50 miles away. Bryce once told former agent Bob Oswalt that he could actually see a bullet leave the barrel of a gun and follow its trajectory to the target. Others have said that a decade after his retirement and regimen of giving firearms demonstrations, in his sixties, Bryce could still demonstrate the same level of skill as he had in his prime. One writer compared him to "an aging Samurai (who had) transcended the need for practice of any kind."

But there was a lot more to Jelly Bryce's eyes. Emerson's quote about "the antiquity of the soul" comes to mind.

Bob Wilder, the son of Bryce's old partner H.V. Wilder, described them as "a clear, vivid blue—but cold, hard. They'd cut right through you." One of Smokey Hilbert's nephews described him as having "the aura of a killer." An agent who served under him in Oklahoma City said he had "the eyes of a killer." Another agent called them "chilling— piercing— penetrating..." Another remarked that Bryce could discomfit almost anyone just by looking at them. Even among friends and colleagues, his stare was a habitual, cold, calculating threat assessment. It was uncomfortable to those who knew him because they couldn't help but factor in the unspecific but general knowledge of what those eyes had seen and this man's proven capability for deadly violence. It was especially chilling for those who didn't know him as well because of the primal danger signals it sent out. Sort of like looking in a caged tiger's eyes in a zoo and facing the sudden realization of what might happen if that cage wasn't separating the two of you.

Bryce's eyes were like the tiger's. As far as he was concerned, he was just looking, watching. From his perspective, they didn't threaten. They didn't have to.

More than once, at relaxed dinners or meetings among law enforcement colleagues, Jelly Bryce would tell stories about killings colored with the veteran law enforcement officer's black sense of humor. He told one of a search for a local fugitive while he was with the OCPD. The fugitive was traced to a gambling game going on in the basement of a house. As the officers crashed through the door, the man drew a gun and fired at the officers. Naturally several of the officers returned the fire and the man was riddled with bullets.

Once the smoke cleared, they dragged the body outside and propped him up against a tree. All of the officers looked at the man but none could be positive he was the fugitive they had been after. One got the idea to take a photo of him, have it developed and take it to the man's mother to get a positive identification. Since he was riddled with bullets, they covered him from the neck down with a sheet borrowed from a nearby house.

Taking the photo and getting it developed in the police photo lab, some of the officers took the photo to the fugitive's mother's house. They showed her the picture and asked her if that was her son. She said it was but asked why he had the sheet around him. As they were leaving, the officers told her it was because he was cold. The table erupted in laughter and moved on to the next war story.

From the beginning of his career until his death, Jelly Bryce was notoriously reticent about talking about his own adventures, especially the killings in which he had been involved. In telling these stories, like most officers, Jelly Bryce was much more likely to tell stories of events he had witnessed or learned about from the participants or other witnesses.

A number of the people I talked with got the unspoken impression that Bryce was bothered somewhat by the people he had killed. Few of them ever broached the subject with him and he rarely spoke about it with any of them. From what I have learned about him, I doubt he would have ever discussed it with his wives, children or family members. He may have talked about it with his closest personal friends like H.V. Wilder, Smokey Hilbert, Clarence Hurt or Mickey Ryan, men of similar backgrounds and experiences, who had walked in his shoes. But again, I doubt it. Jelly Bryce was too introspective, too self-contained for that to be either necessary or beneficial.

I have known many men who have killed, either in war or police work. I have known many more who have crossed the divide of making the decision to take a human life and have tried to kill, unsuccessful only by an accident of marksmanship. Some adjusted to it better than others and some adjusted remarkably well. Some of the former were very shaken by the experience. Some of the latter were shaken by the realization that they were capable of emotions and actions that they had not faced about themselves previously. Most were resentful that they had been forced into those actions. None actually enjoyed it. About the best that any of them could say was "I'm glad he's dead and I'm alive." That's not the same as enjoying it, even when there was a realiza-

Jelly Bryce, 1953 (photo courtesy of Ray Kissiah)

tion that some final justice had been done, even though inadvertently.

During his career, whenever Bryce was asked by reporters if he had ever been forced to shoot a man in the line of duty, he always replied "No comment." When asked if he tried to bring his prisoners in alive, he said he was more concerned with bringing himself back alive.

Although he never heard the term, Jelly Bryce almost certainly suffered from a certain amount of Post Traumatic Stress Syndrome. In his world and in his time, you didn't get counseling, therapy, medication or sympathy for it. You either went into another line of work or you lived with it and went on with your life and career. He once privately remarked to a friend that he didn't think anyone could take another person's life, even to protect another's, and ever sleep well again.

One example that Bryce's attitude toward his shooting skills was based on survival and not showmanship was his ever-vigilant paranoia. Without doubt, the man had made many dangerous enemies in his time and he always took them seriously. It might be unwise not to and only one misjudgment could be fatal. Even in his leisure time, after retirement and right up to his death, no one can ever remember a time when a gun was more than arm's reach away from Jelly

Bryce. Even with as much shooting as he did, Bryce never allowed anyone else to clean his guns.

His reflexes were also a constant. His agents universally described him as "quick—fidgety—lots of nervous energy—his hands were never still—always moving—always walked, talked, moved, thought and acted quickly—." His movements had a natural stealth about them also. More than one former employee told of being startled by Bryce. They would be standing alone in the office and "suddenly he was just there," standing next to them. Obviously he had long since learned the advantage of not advertising his movements to people he was approaching, always giving himself the advantage of surprise, and it had developed into an automatic response.

Regardless of where he went and under all circumstances, he made it a point to always sit with his back to a wall and never to an open room or doorway. In any room, he would always seek out the seat farthest from the front door with the widest field of view. If he went in a restaurant and there were no seats available like that, he would leave without seating himself. His friend Elmo Black once visited him in his office and, as a game, tried to subtly get behind him. Every time Black would try to sidle out of his peripheral vision, Bryce kept automatically turning to keep facing him. Even in the most secure locations surrounded only by friends and colleagues, it was an ingrained, unconscious habit.

The habits didn't relax at home, either. Realtor Bob Graham once went to Bryce's home on North MacArthur. Ringing the front door bell, he waited for a few seconds. He was startled when Bryce spoke behind him. Bryce had gone out the back door, circled around the house and come up behind him in total silence.

On their hunting trips, Graham noted that Bryce always had a second pistol in the glove box of the car. After one lunch they had at the Huckins Hotel, Graham noted that Bryce's suit didn't seem to fit him as fastidiously as usual. Bryce showed him that he was wearing a bulletproof vest that day. They walked outside and four FBI agents in a car with a whip antenna on the trunk pulled up to pick him up. Bryce casually mentioned that he'd recently "had some threats." Graham noted that during these periods, Bryce usually surrounded himself with a select clique of agents from his office, men that he had the utmost confidence in, men he could count on in any circumstances or situation. These usually included John Rice, Wilson "Skip" McCully and Weldon "Spot" Gentry.

Bryce was also extremely paranoid about his enemies seeking

vengeance upon his family. In the early City Directories, he was boldly listed at his addresses as "city detective" or "police officer." Later as an FBI agent, he was still listed but under the demure occupation of "salesman." In the 1948 Directory, he is listed on North MacArthur as "Special Agent in Charge-FBI." From 1949 on, he is totally absent from the Directories.

As an additional precaution, he always carried a shotgun in the trunk of his car, even into retirement. This was a personal weapon, not issued by the FBI. It was a Number O Riot Grade Remington Model 10 twelve-gauge pump shotgun with a twenty-inch barrel specially engineered to fire buckshot rounds. The serial number, U68713, is stamped just forward of the loading port in the bottom of the receiver. A well-worn but also well-cared-for walnut stock ends in a thick rubber recoil pad. A magazine extension under the barrel allowed it to hold six shells instead of the normal four, not counting one in the chamber. This particular model was only manufactured between 1907 and 1929 but this one is even rarer than that indicates.

One of the earlier models, this one was made in 1910. Its original price was $27. It appears to be made of stainless steel but it is actually only the natural patina of the metal with not a single speck of the original bluing remaining. With only a small bead front sight and none at the rear, it is obviously intended as a point-and-shoot weapon. The sides of the receiver are totally smooth, the normal stampings absent. The only other stampings on the weapon are the "Remington Arms Company" and patent dates on top of the receiver.

The legend behind the gun is that only ten like it were made, especially for the Oklahoma State Penitentiary. Although neither the OSP nor Remington Arms can verify this, it is very definitely a special shotgun, unlike any I've ever seen before. With its short barrel, magazine extension and bead sight, it is also obviously not meant for hunting—unless you're hunting men.

A feature of the weapon that didn't require modification was that if you held the trigger back, the gun would fire every time you slid the pump action forward and chambered a shell. Therefore the only limitations on how fast it could fire was how fast the shooter could pump the slide. It was this type of action that allowed Jelly Bryce to outshoot automatic shotguns every time.

On one occasion while he was the SAC in Oklahoma City, Jelly had to go out to Tinker Air Force Base in Midwest City. In the Cold War of the Fifties, security at military bases was taken very seriously. At the main gate, the Air Force Policeman on duty asked him to open his trunk. He did and the AP was aghast when he saw a shotgun, a 30-06 rifle and a Thompson submachine gun in the trunk. He said "You can't bring all those weapons on this base!" Bryce showed the AP his identification and said "Yes, I can." And he did.

When Bryce was living in the house on his 80 acres southwest of Mountain View, he told people that he had his favorite chair in the living room situated in such a manner so that, by using strategically placed mirrors on the walls, he could view every entry into the room.

After buying one of the first commercially available microwave ovens in the early 1970's, Bryce was trying to cook an egg in it when the egg exploded. Bryce said that when he heard the unfamiliar "pop", he thought someone had gotten into the house and shot at him.

Only a few years before his death, while living in his final home at 600 South Fourth Street in Mountain View, Bryce approached a neighbor and asked to see his automatic garage door opener. The neighbor was somewhat surprised since Bryce was not usually the neighborly type. Prior contacts had given the neighbor the impression that Bryce was a gruff, stand-offish man with a very hard exterior. He attributed this to Bryce's background in law enforcement. Nevertheless, he showed Bryce the garage door opener and let him operate it.

When asked about his interest, Bryce explained that when he got out of his car to manually open his garage door, he "couldn't imagine being in a more exposed position." The neighbor thought that was being excessively careful especially in their small, peaceful hamlet but figured "maybe the man had made a lot of enemies."

After Bryce's death, while inventorying the possessions in his home, relatives found a loaded sawed off shotgun behind the night stand next to his bed.

IX
Shooter

Bryce's original recruitment and entry into the Bureau had been directly related to his combat shooting ability. Those talents had originally been exploited as a member of the Bureau's "special squad" going after extraordinarily dangerous criminals. But his firearms talents were not only for use in the field.

His original interests in firearms and marksmanship as a boy had been rooted in hunting. In a sense, Bryce had been giving firearms demonstrations nearly all his life. They just started with spontaneity around friends.

Smokey Hilbert's wife's nephew, Tom Tate, recalls a hunting trip when he was a boy. Hilbert and Bryce used to hunt rabbits on Hilbert's farm in Harrah, east of Oklahoma City. They used pistols and the objective was to hit the rabbit in the head so the shot didn't spoil the meat. He remembered Bryce shooting one rabbit and when Tate went to fetch it back, he showed them that the rabbit was shot in the head. He recalls Bryce was displeased because he "was aiming at his eye."

On another occasion years later, Bryce and some FBI agents went to visit OHP Trooper Jack Roberts at his rural acreage in far northeast Oklahoma City. Roberts invited them to stay for dinner, saying they'd have fried chicken, gesturing toward the chickens running around in the front yard. Bryce agreed, walked out on the front porch, drew a .22 pistol and fired four shots. Four chickens lay dead in the yard, each hit in the head. That was only one of many instances in which witnesses noted that Bryce seemed to have a gun for every occasion with him.

Other friends remember that Bryce's phenomenal eye-hand coordination wasn't limited to firearms. With a rod and reel, he could also drop a fly in any spot in the water with unerring accuracy. Bryce brushed it off, saying it was a "God-given talent."

He once attended a gun show with another FBI agent and stopped to look at a crossbow. Saying he'd never seen one before, Bryce asked the vendor to show him how it worked. After a few minutes of handling it, Bryce asked the man if he could try it out. The vendor agreed and Bryce walked outside with it. Loading the crossbow with an arrow, Bryce threw an apple up in the air and skewered it with the arrow on the first try.

From the very beginning of his career, Bryce was periodically recalled to Quantico, Virginia, to participate in matches for the Bureau's pistol team and teach new agents as part of the Firearms Training Group. He would attain legendary status in these assignments, tales of his prowess repeated long after his retirement. He was a member of the Bureau's elite "Possible Club", marksmen who had shot the maximum possible score on the pistol course. Bryce's personal innovations also made inroads into firearms training. He had long since modified his own personal holster. He showed it to his step-brother Raymon Kasbaum and they had discussed Bryce's reasons for the modifications.

The belt hole was smaller in the back and larger in the front. This gave the holster and the gun a natural forward tilt. There was no thumb-break or retaining strap. Kasbaum noticed that the holster pivoted very loosely on the belt and it looked like the gun could have easily fallen out. Bryce admitted the holster "didn't have a real good hold on (the gun)" and that "you had to be real careful with it." Bryce said that the purpose of the modifications were, naturally, for the holster not to impede drawing the gun quickly and the belt hole arrangement was so the motion of the hand was altered from up and down to front and back. The hand didn't come up, grab the gun, draw it out upwards and then point it forward. Instead the hand literally slapped the gun backwards and it rocked backwards out of the holster, pointing forward the instant it cleared the holster. Then, if an extremely quick shot was necessary, the trigger could be pulled as soon as the gun reached horizontal. If necessary, the gun could be fired with the muzzle even with the shooter's side without taking the extra fraction of a second to extend it forward. If followup shots were necessary, they could be accomplished while extending the gun forward. But, as Bryce had proven in combat situations before, the first shot was all-important. Bryce revolutionized the Bureau's fire-arms training and taught them his method for drawing quickly. This became a standard technique taught to all Bureau agents.

His unique abilities were also rapidly utilized for demonstrations to law enforcement officers. The first mention of his firearms-related duties in his FBI file is a letter from Hoover on October 14, 1935, barely eleven months after he joined. Sent to Bryce's office in Chicago, it included a medal awarded by the National Rifle Association to the Bureau's pistol team for competing in the Police Pistol

Matches at Camp Perry, Ohio, the previous September. The rest of his file is peppered with commendations from Hoover for firearms demonstrations given to groups as diverse as the International Association of Identification, the International Chiefs of Police, the FBI National Police Academy, Boy Scout Troops and the Rio Grande Valley Mayors and City Officials Association. These demonstrations weren't always at Headquarters and even extended internationally. Two were specifically for exhibitions given in Mexico City and Monterey, Mexico. One commendation was for continuing an exhibition in a downpour of rain.

The exhibitions didn't cease with his promotion to a supervisory position. On the contrary, no longer burdened with a regular agent's daily caseload, their number and frequency increased.

As previously noted, the position of Special Agent in Charge of a FBI field office was and remains a position of unique responsibility. During the tenure of J. Edgar Hoover, it was even more. Every local SAC was envisioned as Hoover's personal, hand-picked representative of the Bureau and all things relating to it in that area of the country, quite literally Hoover's alter ego. An inherent part of that job was public relations, simultaneously propagating, protecting, defending and extending the FBI's public image.

One of the young agents who left the Bureau on military leave during Wold War II was Cartha "Deke" DeLoach. He joined the Navy to see action. Turning down his request for combat duty, the Navy instead assigned him to a Naval Air Station in Norman, Oklahoma. While stationed there, he naturally visited and became acquainted with the local SAC, Jelly Bryce.

Although "just another young agent" to Bryce, DeLoach recalls him as a man of "stern visage, reserved personality and not very talkative." He recalls that Bryce "reluctantly" gave shooting demonstrations for various law enforcement and civic groups. At that time, SAC's were required to participate in a certain number of public speaking engagements each year to various groups. Bryce disliked public speaking, something he overcame and became quite polished at later. Firearms demonstrations counted towards his required quota of speeches so they were substituted whenever possible. DeLoach also recalls that, in a more practical use of his talents, Bryce insisted on personally participating in all raids and dangerous arrests, not because of Hoover's directives and "not for glory, but (because he) loved the challenge."

Following his discharge from the Navy and return to the Bureau,

DeLoach would complete a stellar career, becoming the Number Three man in the FBI in the 1960's and a close personal confidant of President Lyndon Johnson.

As a senior member of the Bureau and one who had shown himself worthy of promotion and leadership, another of a SAC's regularly expected duties was to make suggestions to improve policies, procedures and operations in the Bureau. Bryce made a number during his tenure in each office and a number were related to his expertise with firearms. One suggested the Practical Pistol Course (PPC) taught to agents be modified to include shooting from sitting, standing and prone positions. These modifications were adopted by many police agencies including his alma mater, the OCPD. This version of the PPC was taught to fledgling police officers well into the 1970's. Another suggested a method for improving the efficiency of firing ranges by the construction of collapsible barricades.

There are many disadvantages and opposing dichotomies in law enforcement. One of them involves carrying a gun. Police officers have to gauge their actions toward suspects as though they are unarmed until they see evidence to the contrary. It is almost the equivalent of the old principle of "letting the other guy draw first", a principle fostered more by Hollywood than the actual gunmen of the Old West. When trying to arrest an unarmed suspect, the suspect will sometimes try to grab the officer's gun so lawmen are taught to be aware that they might be providing a weapon to an unarmed suspect. To this day, several officers are killed every year in this manner.

Some officers become obsessed with the idea of having their own weapon used against them and individual officers have reacted to this problem with various strategies. Some carry a backup weapon concealed in a pocket, shoulder holster, ankle holster or in a boot. At least one officer used to carry his exposed holster weapon unloaded while his backup gun was loaded. His theory was if someone grabbed his weapon out of his holster, he'd draw the loaded backup. The problem with that tactic was remembering to go for the backup instead of the automatic reaction to draw the holster weapon when confronted by one of those instantaneous emergency situations that crop up now and then in police work. Sometimes you don't have time to think, just react. That's where training comes in and you're trained to draw from your holster.

Another officer carried his holster weapon with the first chamber empty and the other five loaded. He figured if a suspect grabbed it and pulled the trigger, the "click" on the empty chamber would give him time to draw his backup weapon. This was predicated upon the assumption that the suspect would only pull the trigger once or that the officer could draw his backup and fire before the suspect could pull the trigger again.

Another officer used to carry a .357 Magnum revolver with the first chamber loaded with a low-powered .38 "wadcutter" or target ammunition and the other five chambers with full power .357 hollow point bullets. He figured that the lower powered round would wound him less severely than a hollow point round and give him time to draw his backup weapon. One problem with that is the assumption that the suspect would be satisfied with shooting him only once. Another is the fact that, depending on where it hits, a wadcutter can be just as deadly as a hollow point.

In the summer of 1944, Bryce became aware that some agents were carrying .357 Magnum pistols loaded with a mixture of Magnum ammunition and lower powered .38 caliber loads. On his own initiative, he personally ran tests of a Magnum pistol loaded with five Magnum rounds and one .38 round. He found that the heavier recoil from the Magnum rounds jarred the bullet loose from the .38 round, jamming the pistol's cylinder and preventing it from turning, effectively locking the gun up.

He referred this problem to the Firearms Instructors at Quantico for further testing and possible dissemination to other police agencies throughout the country. Bryce's suggestions weren't just bureaucratic toadying or ticket-punching. They were original, well-considered and useful. Some were even prophetic. Less than a year after Bryce forwarded his Magnum test to Headquarters, an agent was disarmed by a suspect and shot with his own weapon. Luckily he survived but Bryce took the occasion to fire off another suggestion to Headquarters.

It seems the agent had his suit coat off and was in shirt sleeves at the time his gun was taken from him. Bryce was convinced that the agent's weapon was more easily accessible to the suspect because the agent's coat was off. Bryce had made it a rule in every office he supervised that agents had to keep their coats on and their weapons covered when on field assignments. The only place they could remove their coats was in the office and then only if their weapon was locked in the desk. That would become dangerous in the future but this was before the days when deranged people charged into police stations or federal offices spraying bullets. He recommended that it be made a Bureau-wide policy and shortly afterwards, it was.

Near the end of World War II started the heyday of Bryce's firearms demonstrations and was, to some degree, his own fault. Truth be known, he was probably trying to accomplish the exact opposite.

On April 15, 1944, he forwarded another suggestion to Headquarters. In it, he suggested that the Bureau's firearms instructors "be on the alert for potential trick shot artists" within the agent force. The proposal was to train "15 or 20" of them so they "could fulfill all the requests from Quarterly Police Conferences and State Conferences, etc. for exhibition shooters." In other words, one is led to suspect that Bryce was saying that he was doing too many of these shows and wanted some help.

In every suggestion, the SAC had to provide a list of both advantages and disadvantages in adopting it. The advantages he listed were that it would increase all agents interest in firearms and would also tend to convince people that all FBI agents could shoot that well. It was the two disadvantages he listed that were his undoing. One was contradictory to established policy and the other was too truthful.

In the first, he said that "the Bureau should not get into the habit of trying to publicize that kind of shooting." Obviously the Bureau, meaning Mr. Hoover, already felt that they should or Bryce wouldn't have been doing so much of it for the last decade. If any agent did anything that generated publicity, for himself or the Bureau, and did it more than once, it was an accepted fact that it had the Director's approval.

The second disadvantage and its honesty sealed his fate, although if he had omitted it, he wouldn't have been concealing anything the administration didn't already know. He said "There is not one man in a hundred, although good shots, that can get up and really put on a demonstration and do it in a professional manner." The Bureau already knew that and they already had their man. Jelly Bryce.

In the fall of 1945, Jelly Bryce was in New York on official business. His old friends from El Paso, Don and Jean Eberle, had since been transferred to the New York office. While he was there, Bryce looked them up. He cajoled Jean into going shopping for him to pick up a present for his son's first Christmas, explaining it "just wasn't his thing."

In late 1945, Life Magazine was starting its ninth year as America's premier picture magazine. Published weekly, it sold on the newsstands for ten cents a copy or you could subscribe to it for $4.50 a year. The cover of Life told you what or who was happening in that particular week. By mid-November, millions of people across America knew what Jelly Bryce had been doing in New York.

The issue of November 12 of that year featured actress Ingrid Bergman on the cover. Her cover was the result of successes in three big movies that year; Saratoga Trunk, Alfred Hitchcock's Spellbound and Bell's of St. Mary's. She had been the lead actress in 1943's Best Picture, the classic Casablanca, and was nominated for Best Actress for her work in For Whom The Bell Tolls. In 1944, she had won the Best Actress Oscar for Gaslight and would get her third consecutive Best Actress nomination for Bells of St. Mary's which would also be nominated for Best Picture. Her six-page spread may have been the biggest article in the magazine but it wasn't the lead article.

The first 11 pages trumpeted the victory of the capitalist system and an end to wartime rationing and austerity to avid consumers with advertisements from B.F. Goodrich, A&P Coffee and the new 1946 Oldsmobile with Hydra-Matic Drive (There's not even a clutch pedal in the car!).

Turning to page 12, under the bold headline "SPEAKING OF PICTURES...G-MAN CAN DRAW A GUN FASTER THAN YOU CAN READ THIS", the reader's eye was caught by something they wouldn't expect in America's premier picture magazine...blurred photographs. Photos of a handsome man, nattily dressed in a suit with vest and tie but still blurred.

They were stroboscopic time-lapse photos taken by Gjon Mili. The first, covering a full page, showed Delf Bryce dropping a silver dollar at forehead level and drawing his gun with the same hand before the coin dropped to waist level. The photo on page 13, nearly as big as the first, showed three superimposed photos of Bryce drawing over the caption "Delf Bryce shoots from crouching position, uses footwork of basketball player to aim both body and gun. He draws in two fifths of a second." They erred slightly by saying that he had "spent nine of his 39 years on the Oklahoma City police force."

The short narrative labeled Bryce as "the FBI agent most likely to live longest." Admitting that the speed of famous gunmen such as Billy the Kid had never been measured, they theorized that "Mr. Bryce could easily have outdrawn them." Bryce was touted as the best of the FBI's 4,000 marksmen, doubtlessly an overblown compliment to the other 3,999 when comparing his talents to theirs. They had Bryce explain his revolutionizing the FBI technique. He oversimplified by saying the old style "was a four-count draw: one, reach for the gun; two, pull gun from holster; three, aim gun. The fourth move was to fire, but the man wasn't alive anymore by that time."

Bryce had simplified the training to a one-count, "swooping, circular motion."

The two final photos on page 15 showed Bryce in his crouched position, facing his target head-on "so he will fall forward if he is hit (and) can keep right on shooting." They also said that Bryce still takes short pistol courses in which he concentrated on "maiming instead of killing." They said the FBI had only killed 23 men in 100,000 arrests. The last photo showed Bryce's man-sized silhouette target with all six rounds grouped tightly in the center of body mass, what cops refer to as the "X-ring or ten-ring" for the number of points given for each hit in this area.

The article was obviously a positive public relations piece. Just as obviously, it would never have happened without the full personal approval of Mr. Hoover. It concluded by stating vaguely that Bryce "is a special agent in the Southwest (and) spends much of his time instructing other FBI gunmen."

Less than four months later, Bryce would get his own cover story. The Picture Post magazine of March 2, 1946, featured another stroboscopic photo on Bryce on the cover under the byline "Quickest Man on the Draw".

Flash forward half a century. The skills that Jelly Bryce used to stay alive have been turned into a sport. There is even a World Fast Draw Association for aficionados. The champions in that sport have bested Bryce's draw-and-fire times by several thousandths of a second but it's a lot different. It's as different from a gunfight as sport karate is from a man fighting for his life.

The sport version uses specially modified holsters and they would never consider drawing from under a suit coat. There are cutaway holsters that just barely hold the gun and swivel holsters that allow the gun to be rotated and fired from the hip without even drawing it. They also used modified single-action revolvers, ones that must have the hammer cocked before they can fire. These revolvers can also be "fanned" for faster shooting. Bryce's double-action revolvers must have the trigger pulled every time they fire.

Other modifications include replacing the barrels with ones of aluminum to reduce the gun's weight and reshaping the hammer to allow easier, faster cocking. The barrel replacement is possible because these guns aren't intended to fire real bullets. They use specially loaded ammunition, blanks and wax bullets. The wax bullets are fired at steel plates for distances up to fifteen feet. The plates vary from fourteen to thirty inches in size. The blanks are loaded with an extra-large charge of gunpowder, so much that all the powder cannot be burned when the gun is fired. These rounds act like shotguns, blasting a cloud of unburned powder grains at targets that usually consist of balloons in diameters of four or nine inches, usually from distances of eight to twelve feet. At that range, the blank cartridge charge expands to the diameter of a dinner plate.

Jelly Bryce's draw was timed at four-tenths of a second and that was during a demonstration, not under combat conditions or in a real life-or-death situation. He always used live ammunition, both in his work and his demonstrations. Blanks and wax bullets are nowhere comparable in either blast, power or recoil, all of which make aiming more difficult. Not to mention that balloons don't shoot back at you and there is nothing on the line beyond winning or losing a contest.

A policeman once said it was very hard for a policeman to impress other policemen and he was right. Jelly Bryce impressed an awful lot of veteran policemen with his shooting. The civilians and non-shooters in his audiences must have been nothing less than astounded. Over time, his exhibitions became more polished and witnesses still speak of them with awe many decades later.

His early demonstrations were usually conducted with a .38 pistol, a twelve gauge shotgun and a .220 Swift rifle. The Swift .220 was a caliber, not the brand name of a rifle. It was a so-called "varmint" rifle meant for hunting crows, coyotes, prairie dogs and woodchucks, not big game. The cartridge was developed by Winchester in 1935. It was essentially a six-millimeter rifle casing necked down to .22 caliber. Using a 50 or 55 grain bullet, it was a long shell containing a lot of powder. Try to envision a 30-06 shell with a .22 bullet in it, almost the precursor of the .223 round developed for the later M-16 rifle.

This gave the bullet a very high muzzle velocity, over 4100 feet per second, four or five times faster than the average pistol round. It was the fastest factory-produced sporting round ever manufactured and had the flattest trajectory. Besides making it one of the most accurate cartridges in history, the tremendous speed also caused the bullet to completely disintegrate on its first contact with a target. This was supposed to eliminate the possibility of ricochets and, while it didn't totally eliminate them, it did minimize them considerably. Simply stated, this made the bullet get to the point you were aiming at very soon after you pulled the trigger. Typical three-shot groups at a distance of one hundred yards usually measured less than three-quarters of an inch, the size of a penny.

Bryce would hold his arms out in front of him at shoulder level, an unloaded pump shotgun lying on his outstretched palms. Three clay pigeons would be balanced on the stock and he would hold three rounds in his left hand. He would flip the three targets up in the air, load the shotgun and shoot all three targets before they hit the ground. In later years, he increased the number of clay pigeons to five, having a spectator or another agent throw the additional two into the air at the same time he threw his. And he would get all five before they landed.

Bryce always favored pump shotguns over automatics. Accuracy aside, he said he could shoot a pump shotgun faster than another man could use an automatic and proved it on more than one occasion. If you were familiar with firearms, it wasn't any mystery, just basic physics. An automatic can only fire as fast as the gas from the fired shell pushes the slide back, ejects the expended shell and slides forward to load a new one. There isn't anything an individual shooter can do to speed up that process. Bryce also had his pump shotguns specially modified. If you stood one up vertically resting on its butt, the slide would just fall back to the open position with no resistance. Thus the only thing controlling how fast it could be loaded and fired was Bryce's reactions. This explanation of the mechanics of the operation takes nothing away from the feat.

Ed Clark provides more memories of Jelly's firearms abilities. A former OCPD officer who was largely responsible for the modernization of the OCPD Training Division, he later became Chief of Police in the Oklahoma City suburb of Nichols Hills. Clark is an extraordinary shot himself, attended many periodic shooting matches in Stringtown with Bryce and used to perform firearms demonstrations contemporaneously with Bryce but never really enjoyed doing them because he didn't savor the attention.

He was unlike Bryce in that respect, he recalls. By that time, Bryce was relaxed and very much at home in front of crowds. Clark describes him as "a first-class showman." Contrary to his earlier days, Bryce eventually also became an accomplished and entertaining speaker. In his speaking engagements before law enforcement groups, the talk was usually pretty rough. There were virtually no women in law enforcement then so the profanity wasn't out of place.

His speeches almost always centered upon his expertise in combat shooting and were usually a combination of good advice punctuated with humor. Many men can still remember quotes from them;

—"Never shoot to wound—only to kill."

—"Aim for the belt buckle. If you hit anywhere in that area, it'll take him down."

—"If you can reliably hit a man-sized target at ten yards, you can shoot with anyone in this business."

—"The loudest sound you'll ever hear in a gunfight is the hammer falling on an empty chamber."

—"If you run out of ammo, don't reload—use the gun as a quirt to whip yourself in the ass and get the hell out of there."

—"It's good to have a partner because sometimes you need a reliable witness."

He would contrast the ways everyone is taught to shoot, either in law enforcement or the military, and the differences in combat shooting. He would discourse on the merits of jerking a trigger as opposed to squeezing it smoothly, the effect that had upon your point of aim and when it mattered or not. In a pistol match, it might mean the difference between getting ten points and no points. In a gunfight, when it meant the difference between hitting a man in the stomach or the chest, it was just more important to hit him—first. He disliked automatic pistols and considered them unreliable. It always took two hands to clear a jammed or misfired round in an automatic. In a revolver, you just had to pull the trigger again. Those fractions of a second could cost you a trophy in a match. In a gunfight with another man, they could cost you a lot more.

During one demonstration held for a class of new agents at Quantico, one of the fledgling agents asked Bryce how much chance he thought some of the Old West's famous gunmen would have had against him in a gunfight. Bryce's reply was "About as much chance as a one-legged man in an ass-kicking contest."

Clark unabashedly admits being in awe of Bryce's firearms abilities. Many times he saw him start his demonstrations by throwing grapefruits up in the air and shooting them with a pistol. He would then make the demonstration progressively harder by shooting potatoes, then thrown quarters and grapes. For those who have never measured one, a quarter is slightly less than one inch in diameter and most grapes are about half that.

He saw that Bryce was very good at sleight of hand and could easily make quarters disappear while handling them. He saw some of this talent incorporated into the demonstrations. To demonstrate his fast draw, Bryce would ask for a volunteer or have an assistant stand in front of him like a suspect. He would use his left hand to flip the gun out of the holster on his right hip and throw the gun into his right

Evidence of Jelly Bryce's firearms abilities during demonstrations. Top left: Bryce shooting his revolver upside down, using his little finger to pull the trigger. Top center: Bryce aims at targets 25 yards away through a mirror held between his legs while shooting backwards and upside down. Top right: Bryce's fast draw viewed from the business end. Bottom left: Bryce shooting skeet with a shotgun. (photos courtesy of D.A. Dawson Collection) Bottom right: British coins shot out of the air by Bryce. Both coins appear to have been hit at least five times each. (photo courtesy of Bob Gentry)

hand while simultaneously shoving his suspect in the chest with his left hand. The motion would cause his coat to flip back and the gun seemed to materialize in his hand faster than the eye could follow. Bryce told Clark that he used to practice his fast draw while standing on a mattress, presumably to cushion the gun falling before he became sure handed at it.

One agent who worked for Bryce in El Paso said "I watched this demonstration many times and he literally was so fast that you could not see him draw the pistol from under his coat." Retired OCPD officers Jack Garrette and Jack Mullenix saw modifications of this draw. Garrette saw Bryce use his left hand to push his coat back before drawing with his right and Mullenix saw him use his left hand behind him to pull the coat back before drawing. Both said this trick was especially visible on windy days.

Sometimes he would draw and fire at a target while he was walking toward it, then start tossing the gun back and forth between hands, firing alternating shots with alternating hands. All six rounds would be in the center of the target. He would write his name in the air with tracers from a submachine gun, then go back and put the periods behind the "D" and the "A."

He also used clay pigeons in his demonstrations. Some would be shot with a pistol as he threw them in the air. Others would be placed on a clothesline with clothespins. One by one, he would shoot the clay pigeons off, sometimes in small sections, and then shoot the clothespins. Sometimes he would vary this routine or make it progressively harder. First he would shoot the clay pigeons while turned around backwards, bending over and sighting upside down between his legs. Next he would shoot backwards over his shoulder while sighting in his diamond ring. Finally he would shoot while lying on his back and aiming the pistol upside down in a mirror held between his knees. On occasion he was known to perform this final feat with the gunsights covered with cardboard, making it obvious he was only using his eyesight and distance judgement for sighting.

The size of this diamond ring is in dispute. Descriptions of it vary from eight to eleven carats. He told one friend that it had 56 facets that he used as mirrors for his shooting tricks.

As an example of the showmanship he developed, after suitably impressing his audience with his accuracy, Bryce would ask to borrow a pocket watch from one of the spectators. He would carefully mount the watch in the center of one of the clay pigeons, place it on the clothesline and then move off some distance. Either lying on his back or aiming backwards sighting through his ring, he would then shoot pieces off of the clay pigeon all around the watch. Apparently shooting slower and aiming more carefully with each shot, he would eventually have chipped all of the clay pigeon off around the watch. The final round would go directly in the center of the watch, blasting it to smithereens. He would then apologetically approach the frustrated spectator and give him back his undamaged watch. Bryce had palmed the man's watch and deftly replaced it with a cheap one that looked similar.

Combining speed and accuracy, he would also repeat the stunt pictured in Life Magazine, dropping coins or pill boxes off the back of his hand at shoulder level, draw and shoot them before they fell below waist level.

To show the practical side of his exercises, Bryce would invite one of the spectators to come forward. Bryce would give the spectator an unloaded pistol, have him cock it and point it at Bryce's stomach. Bryce would then holster his own unloaded pistol under his suit coat. The spectator would be told to pull the trigger as soon as he saw Bryce move. Bryce would then draw and get off at least two simulated shots before the spectator could pull the trigger. The spectator had just gotten a free glimpse of the lesson J. Ray O'Donnell had died learning at the Wren Hotel two decades earlier.

When retired OCPD Lieutenant Chris Walker once asked Bryce to explain his shooting ability, he said he couldn't except that he "spent an awful lot of money on ammo." More than one lawman mentioned that it was a good thing Jelly Bryce had decided to become a lawman instead of joining the other side.

Johnston Murray became Governor of Oklahoma in January of 1951 and served four years in that office, exactly twenty years after his father, William H. "Alfalfa Bill" Murray, served in the same office. At one time during the junior Murray's term, Jelly Bryce put on a firearms demonstration at the old OCPD Pistol Range on the north side of Lake Hefner. Bryce routinely described the tricks he was going to do before starting the demonstration. As he was talking, he looked over at the audience and said "I see the Governor's here." Smiling, he walked over toward Murray with his right hand extended for a handshake. The Governor stood up and reached out for Bryce's hand but found himself clasping the barrel of Bryce's pistol, the gun having come out from under the suit coat so fast he hadn't seen it. With everyone duly impressed with the speed of his draw, Bryce continued the demonstration.

This was the demonstration that retired OCPD Lt. Bill Mead attended as a young detective. Mead had heard the stories and, with the skepticism of a veteran police officer, assumed they were exaggerated. Like he had the Governor, Jelly Bryce made a believer out of Bill Mead that day.

Bryce began the demonstration by shooting Mexican pesos and other small coins out of the air with his .220 Swift rifle. He would explain to his audience that he always made it a point to use foreign coins since it was against Federal law to deface American money. His old friend Spot Gentry assisted him many times in these exhibitions by throwing the coins up for him. Gentry's son, Bob, also helped in this capacity occasionally.

Just hitting the coin wasn't good enough. The idea, Bryce explained, was to be able to use the coin as a watch fob. Therefore the bullet hole had to be within a sixteenth or thirty-second of an inch from the edge. A hit in the dead center, he considered a miss. And he wasn't perfect. Throwing half a dozen of the coins and shooting them, he hit one in the center and threw it away but the rest were right on the edge.

Bryce then shot a series of clay pigeons, shooting backwards over his shoulder and sighting in the big diamond ring on his left hand. He then moved on to using a twelve-gauge pump shotgun, performing the trick of placing three clay pigeons on the stock of the shotgun and holding two in his hands. Throwing all five into the air at once, he hit all five before they fell to the ground.

Talking to Bryce after the demonstration, Mead said he was "a real friendly guy, very immaculate." Mead noticed that Bryce's hands "shook like a leaf, not rock steady like you'd expect." With a cop's typical directness, Mead pointed it out and asked him how he could shoot so accurately like that. Bryce told him that he just pointed the gun and "waited until it all came together, then fired." His reactions, eyes and adrenaline moving much faster than that of his audience, things just moved slower for Jelly than the observers, a version of the "slow motion" people experience under stress.

At the end of their talk, Bryce let slip a small indication of his fatalistic acceptance of his administrative position and his secret yearnings for the action of the old days; "I'm not a policeman anymore, I just do demonstrations."

X
The Post-War Bureau

Just as the Life article featuring Bryce was hitting the newsstands in 1945, the nation was facing a new Public Enemy Number One and Bryce's Oklahoma City FBI office was right in the middle of it.

When the Kimes-Barker-Terrill gang began robbing banks in Oklahoma, Delf Bryce was a sophomore in Mountain View High School, John Dillinger was a machinist on the U.S. Navy battleship Utah, Clyde Barrow was an incorrigible truant in Houston, Texas, and Bonnie Parker was in grade school.

Beginning in early 1924, the gang's career lasted less than three and one-half years and their bold leader, Matthew Kimes, was in jail more than half of that time. Nevertheless, in slightly more than a year and a half, they robbed at least 13 banks, burglarized two others, committed several other burglaries, robberies and kidnappings, two jail escapes and killed at least three law enforcement officers.

Besides Matt and his older brother George, the gang included Ray Terrill, an old associate of Al Spencer (responsible for the last train robbery in Oklahoma in 1923) and future Kansas City Massacre victim Frank "Jelly" Nash, Wilber Underhill, brothers Roy and Clyde Brandon, and Ma Barker's oldest son, Herman. Some authors have speculated that the exploits of the Kimes gang may have inspired a competitive edge in Pretty Boy Floyd when he heard of them in the Missouri State Prison. It is documented that Floyd showed an unusual interest in their shoot-outs and jail breaks around his home area of Sequoyah County, Oklahoma.

In the society of bank robbers, trying to rob more than one bank at a time was considered to be the ultimate challenge of their professional expertise and machismo. It had been the fatal downfall of the Dalton gang and Henry Starr. But the Kimes gang pulled it off twice! The second time, they were actually trying to rob three banks together but a wrong street clock destroyed their timing. The logistics broke down but they still got away after looting two banks and killing Beggs Chief of Police W.J. McAnnally.

By the summer of 1945, Matt Kimes had served 18 years of a life sentence at the OSP in McAlester. Managing to convince a number of corrections administrators that he was rehabilitated he was granted a 60-day leave of absence from prison on July 23 of that year. One of the conditions of his release was that he remain in McAlester.

Rehabilitated he wasn't. On September 5, he and three other men robbed the First State Bank in Morton, Texas, of more than $17,000. When his 60-day leave expired in late September, an unsuspecting Oklahoma Corrections Department extended it for another six months. In October, he robbed a theater in Wewoka, Oklahoma, of $1,200. On October 26, he was stopped for speeding in McAlester. Apparently it never occurred to anyone to ask where he got the car or how he paid for it. Kimes reported it to his parole officer three days later, perhaps trying to establish the fact that he was still in town or impress the corrections department with his new-found honesty.

It was a case of too little, too late. By then he had already been identified in the robberies and two of his accomplices in the Morton bank job had been arrested. On November 9, Oklahoma Governor Robert S. Kerr revoked Kimes' leave of absence and the FBI issued a warrant for his arrest. Withheld from the press for a week, on November 16, Oklahoma City SAC Jelly Bryce notified the press that his office had been placed in charge of the hunt for Kimes. Reputed to be heavily armed and considering his history, it was assumed he would violently resist going back to prison.

The whole thing ended with an anticlimax. On the evening of December 2, a man stepped out into a street in North Little Rock, Arkansas, from between two parked cars. A passing poultry truck, unable to stop, ran over him. A police officer some yards away ran to the scene and immediately became suspicious. The seriously injured man had a .38 revolver lying at his feet. His pockets contained several .38 caliber bullets and over $1,600 in cash. Initially refusing to identify himself, he eventually produced identification saying he was named Woods and was from Miami, Oklahoma. While he was being treated in the hospital, police found that Mr. Woods was still in Miami and had recently had his car and identification stolen. Confronted with having his fingerprints taken, the man admitted he was Matt Kimes.

Both of his legs were broken below the knee, he had multiple bruises, lacerations and contusions as well as internal injuries. In fact, his face was so discolored and swollen that he couldn't be compared to his photos on the FBI wanted poster. Nevertheless, a force of 30 FBI agents and police officers surrounded the hospital. An anonymous man had already called asking about "Mr. Woods" condition. Matt Kimes had already broken out of one Oklahoma jail and been broken out of another by his gang.

On December 5, the last remaining fugitive in the Morton bank job, Olaf Alvin "Chick" Rogers, walked into the Oklahoma City FBI office and surrendered. Perhaps it was the Bryce Effect. Surrender or die.

Although not voluntarily, Matt Kimes exercised the other option. On the morning of December 14, he died from his injuries, presumably the internal bleeding. It was the end of the era of the Twenties gangsters. When a reporter checked with Jelly Bryce about the news, Bryce said he had just received confirmation of Kimes' death. The reporter noted that "Bryce didn't seem depressed over the report."

One measure of a boss is how hard his subordinates work for him and how effective they are at their jobs. Weldon C. "Spot" Gentry completed a career in the FBI and then became the Director of Security for Kerr-McGee Corporation. He was a close friend of U.S. Senator Robert S. Kerr and was one of Bryce's closest cronies in the Oklahoma City FBI office, one of the "special" men the boss could count on in any situation. According to Gentry, during Jelly Bryce's tenure as SAC in Oklahoma City, there wasn't a single unsolved bank robbery in the state of Oklahoma.

Yet another measure of a boss is his subordinates' willingness to tweak his sense of humor. Many cops are great practical jokers and the ones who like and respect their supervisors are always on a quest to "get something over on them." At one point during Bryce's tenure in OKC, some of his agents found out about him being accidentally shot as a boy in Mountain View. They also found out one of the boys involved had grown up and was now working for the Oklahoma State Tax Commission in Oklahoma City. They approached the man about playing a practical joke on Bryce by sending him a huge overdue tax notice, complete with threats of liens on his property, repossessions and all kinds of fiscal horrors. The man listened to their proposition and then declined nervously, saying "Do you think I'm nuts? I'm the only person to ever shoot Jelly Bryce and live to tell about it."

Having those kind of relationships with your men isn't to say that he can't still be the boss. One day a newly transferred agent reported to Bryce's office but saw that he was on the phone. Without interrupting his conversation, Bryce motioned for him to come on in and have a seat. While waiting and listening to one side of the friendly, casual conversation his new boss was having, it gradually dawned on the new agent that Bryce was talking to Hoover. He later told other agents that "At that moment, I figured I was either in the best place in the world or the worst."

When Bryce hung up, the agent introduced himself. Bryce said "I know who you are and why you're here. It's a disciplinary transfer." In many places, that would have meant he was destined, at best, to be the office whipping boy or, at worst, set up to fail and headed for the fast track out of the Bureau. In typical fashion, Bryce cut right to the chase with his next statement. "If you do your job here, we'll get along fine. If you don't, I'll fire you. Now get out of here and go to work." The agent said they later became close friends and he had immense respect for Bryce.

Another of Bryce's virtues his former agents like to relate is his small-town values of friendliness and consideration toward others, at least when he was at ease among law enforcement colleagues, no matter how wide the apparent chasm between them. Bryce had a way of overcoming chasms. Jelly Bryce certainly had no lack of ego nor any reason to lack it but, as with most things in his life, he controlled it rather than the reverse. Just as he was able to use it when necessary, he was able to dispense with it with equal facility.

He frequently attended meetings and conventions of peace officers, sheriff's associations and other law enforcement organizations. At many of them, some small town marshal or deputy sheriff would be at the very back of the room doing his best imitation of a wallflower, silently but thoroughly intimidated by the big city cops, sheriffs and federal agents present. When Bryce spotted one of these men, he would head straight for him and strike up a conversation, giving him his full and undivided attention. With the automatic draw of Bryce's wide recognition and personal magnetism, a dozen or more officers would soon be drawn into the impromptu "bull session". In record time, Bryce would have the officer from the small agency feeling like he was the most important officer there. Bryce's agents witnessed this phenomenon many times and fully realized that much of the courtesy and cooperation they received on their investigations in local jurisdictions sprang directly from these contacts. Many times the parting words of officers and deputies in small Oklahoma towns were "Tell Jelly 'Hi' for me." Agents who served under Bryce in every office commented that they saw less of the petty jealousies between law enforcement agencies and more cooperation than at any other times in their careers.

Former FBI Agent Dale Williams described Bryce's managerial style thusly: "He was a very considerate individual and would never try to second guess one of his agents if the agent was doing his best and the mistake was one of judgement. He would probably call the agent in and they would discuss the problem and after the discussion was over, it was forgotten about and he would vigorously object to any critics from Washington who may have wanted to second guess."

Williams served under Bryce in both Albuquerque and Oklahoma City but first became aware of Bryce's consideration for others in 1949. Williams was stationed in Newark, New Jersey, and his father was preparing for a serious operation in Oklahoma City. Bryce sent a telegram to the Newark office suggesting that Williams be allowed to report to the Oklahoma City office temporarily until his father was out of danger. Williams gratefully declined the offer but did use it to make arrangements so he could return on short notice if it became necessary.

Later, in Oklahoma City, Williams served as one of the agents who handled routine administrative tasks for his boss. He said "I don't remember that he ever second guessed any action I took in his behalf. I do remember there were two or three occasions when actions I initiated in his behalf were questioned by officials in Washington—in every instance, he would either write or call the official in question and state to the effect that I was acting for him and that if anything was to be questioned about the action taken, then the questions should be directed to him and, had he been present, the action would have been no different. That was always the last you heard of the incident."

Bryce always maintained his reputation for a fastidious dresser and, as in other areas, mirrored the standards he set for his office. He insisted his agents keep their suit coats on in the office and even in the days before the First National Building was air conditioned, Bryce was always neatly attired in white shirt, tie and suit. One of the secretaries who served under him vividly remembers the only departure she ever saw from that standard.

One day there was a particularly notorious kidnapping in Missouri and investigative leads indicated the suspect might be headed toward Albuquerque. It was logical that they might pass through Oklahoma City on their way and Bryce was notified. He immediately mobilized the entire office at 5 A.M. on a Sunday morning and everyone reported for duty.

A little while later, a phone call came in for Bryce and one of the secretaries went back to his office to notify him. Finding his office empty, she started down the hallway calling his name. Bryce stepped out of the bathroom in his undershirt with shaving cream all over

156

his face. Stunned into silence momentarily, the secretary told him of the call, whereupon he wiped the shaving cream from his partially shaved face and went to his office to take the call. She says her overwhelming memory of the moment is "lots of tattoos." The more memorable ones were a cross and a heart with the word "Mother" on his upper left arm and a large horsefly on his upper right arm.

Unfortunately, relations with his own relatives were not always as cordial as they were with his law enforcement colleagues. During the Korean War, his first son, William Delf Bryce, was an undergraduate college student and, like most college students, he faced occasional bouts of financial straits. During one of those occasions, he approached his father for some money.

Bryce was of the opinion that Bill was something of a "namby-pamby" and could use some toughening up. His reply to his son's request was "Join the Marines." No money was forthcoming.

The passage of time did not heal the wounds of a lifetime. Other employees in the Oklahoma City FBI office were told that Bill Bryce was not to be admitted into his father's office in the future. Bryce refused to see him. Rumor circulated that Bryce didn't believe Bill was actually his son although more than one saw a great physical resemblance between the two. As yet another measure of the esteem they held for their boss, some of the agents tried to surreptitiously heal the rift. Some even went so far as to buy Christmas gifts and send them to Bill in his father's name. It didn't work.

Meanwhile, Bryce was doting on his second son, the one he was getting to raise. He frequently brought Johnny up to the FBI office. Often, he had the boy dressed in a fancy cowboy outfit he had bought for him, complete with cowboy hat, tie and toy gun. Bryce hadn't been able to pay enough attention to his first son. The second one would get too much attention.

Understandably, during his assignments in Oklahoma City, Jelly Bryce spent a lot of time down at OCPD Headquarters. Besides his official position as head of the FBI for the state, Bryce had many close personal friendships at OCPD Headquarters. Lee Mullenix had recently retired and his son Jack was on the force. Smokey Hilbert was the Chief of Police, Mickey Ryan was the Chief of Detectives and H.V. Wilder was a Lieutenant until his untimely death from liver disease in March of 1950. Bryce would later have a hand in continuing the Wilder legacy in Oklahoma City law enforcement.

Besides his professional liaisons and personal friendships, Bryce just liked being around policemen including the next generation of young, working street cops. As any old cop will tell you, spending a little time around the next generation can't help but infect you with their enthusiasm, energy, and the sheer fun they're having at doing their jobs. Bryce became a familiar face around the OCPD at all hours of the day or night.

Kenneth A. Nash joined the OCPD in 1952. Hardly your average officer, in a career of twenty years he would graduate from law school and retire at the rank of Major before moving on to another career as the City Attorney for Oklahoma City. In a career of unique experiences, one stands out in his memory.

Traditionally, City Jail trusties have been able to shorten their time in jail and work off their fines by performing labor around the police station. In modern days, they perform construction, housekeeping and janitorial tasks. In days past, they washed and fueled police cars and manned a shoeshine stand near the lineup room where officers had their shoes or boots shined before going on duty.

One evening before going on duty, Patrolman Nash was sitting in the shoeshine stand with a trusty diligently preparing his shoes for inspection. A man dressed immaculately in a very fashionable suit, vest and tie walked by and stopped to watch. Evidently dissatisfied with the job that was being done, the snappy dresser took the shine rag away from the trusty and proceeded to show him how the job should be done. Nash later remembered that amid the popping and snapping of the shine rag, "he really made that rag sing." When Officer Nash went to lineup that night, his uniform shoes had never looked better.

Although we can't be absolutely certain, I strongly suspect that Ken Nash is the only patrolman who ever had his shoes shined by the Special Agent in Charge of a FBI field office.

In the 1950s, the state of Oklahoma coded the first digit of the automobile license plates for its 77 counties according to their population. A low prefix number showed that the tag was issued in one of the more heavily populated counties or one of its adjoining counties. Thus Oklahoma County, the site of the state capitol and the most populous county in the state, had a prefix of "1", Tulsa County had "2", and so forth. The prefix was followed by a sequential number for the tag.

In the days before there was such a thing as personalized license plates, Jelly Bryce used his influence to obtain what may have been one of the first. The Oklahoma license on his big gray Cadillac was "1-2345."

Even as an administrator in charge of all the FBI for Oklahoma, the Bryce legend continued to expand and diversify. Bryce had long made it a habit to be present for all major or dangerous arrests made by his men in his jurisdiction. After getting to know a little about Jelly Bryce, one can't help but feel that is the way it would have been even without Hoover's directives to that end.

Presaging the days of trained hostage negotiators by two decades, whenever a bank robber was trapped in the act and took hostages or a fugitive barricaded himself in a room somewhere, Bryce's men had orders to secure the scene and call him. Bryce insisted on being notified and personally responding to all such incidents.

Without resorting to the telephone or bullhorn negotiations that later became commonplace, Bryce often responded by having a direct and immediate face to face confrontation with the suspect. A few quiet words with Bryce doing most of the talking and the suspect invariably surrendered peacefully. Although no one has been found who actually overheard both sides of one of these conversations, one suspects the gist of it was something to the effect of "surrender or die", punctuated by those cold blue eyes.

It even came to the point where suspects would surrender immediately after Bryce's arrival at the scene of one of these confrontations and sometimes even before he arrived. It came to be known as "the Bryce Effect". It was almost as if the suspects sensed the aura of impending death in the air around them.

One former agent tells of witnessing one of these events in Tulsa. Agents had cornered a wanted fugitive in a motel room and, as per standing orders, notified Bryce in Oklahoma City. Bryce drove up to Tulsa and after arriving at the scene, was briefed by the surrounding agents. Future incidents would merit the activation of a SWAT Team, hostage negotiators and telephoning the suspect to conduct negotiations. Bryce had a simpler method.

He walked up to the door of the motel room and beat on it with his fist. Loud enough to be heard inside the room, he then yelled "This is the FBI. Open the door and come out or I'll kick the goddam thing down." The fugitive immediately came out with his hands up.

After eight years as SAC in Oklahoma City, Jelly got caught up in another "career enhancement transfer" in late April of 1953. In what was described as a "routine reorganization which is periodic in the FBI", Bryce was ordered to switch posts with the SAC in Albuquerque, New Mexico. Albuquerque SAC James C. Ellsworth would replace Bryce in Oklahoma City. Ellsworth, an Arizona native, was an 18-year veteran who had already served in seven other field offices, mostly on the eastern seaboard or the far northwest. The newspaper termed the reorganization as "a general shakeup which has already affected more than half a dozen agents."

Although he doubtlessly regretted leaving Oklahoma City, Bryce was hardly being punished. He had been in charge of the same territory when he was in the El Paso office over a decade earlier, before there was a separate field office for Albuquerque.

Back in the New Mexico mountains again, Bryce continued to make his reputation as a firm but fair boss who was generally well respected and well liked by his men. On one occasion, he had twenty agents assigned to him from other offices on a special assignment. He monitored the investigation closely but didn't interfere. At the end of the assignment, he hosted a barbeque at his home for all the agents in appreciation for a job well done.

One of the amusing stories Bryce later liked to tell of his adventures during this assignment involved a bloodhound. Bryce never was reticent about letting it be known that he had no use for the dogs in spite of their long reputation for use by law enforcement in tracking fugitives. Bryce told of one case when they were hunting for a man wanted in a New Mexico bank robbery. He had run into the rugged mountains and some of the local officers insisted on using a bloodhound to try to locate him. Bryce didn't approve but didn't try to make a major point out of it. Bryce later said that they had arrested the suspect in 27 hours but it took them 47 hours to find the bloodhound. Apparently the dog had run across the scent of a mountain lion and, discretion being the better part of valor, lit out in the opposite direction.

A year after his transfer, Bryce got some news from home about one of those odd twists of fate that occur in law enforcement sometimes. His old boss from the Raiding Squad, Lt. Robert Hurt, had long since resigned from the OCPD and become a local constable. In May of 1954, Hurt was arrested in Oklahoma City for complicity in a scheme involving an extortion and two armed robberies. Convicted, he was sent to the State Prison in McAlester. In another twist of fate a few years later, his brother Clarence would retire from the FBI and become elected as sheriff of Pittsburg County, Oklahoma, the county the State Prison is in. Sheriff Hurt requested and got his brother assigned to his office as a trusty.

A few weeks later, Bryce was back in the news in Oklahoma City but in a more positive light. Smokey Hilbert was in trouble in the summer of 1954. The OCPD had been having its troubles in the past year and, as the Chief, Smokey was in the center of the bullseye. First he had fired the Chief of Detectives for accepting an improper loan from a gambler. Then he had to deal with some black officers extorting money from east side tavern owners. Then there was a scandal about accounting irregularities in the jail food service. A grand jury investigated the Vice Bureau and removed its control and reorganization from under the Chief. The last straw was a "bad judgement" arrest by one of his officers that resulted in a Tinker Field officer getting his jaw broken. Smokey, who came up through the ranks in the rough old days of police work and was never known as a stickler for discipline, delivered what was considered a "wristslap" to the offending officer.

On June 25, six of the eight City Council members held a secret meeting at the Skirvin Hotel and drafted a letter to the City Manager requesting Chief Hilbert's dismissal. The next day, a Saturday, Hilbert sent City Manager Ross Taylor a letter asking to be relieved of his duties as Chief and reassigned. The request was approved but only temporarily.

The following Tuesday, Ward One Councilman James Norick, one of the two councilmen not invited to the star chamber meeting in the Skirvin, read a statement during the weekly council meeting lambasting the other council members for their improper interference in the internal workings of the OCPD. In spite of Norick's protests and doubtlessly influenced by the majority faction on the council, City Manager Taylor reconsidered his previous decision and dismissed Hilbert on July 17, stating that he would be removed from the payroll at midnight on July 20.

Smokey Hilbert had been Chief of the OCPD for almost eleven and one-half years, the longest tenure of any Chief in the history of the department and a record which will probably never be bested. He had been one of the most respected and probably the most popular Chief in department history. Many tough old cops said that the first time they had ever seen some of their colleagues cry was the day Smokey Hilbert left the Chief's job.

In the midst of all this furor, the Oklahoma City Times printed a story on July 1 wondering if Jelly Bryce would seek or be offered the OCPD Chief's job. The City Manager denied the report that Bryce was among the candidates, saying "He's not among the ones I've attempted to contact and there's nothing in my study at this time to indicate he's a candidate for the job. I don't have an application from him." The reporter's attempts to reach Bryce in Albuquerque were met with reports that he was out of town.

It was all a tempest in a teapot. Roy Bergman got the Chief's job on July 30.

Jelly Bryce continued with his job in Albuquerque but didn't neglect his love for sporting pastimes. During the first weekend of December, 1955, permits were issued to 25 people in New Mexico for the first legally licensed hunt for barbary sheep in history. On the first day of the hunt, one of the first seven hunters to bag one was Jelly Bryce. Bryce killed a 200-pound ram in the Canadian River canyon near Roy, New Mexico. The animal had to be packed out of the canyon on horseback until it could be winched onto a truck on the canyon rim.

Patrolman Jack Garrette joined the OCPD in 1951, the year before Ken Nash. Early in his career, Garrette met Bryce and they became acquainted through their mutual interest in shooting. Jack Garrette wasn't Jelly Bryce but he was a very good shot in his own right. It was a good thing.

On the afternoon of January 27, 1956, Harold Lee Kersey and Harry Eugene Bush tried to hold up a grocery store in Tulsa but it didn't work out. They should have quit while they were ahead but instead decided to try their luck a hundred miles south down Highway 66. Their luck wasn't very good to begin with and it would only get worse in Oklahoma City.

About 8:30 that night, they burst into Scott's Supermarket at Southeast 25th and Central. Brandishing their pistols at 50 customers, they yelled for everyone to get down on the floor and not to look at their faces. As the robbers collected almost $1,500 from three cash registers and started to make their exit, the owner and security guard ran up from the rear of the store. The security guard was off-duty OCPD patrolman Jack Garrette.

Drawing his weapon, the five-year veteran officer yelled at the two men to stop. Bush bolted out the front door but Kersey stopped and turned toward the officer with a cocked .38 revolver in his hand. Garrette fired one shot, striking Kersey in the heart and killing the 28-year-old Los Angeles native almost instantly. Over $1,000 of the loot was recovered from his body.

A shaken and disoriented Harry Bush spent the next hour driving around and trying to find his way out of town. He finally did but it was only a short reprieve. Five hours later, Bush was arrested in his Tulsa apartment where officers recovered the other $400 taken in the

162

robbery. Bush went to jail and Jack Garrette would go on to complete a 27-year career with the OCPD. Later promoted to Sergeant, he would spend over a decade as Rangemaster of the OCPD Firearms Range, teaching another generation of officers to defend themselves until his retirement in 1978.

The same week as Jack Garrette's shooting, Jelly Bryce made his last move in the FBI. On February 1, 1956, he was transferred back to Oklahoma City. He swapped SAC jobs with N.R. "Nat" Johnson. Johnson had been the ASAC in Pittsburgh, Pennsylvania. When James C. Ellworth was transferred to Kansas City in December of 1953, Johnson had been promoted to SAC in Oklahoma City. Now he would be moving to Albuquerque to replace Bryce.

The fact that Jelly had already made the decision that his FBI career was winding down was evidenced by the fact that he didn't move his family back with him. Shirley and Johnny were moved back to the ranch in Mountain View and Bryce would spend the last two years of his career commuting between home and the capital city. Even in the days of two-lane highways and 65 mile-per-hour speed limits, it was a two-hour drive at best. That time could be shortened even more by the big Cadillac along roads patrolled by friendly OHP troopers and it would have been a rare one who didn't know Jelly Bryce.

Also evidence of his winding down was the fact that for his last two years, he would sometimes spend as little as two days a week in the office. When he was in the city, he rented a room at the Roberts Hotel at 15 North Broadway. One of the better hotels in the downtown area, the ten-story red brick building boasted of 200 air conditioned rooms with a free radio in every room, a coffee shop and the Oak Room Club for nightcaps and relaxation. Just how well built the hotel was didn't become evident until January 14, 1973, when it was demolished by explosives during an urban renewal project. Although the dynamite severed the building's steel support frame, it remained standing after the explosions. The outer brick walls accepted the strain and supported the building for more than ten minutes before finally collapsing.

Five minutes away from the Roberts, it was a short two-block walk to the FBI office in Room 940 in the First National Bank Building at 120 North Robinson.

By the Spring of 1956, complaints were coming in to OCPD Headquarters about "short Broadway", the two blocks of that street north of Grand Boulevard. When the city was first founded, that sec-

163

tion of street was a solid phalanx of saloons and brothels that soon gained the nickname Battle Row for the nightly combat it promoted. More than half a century later, it had only marginally improved.

In between the fashionable spots like the Roberts and Huckins Hotels, and Bishop's Restaurant, most of the rest of the street was populated with notorious beer joints like The Little White Cloud That Cried, the Talk of the Town, the Playhouse and others. Drunks were roaming the streets at all hours, women were being accosted and fights were breaking out. Two beat officers were assigned to foot patrol in the area. In the next three months, they solved the problem by making over 900 arrests. One of the men walking that beat was Jack Garrette.

Away from his family and apparently bored, on some nights Bryce used to come down and walk Garrette's beat with him. One evening, they happened upon an extra large drunk leaving one of the bars. The man was about 6'6" tall and weighed about 260 pounds. The drunk was a lot bigger than Jack Garrette who was a lot bigger than his FBI friend. Garrette arrested the man and asked Bryce to go in one of the hotels and call for the Paddy Wagon to transport him to jail. Bryce deferred, telling Jack to go make the call and he would stay with the prisoner. Garrette had his doubts about leaving the huge drunk with the much smaller man but Bryce convinced him it would be all right so he went in and called for the wagon.

Coming back outside a few minutes later, Garrette found the drunk face down on the sidewalk. Bryce was sitting on the sidewalk next to him, holding on to one of the drunk's arms, had one foot placed against his neck and the other against his side, having him stretched out and immobilized. Bryce said they'd "had a little trouble." Obviously, Bryce's physical courage wasn't limited to gunfights. He was "a wiry little bastard who'd fight anybody." As with Ken Nash's shoeshine, I'd venture a guess that Jelly Bryce was probably the last FBI SAC to walk a beat in a major city.

Leon Cleary saw another example of the man's selective ego on a trip they made together to Lawton. Bryce needed some shirts so they pulled into a K-Mart store. Bryce picked out his shirts and they went to the cash register. Bryce tried to pay for his purchases but, not a believer in credit cards, all he had on him was $100 bills. Unknown to them, Lawton was having a problem with counterfeit $100 bills being passed. The young clerk, unable to tell if the bills were real or not, refused to accept them for the merchandise. Another man might have called for the manager and flashed his identification as the head of the FBI for the state. Not Jelly Bryce. He anonymously left without the shirts.

Law enforcement was a much smaller family in those days but still a family. Bryce liked to keep his law enforcement family close so he often hired the sons of friends and colleagues as clerks in the FBI office. He hired Spot Gentry's son, Bob, as a clerk soon after the young man came home from his service with the Marines in the Korean War. Another was Douglas Hilbert, one of Smokey's nephews. He was the son of Howard Hilbert, known as "Little Smoke", one of Smokey's brothers and also an OCPD Detective. Yet another was Robert Vard Wilder, son of his old partner H.V. Wilder.

Barely past his eighteenth birthday, Bob Wilder would keep the job for the next two and a half years until he was hired by the OCPD the day after his twenty-first birthday in 1960. He would go on to a thirty-year career, serving the last five years as Chief before retiring in 1990. He would then start another career as the Sheriff of Marshall County in southern Oklahoma.

Having virtually grown up around Jelly Bryce, Wilder had an unusually familiar relationship with his new boss. Like many others, he wondered about the legends and the truth behind the legends. At one point, he asked Bryce the question many would have liked to but few would have dared; how many shootings he had actually been involved in. Bryce told him "Nineteen." Wilder assumed that meant that Bryce had killed that many men in the line of duty because, to anyone who had seen him shoot, it was incomprehensible that Bryce would merely wound anybody.

Unfortunately, things were not running as smoothly with Bryce's other family. During one visit to the Bryce home, one of his agents witnessed Bryce damage one of his diamond rings when he hit it on a table "taking a swipe at Johnny's ass for something as he went by."

On one occasion, a FBI Inspector came into town. Director Hoover had a policy of having his Inspections Division conduct surprise inspections of every field office every year. Following the inspection, Bryce took the Inspector to his home on North MacArthur for dinner.

It was common knowledge among the agents who were invited to Bryce's home that his young son Johnny, in spite of not even being a teenager yet, "swore like a trooper." After dinner, Shirley served them all cake. Johnny was walking away from the table with his when the piece of cake fell on the floor. The boy let go with a startling stream of profanity. Shirley then said to her husband, "Delf, we've got to do something about that." Whereupon the Inspector said, "Yeah, get him another piece of cake."

On another occasion, Bryce had scheduled a vacation to Colorado with his family to go on a hunting trip with an agent who had worked for him in El Paso. Bryce called the agent and apologized, saying that he was not going to be able to make the trip "because of that wild boy of mine." The agent didn't ask further questions and Bryce didn't elaborate.

As early as 1953, Bryce had been spending most of his time out of the office, visiting other law enforcement agencies, arranging training schools and giving firearms demonstrations. Some agents estimated he spent as much as three-quarters of his time away from the office. Always present to handle major administrative matters and on the scene of all major investigations or hazardous arrest situations, he left routine administrative matters to a designee. Among others, two agents named Tully and Scruggs had been handling many of the more mundane administrative matters for him. One of his last public appearances as a SAC was in mid-November of 1957 when he and Oklahoma County Sheriff Bob Turner presided over the exhumation of a missing bootlegger's body from a shallow grave in southwest Oklahoma City.

On the last day of 1957, Bryce wrote a letter to Mr. Hoover. He stated that his last day of active duty would be January 10, 1958, and he requested leave without pay until February 1 when his retirement would commence. He confirmed that he intended to become a candidate for Governor of Oklahoma and another statement indicated that he had discussed this plan with Hoover the previous June. Hoover replied on January 2, the letter sent to Bryce's home in Mountain View. Hoover was effusive in his praise in spite of the official nature of the communication;

"I must take this opportunity to express my personal regret at your departure from our ranks though I can well understand your motives. Your service with us, spanning the decades of our greatest achievement, has been long and devoted, but more than that it has been performed with real distinction. You have been in the thick of our combat with crime and have acquitted yourself in a manner of which both you and the Bureau can be proud.

It is my warm hope that you and your family will find satisfaction in any future endeavor you may undertake and my best wishes go with you. I thank you for the cordial expressions in your letter and trust that you will keep in close touch with us in the years to come.

Sincerely, J. Edgar Hoover."

Bryce had indeed seen the Bureau through the quarter century of its formative years, its greatest glory and achievements during the gangster era, the greatest war in history and the beginnings of the cold war against communism. In 1934, he joined an agent force not much larger than the OCPD he was leaving. He was one of 391 agents supported by 451 civilians in a bureau with an annual budget of slightly more than $2.5 million. When he retired 24 years later, there were 6,147 agents supported by 7,839 civilians with an annual budget of over $105 million. He had been an unsurpassed gladiator for federal law enforcement and had survived a multitude of encounters with criminals but now he was entering an unfamiliar arena against unfamiliar adversaries. Smarter, more cunning, more devious and, in many cases, less principled adversaries. Politicians.

XI
Politics-A Lamb in the Hyena's Lair

Oklahoma had problems with alcohol from Day One. When it was Indian Territory, the U.S. Congress passed prohibitory laws against the introduction and sale of liquor. Making no provision for territorial government, enforcement was left to the U.S. Army and Deputy U.S. Marshals which naturally proved an impossible task due to their small numbers and the vast expanse of territory they were expected to police. The laws continued through the territorial stage and local law enforcers found the control of illegal spirits just as foreboding as had the federal authorities.

The situation was constantly railed against by organized religion and groups such as the Women's Christian Temperance Union (WCTU) and the Anti-Saloon League. In fact, a branch of the WCTU was formed in Muskogee a year before the area was opened to white settlement. It was just as consistently supported by business interests who knew most of the rougher pioneers flooding into the area didn't want to move to Paradise, much less spend their money there. One early City Council meeting during Oklahoma City's first year dealt with a stampede of horses and an early day traffic accident caused by a young woman with the Salvation Army beating her drum loudly on a corner. One councilman criticized the relentless do-gooders who wanted to "Kansasize the whole damned town."

Hatchet-wielding Carry Nation moved her headquarters to Guthrie, then the capital of Oklahoma Territory, in 1905. Along with the persistence of the other anti-liquor movements, her relentless filibustering and proliferation of the WCTU had a profound effect. When statehood came in 1907, Oklahoma came into the Union with the longest State Constitution in the country, 45,000 words and ten times longer than the U.S. Constitution. It was also the only state to have prohibition written into its' Constitution.

It wasn't the first attempt in history of a vocal minority trying to force a principle down the majority's throat and it fared even less well than most. The law was generally ignored, bootleggers, saloons and whiskey were widespread. One publication, speaking to the hypocrisy of the situation, called prohibition "the rankest farce that ever cursed a state" and a "stupendous piece of legislative folly."

Nevertheless, the attempt widened.

In 1908, only 5 of the 46 states were "dry." Eight years later, after the admission of New Mexico and Arizona, 23 of the 48 had adopted prohibition and the number had reached 30 by 1919. When the Eighteenth Amendment to the Constitution was proposed, the Oklahoma Legislature approved it in a single day, a phenomenal achievement for Oklahoma politics.

So Prohibition with a capital "P" became the law of the entire land in January of 1920. The convoluted Volstead Act placed restrictions on the manufacturers, sellers and transporters of alcohol but none on the purchasers. Organized crime had their funding boon for the next 13 years.

Enforcement continued to be a national bad joke but not for the people trying to do the job. In 1920, the Treasury Department's Bureau of Prohibition had 948 agents to enforce the unpopular law on a nation of over 106 million people. The force never exceeded 2,300. Oklahoma, with 2 million people, had 15 agents. Over thirty Prohibition agents were killed in the line of duty in the first four years of the law.

By 1932, almost three-quarters of the population favored abolishing the Eighteenth Amendment. In spite of the machinations of the WCTU, the Anti-Saloon League and a new organization which would become known as the United Drys, the national leadership responded. In March of 1933, Congress altered the Volstead Act to legalize 3.2 beer. Before the year was out, 36 states had ratified the Twenty-First Amendment to the U.S. Constitution repealing the Eighteenth and national Prohibition was over. Oklahoma was not one of the ratifying states.

Oklahoma still tried to maintain as much control over the booze as they could by keeping some of the most restrictive laws in the country. If they couldn't prohibit the demon rum, they could make it as troublesome as possible. They refused to allow liquor by the drink and "BYOB" (Bring Your Own Bottle) became a commonly known abbreviation.

In 1936, 1940 and 1949, elections tried to overturn the laws, always failing. The usual pattern was that the urbanized areas of the state would vote overwhelmingly for liquor but the rural vote would always vote it down.

But times were changing and so were public attitudes among ordinary citizens. Even if they didn't want a drink themselves, they wanted the right to have one. It also meant business, industry and, ultimately, revenue.

Friday, January 10, 1958, was Bryce's last day as an active-duty FBI agent. The next day, Bryce was feted at a barbecue with 400 guests at the Osage County Fairgrounds in Pawhuska. As expected, he announced his candidacy for the governorship in the next election. A registered Democrat, it was generally assumed he would run for the Democratic nomination. That assumption turned out to be premature.

In speaking to his supporters, Bryce cited his 17 years of administrative experience in the FBI and the fact that the Bureau consistently returned operating money to the government. His platform would be based upon reform and progress. Idealistically, he formulated the progress portion first. What could he do for the people?

He intended to make state government more efficient, to "assure the people of Oklahoma that every tax dollar spent will be guarded in such a way that they will receive 100 cents value in service and material."

He wanted to reduce traffic deaths, "to alleviate the present highway slaughter." Periodic meetings with judges and county attorneys could work out innovative and effective programs. A traffic curriculum in the state education system would help, he said, as well as a new system of highways designed to better accommodate the higher horsepower of modern automobiles and the increased traffic.

He also displayed some of his political naivete on this subject as well as providing a peek into his reform intentions. Ignoring the obvious revenue gathering implications, he said he had no turnpike program because he envisioned no more turnpikes in the state's highway system. He then said the first step in his highway program would be "the elimination of the unethical policy in the conduct of road contract letting." He preferred having sealed bids for all road contracts offered at open bidding sessions with the best qualified Oklahoma firm getting the contract. He was openly proposing this in a state where drivers routinely joked about the lousy roads, paved in deteriorating asphalt specifically so they would have to be re-paved every few years because someone in the state capitol had a brother-in-law who owned an asphalt company.

He wanted to encourage industrial expansion, increase job potential and "make it possible for Oklahoma's young people to earn a living wage and remain in Oklahoma."

Stating that the state's youth were their greatest resource, he wanted to personally sponsor and endorse a badly needed and well planned state-wide youth program. He was probably thinking back to the Civilian Military Training Camps he attended as a youth. He also wanted improvements in mental health care and, doubtlessly reflecting back upon his experiences as a State Game Ranger, improve soil and water conservation. He also made a Freudian slip when discussing the latter subject, subtly telegraphing some of his reform opinions. He wanted to promote Oklahoma as a recreational mecca but, claiming no expertise in that area, he wanted to put the program in the hands of "capable, efficient personnel, not politicians."

A little behind the times and perhaps mirroring his former Director's preoccupation with leftist subversives, Bryce told his audience that he knew the name, address and place of employment of every communist in Oklahoma and promised none of them would ever hold a position of trust or importance under his governorship.

He then made several extraordinary departures from normal politics. He intended to campaign on his own merits rather than on the personal indiscretions of the other candidates. No mudslinging in an Oklahoma political race? God forbid! He did, however, warn his opponents that any rocks tossed his way would be adroitly returned. He said he had no personal axe to grind while in the governor's chair. Most politicians would never admit that the idea had even occurred to them. He also declared that he was entering the race with no financing and no commitments. He would prove the truth of these statements in the months to come.

Addressing the wet-dry issue, he was initially a little more politically correct without sacrificing his innate directness. Calling it "the most over-emphasized political football in Oklahoma", he urged "Let's be realistic about the liquor question. Legalized liquor can only be brought to Oklahoma by amending the state constitution. Such an amendment must be made by a vote of the people. When properly presented, any governor would call a vote upon the requested question."

While he was giving some previous governors more credit than was due them and almost certainly knew it, he continued "The governor has the choice of calling a special election or putting the question on the next general election ballot. Other than that decision, no governor exercises any more authority to repeal or retain prohibition than any other qualified voter. We all have one vote, governors included."

He ended his statement on the matter by saying that he would call a special election immediately after a legal petition was presented in order to settle the question immediately. He gave his personal opinion that the most practical liquor laws would "embrace the state-owned package store with careful regulations to safeguard the youth of Oklahoma."

Even at that, it wasn't what the voters wanted to hear. He would tell them a lot more they didn't want to hear in the near future.

The election year of 1958 would be a traditional Oklahoma melee. Eight Democratic candidates announced for the race as well as three Republicans. The hot topic in this year's race, as in many previous ones, would be liquor.

Over the next three months, Bryce became more closely acquainted with Democratic politics in Oklahoma and it left a decidedly bad taste in his mouth. He spit it right back out in what amounted to nothing less than a sweeping indictment of the "old boy network." He kept his pledge of not attacking the other candidates individually. Instead he attacked them as a body.

We don't know who he talked to or who visited him or what was said but we know the result. When the filing period began in late April, Bryce filed as an Independent candidate, not as a Democrat. He must have known the odds against him.

Since its inception, Oklahoma had been a bastion of Democratic politics. Republicans put up a respectable fight in every election but independent candidates traditionally did poorly.

Some of the media speculated that it was political strategy. By not seeking a party nomination, he would avoid the primary races and still be on the general election ballot in November. However, when they interviewed him, he made his reasons clear with typical bluntness;

"If the people of Oklahoma are ready for a change; if they really want to clean up the mess and run the political parasites and unscrupulous characters out of our statehouse; if they want simple, honest, thorough economy and FBI efficiency by a proven administrator in the state capitol, then they will voluntarily support me with their contributions, their energies and their votes. Under these conditions, and no other, will I be the next governor of Oklahoma."

Warming to his subject, Bryce said that he had always been a loyal member of the Democratic party but the realities of politics in general and Oklahoma politics in particular had disillusioned him. His comments would seem to be no less relevant more than four decades later. In fact, the realities of present day politics and a well-earned national cynicism among the populace give them fresh meaning.

"Quite simply, I cannot and would not under any circumstances buy the Democratic nomination. I will not allow my friends to pay the price tag of over $300,000 for the Democratic nomination, nor will I accept money from disreputable sources.

A few political opportunists have so undermined the principles of the Democratic party that an honest man finds it virtually impossible to retain his integrity and successfully seek the Democratic nomination. I have already been approached with several unsavory offers concerning my candidacy, which I promptly rejected.

This situation has led me to conclude that the only way to clean up Oklahoma's quagmire of political corruption is to defy the professional politicians and elect a governor who has no political ties or personal ambitions beyond serving the people. I alone of all the candidates can offer the people of Oklahoma such an administration, and I feel that I can best do so by campaigning as an independent candidate.

One has only to look at some of the past administrations to see the type of government the one-party system has given our state. I personally favor cross-filing as a means of partially eliminating the present deplorable situation.

As an independent governor, I can eliminate such things as the Selected Investments scandal—a direct result of backroom politics. Under my administration,, there will be no more kickbacks, no more

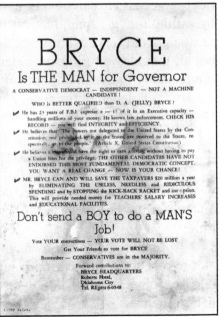

An original campaign poster (front and back) of Jelly Bryce's run for governer.

bribes for state contracts and no more political favors which cost the taxpayers thousands upon thousands of dollars every year."

Bryce also became much more direct in his intentions for reforming government if elected. He said his proposals and statements would not be a series of exaggerated promises that look good on paper, sound good in a speech but amount to little more than political poppycock. He would cite examples of graft, inefficiency and grossly inadequate political leadership.

"Oklahoma's next governor must, above all else, bring a sincere dignity to the state house. He must gain the faith and respect, not only of his fellow Oklahomans, but of all those persons who presently regard the conduct of Oklahoma governmental affairs as ludicrously corrupt. By ignoring the present traditions of blatant dishonesty and carving a course of scrupulous administration through the problems I will face in the next four years, I hope to bring a new concept of honesty to Oklahoma politics."

While the particular problems facing the next governor would differ with individuals, the problem of diplomatically revising the present attitudes of those who consider public service a vehicle for personal gain looms as the major hurdle for any governor sincerely desirous of giving the people of Oklahoma an honest, efficient, economically administered state government."

His idealism laid out on the table for all to plainly see, he accurately forecast virtually every political race for the rest of the century by calling for "a strong, fearless leader of undeniable integrity" to campaign and serve with something other than "hackneyed political hot air that blows furiously at election times but loses itself almost immediately in a rash of political shenanigans."

He even declared his sympathies for the "great many honest people(who) find themselves forced to engage in unethical practices in order to survive against those few who callously perpetrate corruption..."

Bryce listed the first three laws he would like to see passed if he were elected. Overlooking the 1950's terminology and looking back on them from the last decade of the century, they were ahead of their time.

"1. A law requiring known convicted sex perverts and degenerates to register with the proper authorities within 24 hours after their release from a state institution or upon entering Oklahoma to establish residence.

2. A stringent, effective system of controlling dope addicts and

peddlers, with particular emphasis upon preventing these persons from preying upon teenagers.

3. A sweeping law that will make any "kickback" procedures criminal offenses and that will insure conviction of those who practice such procedures."

This was in 1958. Looking back on it from a 21st Century perspective, reader, what do you think?

Bryce was being as honest as he knew how, calling a spade a spade and refusing to straddle fences but he was violating the first rule of politics. He wasn't making many friends and he was embarrassing his opponents with the dirtiest weapon they could imagine—the truth.

On April 26, 1958, Bryce filed a petition in Kiowa County District Court to legally change his name, incorporating his longtime nickname into his name. He was now D. A. Jelly Bryce, no parentheses, no quotation marks.

The primary election was held between the eight Democratic candidates and the three Republicans on July 22, 1958. The Independent candidate, Delf A. Bryce, got to sit at home on his 80-acre ranch three miles west of Mountain View and watch the furor. When the smoke cleared, the Democratic nominee was J. Howard Edmondson, a 32-year-old redheaded county attorney from Tulsa. His Republican opponent would be Phil Ferguson, a rancher and banker from Woodward.

Edmondson had won the primaries with a huge margin of more than 200,000 votes. Young, handsome, energetic, innovative, perfectly coifed, he was the picture of progressive liberal politics—an Oklahoma version of a vigorous young Massachusetts senator named John Fitzgerald Kennedy who had almost captured the Democratic nomination for Vice President of the United States two years earlier. He was the favorite from the outset and his opponents did everything they could to help him.

Ferguson was a former Democratic congressman who had changed party affiliations to the Republicans. This had automatically alienated a large segment of the voting population, giving him at best a wishy-washy reputation in their eyes or, at worst, one as a wolf-in-sheep's-clothing. He alienated even more by coming out against homestead tax exemption in a largely rural state. Then, as a self-administered coup de grace, he joined his Democratic opponent in announcing that he was for repealing prohibition. With both of the major party candidates promising repeal, it seemed Oklahoma's liquor laws were doomed to be dragged into the Twentieth Century. The sole holdout was the Independent candidate, Jelly Bryce.

Some of Bryce's campaign literature advertised himself as "An honest citizen-not a politician" and "Not a machine candidate." He also took a shot at Edmondson's youth by saying "Don't send a BOY to do a MAN'S job!" But if it gained him any yardage, he lost it just as fast.

In the last few months, Bryce had stiffened his opposition to liquor, saying "Every major crime I investigated as agent in charge of the FBI (in Oklahoma) was traceable in one way or another to the beer joint or the walk-in whiskey joint." This somewhat naïve piece of overstatement (if he really believed it) allied him with some of the dry contingent. Dr. Max Stanfield, president of the United Drys, and Dr. Stanley Niles, their executive secretary, both endorsed Bryce for governor. They couched it by saying it was not the endorsement of the organization, however, just their personal choice.

For all the talking he was doing with the press, Bryce was still being uncharacteristically reticent with them…characteristic for Bryce but uncharacteristic for a dark horse political candidate, that is. Perhaps unable to break the old Police Department and Bureau penchants for generally keeping your mouth shut about what you know, he told reporters he would be meeting with some potential supporters soon but refused to name them, say what they would talk about or where he stood on some issues. As late as the primaries and three months before the election, he declined to discuss some points of his platform and even refused to identify his campaign manager (it was George Dane, a former agent who later became a security specialist for the Federal Aviation Administration).

In the next three months, he would carry his reticence to even greater heights, to his own detriment. He made few campaign speeches, preferring to get his message out through general press releases or reporter interviews. Even when invited to participate in debates or question and answer sessions set up by the media on television and radio, Bryce refused to participate in them. For a modern politician to turn down this kind of (then) free exposure to the voters is unheard of.

One person close to his campaign felt that part of the reason for these refusals was a silent admission of his own ignorance. During his Bureau career, Bryce had occasionally been intimidated or defensive when confronted with the higher education of some of his agents. In discussions, as in all other situations, Bryce liked to have the high ground, an edge or a dominating position over any opponent. The campaign worker felt that Bryce was actually quite ignorant of the actual problems of state government, the specific mechanics of how to go about solving them and failed to educate himself on those finer points. He would have been at a decided disadvantage in any public debate on specific issues and solutions with any experienced, professional politician and he knew it.

His solution was to avoid these public forums, oversimplify the morass of problems by blaming them all on corrupt officials and practices, staunchly adhere to the unpopular cause of prohibition and offer the citizens nothing as a candidate but his integrity and good intentions. It wasn't enough.

The populace had separated into those factions favoring and opposing prohibition repeal, the so-called "wets" and "drys." The drys were a shrinking but staunchly vocal segment of the population. The political pundits immediately began predicting Edmondson as the runaway winner but, while giving him no chance for victory, allowed for the possibility that Bryce might get a surprising number of votes.

The ardent drys would vote for him in a block, they said, as a protest against the repeal stance of Edmondson and Ferguson. He could pick up other votes from disenchanted members of both parties who didn't like either of the other candidates. The Daily Oklahoman pontificated that Bryce might garner as many as 25,000 votes which would be "a tremendous number for an Independent candidate."

Although he was campaigning for the office, Bryce wasn't campaigning with the fervor, relentlessness and singlemindedness associated with modern politicians or even with determined politicians of the Fifties. He had been passing out personalized business cards colored a patriotic red, white and blue. The front said "Vote for D.A. "Jelly" Bryce, Governor, 23 years with the F.B.I." and listed his state headquarters as both The Roberts Hotel in Oklahoma City and his home in Mountain View, giving both phone numbers. The back of the cards carried the catchphrase "Get out of a Jam with 'Jelly' for Governor" and listed what he evidently considered his four primary qualifications:

"*Recognized Racket Buster

*Unquestionable Integrity

*Voluntarily Retired from the FBI at age of 51

*Will bring Honesty, Efficiency and Economy to State Government."

He also evidently wasn't campaigning with the backing and

funding of experienced politicians. Although some contributions had been coming to his home in Mountain View, Bryce admitted he was "handicapped by a lack of campaign funds." The state of his financing was obvious from the statement that his Oklahoma City campaign headquarters was temporarily closed because his secretary was ill. Presaging another future political controversy and policing his own campaign financing, he said "I will not take any money from people who expect commitments in return and I cannot take large amounts of money from anyone." It is hard to imagine a quicker way to doom a political campaign in Oklahoma.

Perhaps he was feeling some guilt for all the years his family had suffered the absences made necessary by his law enforcement career. Now he was putting his family first and told the reporters so. In mid-August, he cancelled an appearance before a Tulsa civic group because he wanted to take his family on a trip out of the state. He asked the Tulsa Chamber of Commerce to postpone his appearance but said the trip wouldn't wait because his son had to go back to school soon.

Asked if either of the major party candidates had approached him to withdraw from the race in their favor, he said "No representative of either man has talked to me." Obviously, neither candidate took him as a serious threat and he knew it. "I have known all the time it would be an uphill battle with a short stick. But I have fought that way all my life. I know it will be rough. I kind of like them rough."

By mid-September, obviously discouraged, he even hinted to the press that he might drop out of the race, saying "If I can't get enough clean, honest money to wage a fighting campaign, I won't make any campaign." Although they evidently caught him in a down moment, Jelly Bryce wasn't a quitter. He had already changed his tune within the week, telling another reporter that he was going to release some "very revealing information" in mid-October. Although admitting he was still handicapped by a lack of campaign funds, he gave a little hint when he renewed his pledge not to withdraw from the race but base his campaign on a promise to end "the kickback racket."

Bryce's FBI file provides another hint but it slams quickly into the wall of bureaucratic red tape and black magic marker. A memo from Assistant Director G.A. Nease to Associate Director Clyde Tolson dated October 16, 1958, says "My memorandum earlier today set forth details of the visit by (redacted) and his concern over the allegation that former SAC Delf Bryce had told (redacted) that the Bureau has a fat file on (redacted).

The next three paragraphs fill the rest of the page and are all blacked out. The closing paragraph says "I am still checking with the Oklahoma City office to determine if we have a file on (redacted) after which appropriate recommendations will be made."

The obvious conclusion is that Bryce intended to use his knowledge of local FBI files and investigations to shed some light on someone involved in the Oklahoma governor's race having something to do with kickbacks. J. Howard Edmondson? Phil Ferguson? Someone associated with one of them? Or one of the unnamed people within the Democratic Party who had approached him before he switched to an Independent? Whoever it was, they were very concerned and they or friends of theirs got the message to Washington and all the way to the top of the Bureau's hierarchy. Bryce never returned to the subject and no information was made public.

Jelly didn't let up with his rhetoric even on the eve of the election. He was still conducting his campaign from a rented two-room suite in the Roberts Hotel in downtown Oklahoma City on the beat he used to walk with Officer Jack Garrette on boring evenings. One room served as an "office" while the other was where he slept when he was in town. The local newspaper characterized his campaign as having "little organization and less money." They were right. Conducting essentially a one-man campaign, he spent much of his time on the telephone, making personal contacts throughout the state. Most of his fund-raising attempts were simply letters sent to individuals and organizations throughout the state.

In the text of a speech released on November 1, Bryce kept driving nails in his elective coffin. The original copy is typed on cheap bond paper, now yellowed and stained with age. The format and wording looks like an investigative report written in the first person and, given the state of his campaign finances and inconsistent punctuation, I wouldn't be surprised if he typed it himself. Moreover, it reads like he talked, without any mincing of words:

"LADIES AND GENTLEMEN

I am D.A. "Jelly" Bryce, the man the professional politicians told he had absolutely no chance of ever becoming Governor of Oklahoma.

Be this true of false, I am a native born Oklahoman and as stubborn as the blackjacks that dot our hills.

In its 50 years since statehood, Oklahoma had tried many types of men as governors. There have been the proverbial butcher, the baker, and the candlestick maker, but never an honest law enforcement officer.

For the past 23 years, I have been an agent of the Federal Bureau of Investigation, voluntarily retiring from that organization January 10 last for the specific purpose of entering this Governor's race.

I sincerely believe that my long experience as an administrator of the honest policies of J. Edgar Hoover insure my capabilities to serve as chief executive of my native state.

I have been told by friends and enemy alike I could never beat the well-entrenched, well heeled political machines that have dominated Oklahoma since statehood.

I am just stubborn enough to believe that you, the tax paying public, are tired of the professional politicians keeping their hands in your pockets and living off your hard earned dollars.

What Oklahoma needs, among other things, is a four-year, non-partisan administration.

It needs a Governor who will represent all of the people regardless of their political affiliations, their color, creed, or religion.

I am the only candidate in this race for governor who can give you that kind of administration.

I have been keeping records of what has transpired concerning the embezzlement of your tax paid dollars.

I have been keeping records of the under-handed and under the table methods of many of our self-styled political leaders.

As a veteran peace officer, I know how these frauds, embezzlements and kickbacks are perpetrated upon you, the tax paying public.

I know the majority of those in Oklahoma who are responsible for these acts of thievery.

As an F.B.I. trained man I know how to stop this skull-duggery.

I have the intestinal fortitude to stop it and in the future when these felonies are committed, I will do everything in my power to see that the guilty persons are prosecuted and placed behind the bars of the State Penitentiary in McAlester.

Do not misunderstand me. I do not infer that all politicians or public servants are crooked, but to the contrary we have proven from statistics that 95% of all people are basically honest.

However, I know from experience that one dishonest person can steal more money – your tax dollars – in one week that a thousand honest people can count in a month.

As your Governor, I can save you, the taxpayers, a minimum of 20 million dollars a year for the next four years, or I will ask to be relieved of my responsibility as your Governor.

In other words, ladies and gentlemen, if I cannot stop waste and corruption, I will resign.

Compare this with the statement made recently in Tulsa by the incoming speaker of the House of Representatives.

He said, 'The legislature has been very lenient with the taxpayers of Oklahoma, but come January we will get into your pockets.'

With a Governor who is determined to stop the kick-back racket, the waste, needless spending, regardless of whom it might affect, I cannot foresee the necessity for any increase in taxes, and I will bitterly oppose any such measures.

With the money I am able to save as your chief executive, we would be in a position to raise the salaries of school teachers and other state employees. In addition we would have money left over to give further assistance to the mental health program, the physically handicapped, and Old Age Pensioners.

The only issue of any consequence that has been discussed with you during this entire campaign has been the repeal of prohibition.

Somehow I do not feel that the repeal question is the one and only major issue, and unlike the other candidates, I am not personally convinced that the people of Oklahoma are clamoring for repeal of the dry laws..."

Bryce forgot that he didn't get to pick the issues, the voters did. Contrary to both of his major party opponents, he promised not to insist on a repeal vote. If he were to be forced to call a repeal election, he would insist on a nine-man commission with state-owned package stores for both whiskey and beer.

He again promised to end corruption in government and save the taxpayers at least $20 million a year "in spite of the fact we would have to build a new wing on the state penitentiary. We would need the new wing to house all the crooked politicians I would send down there. And I wouldn't want the honest convicts to have to live in the same cell block with them."

Unfortunately, he had overestimated the voters.

The general election on November 4 was both an upset and a reaffirmation. Edmondson tallied 401,232 votes to become the state's youngest Governor at age 33. Ferguson had 107,692 to make the worst showing for a Republican candidate in the last four decades. Jelly Bryce got 32,536 votes, the highest number and percentage ever given to an independent candidate in Oklahoma's history. In what was described as a "relatively light voter turnout", the election still produced the highest vote total ever cast and the largest winning majority in any previous Governor's race. More than a quarter

of Bryce's tally came from Oklahoma County, the primary population center in the state and his professional home base, giving him
over 8,500 votes but still giving more than 53,000 to Edmondson and
a little over 15,000 to Ferguson. The bottom line was Oklahomans
wanted whiskey.

And they'd get it, if by a circuitous measure. Governor Edmondson started an unusual strategy for someone who had campaigned
on a platform of prohibition repeal. He started a campaign of strict
enforcement of the existing law. It worked. It showed the citizens
just what happened when laws were scrupulously enforced. J. Howard Edmondson got his point across—there would be legal liquor or
no liquor at all.

On April 7, 1959, the voters went to the polls and for the first
time in 52 years, approved the repeal of Oklahoma's prohibition
laws. Even so, it passed by only 80,000 votes out of nearly three-
quarters of a million cast.

One former FBI associate who helped in Bryce's campaign felt
it was complicated by the fact that he didn't adjust quickly enough
from his former job. Moving from Special Agent in Charge of a FBI
field office to private citizen running for public office was too drastic
a transition to happen overnight.

A SAC was a King in his own private little fiefdom, the ultimate
power and authority over a lot of people and a large jurisdiction. He
wasn't used to being told no by anyone and always received a certain
amount of adulation, from local law enforcement, his own employees
and local citizens. His personal integrity had to be above reproach.

It never occurred to Bryce that anybody would disbelieve him
or any of the charges he made against his opponents. It also never
occurred to him that the vast majority of private citizens could fail
to be as outraged as he was by the commonly accepted definition of
"politics as usual."

Jelly Bryce retired to his home in Mountain View to supplement
his retirement income with private investigations.

XII
"Deef"

One of the first people I contacted when starting the research for this book was retired OCPD Sergeant James H. Garrette. An officer from 1951-1978, Jack Garrette served over a decade as a member of the OCPD Pistol Team and as Rangemaster for the OCPD Training staff, training hundreds of young police recruits to shoot, this author included. As the earlier story about his battle with armed robbers testifies, the lessons he passed on to us were as hard-learned as Delf Bryce's had been. Jack Garrette was as good as any I've ever seen at putting bullets in the ten-ring.

The first day I called him, I had to leave a message on his answering machine. When he returned my call, he apologized for missing my call because he had to go into the small rural town he lives near to buy some batteries for his hearing aids. When we started talking about Jelly Bryce, the conversation also turned to a number of other renowned pistol shots of those days; former Border Patrolman Bill Jordan, Oklahoma Highway Patrol Captain Dan Combs and others. To quote Jack, "All those old pistol shots are deef," himself included.

Police officers using hearing protectors when firing their pistols during training only came into vogue in the 1960's. Before that, their unprotected ears just had to suffer the bombardment of the explosions from their pistols, rifles, shotguns and machine guns. For the average officer who had to renew his pistol qualification a few times a year, those explosions numbered a few hundred a year. For officers who practiced a lot, the number could reach the thousands. For members of the pistol teams and range training officers, they could reach the hundreds of thousands. The unprotected human ear was not designed to absorb that kind of unremitting punishment.

The Army has a joke based upon a similar principle. It says you can always tell an Infantry officer from an Artillery officer. The Artillery officer is the one who's always saying "Huh?"

The OCPD didn't require very sophisticated physical examinations to go to work for them in the 1920's. If you were healthy enough to show up when you were supposed to and do the job, you were hired. If you didn't, you were fired. It was as simple as that.

The FBI, on the other hand, required a fairly comprehensive entrance physical and periodic re-examinations. Almost from the beginning of his career, Jelly Bryce's FBI physical exams showed deterioration in his hearing.

His first exam, conducted in September of 1934, two months before he was hired, shows normal hearing. It was recorded like vision, 20/20, the denominator showing the normal distance and the numerator showing the actual distance heard. The second exam two years later still showed normal hearing but recorded a perforation of the right eardrum.

In 1938, he could hear whispered speech from 15 feet with the right ear but only 10 feet with the left. The doctor noted nerve type deafness in the left ear. In 1940, his hearing was 12/15 in the left ear and 7/15 in the left. By the next year, it had deteriorated to 7/15 in the right and 1/15 in the left. With the constant bombardment of gunshots from his qualifications, demonstrations, hunting and sport shooting, it wasn't likely to improve.

On January 9, 1963, Jelly Bryce forwarded a sheaf of government forms to his old boss, FBI Assistant Director John Mohr. The cover letter addressed him familiarly as "Dear John" and was signed with a handwritten "Jelly."

The forms were an Employee Notice of Injury or Occupational Disease and Claims for Compensation. Copies had been sent to the U.S. Labor Department's Bureau of Employee's Compensation in Chicago. They certified his continuous assignment as a FBI agent for 24 years and claimed a "loss of hearing due to gunfire— condition progressive." Filed from Oklahoma City, he listed his home address as Mountain View and his status as "self-employed."

An examination form from Dr. J.V.D. Hough dated 12-7-62 attested to Bryce's loss of hearing—"diagnosis of bilateral sensorineural deafness"—due to "continued use of firearms from 1934 to 1958 in training and as exhibition shooter." The doctor said the effects were permanent and there was "...no treatment, medical or surgical, available at present time for this type of deafness."

The Bureau provided the Labor Department with Bryce's application for employment and his subsequent physical examination reports but had no record of his sick leave usage due to the period of time since his retirement. Under his own signature, J. Edgar Hoover personally attested to his status as an "administrative firearms expert (who) gave shooting demonstrations to various groups."

On April 23, a followup letter from the FBI Personnel Office stated that Bryce had, among other duties, "been responsible for establishing and maintaining effective relations with local law enforcement agencies...supervised Firearms Training at various intervals during his FBI career...From time to time he performed firearms demonstrations and he was rated as a qualified expert in respect to firearms ability...It is not possible to accurately reconstruct the exact number of such occasions." The letter ended with a typical bureaucratic disclaimer by saying "This Bureau is unable to state whether the investigative or supervisory duties he performed were in any way more strenuous than those performed by other employees engaged in similar work."

Time passed and on August 16, 1965, a final settlement was made by the Bureau of Compensation on Case Number A10-62086. They found that Bryce had suffered "a permanent disability equivalent to a 7.9 per cent loss of hearing in both ears due to sustained personal injury in the performance of duty." He was entitled to 15.8 weeks of compensation at $121.15 per week for a total of $1,914.17.

XIII
Twilight

Jelly Bryce settled into a comfortable retirement in Mountain View. With his Bureau pension and his compensation settlement for his hearing, he could have probably gotten by just fine with no supplementary income at all. He and Shirley lived on their own 80 acres southwest of town and he kept a small herd of Black Angus cattle which provided some continuing income not to mention a supply of steaks and calves. Leon Cleary helped him with the cattle so he had plenty of free time. He also had a place on 160 acres north of town. They called it The Ponderosa, probably after the ranching empire on the popular TV western Bonanza. But Jelly approached retirement from the standpoint of it didn't have to mean doing nothing, just doing what you wanted when you wanted. That was the same way he approached his private investigations business.

Bryce did a lot of investigations work for a Tulsa oilman named Arthur Olson whom he had become acquainted with during his time as SAC in Oklahoma City. Olson had become wealthy owning the second largest oil drilling company in the nation and boasted that he had drilled oil wells in every state in the Union. The consummate high roller, Olson was often spontaneous in the distribution of his wealth. On one occasion, he hosted a party in his hotel room for Bryce and most of the Oklahoma FBI contingent. Olson ordered steak dinners for all his guests from room service. The dinners arrived but were generally ignored as the men were more interested in their conversations. After a while, Olson noted that the steaks were cold, and called room service, ordering the dinners removed and replaced with fresh ones. He would randomly approach military servicemen on the streets of downtown Oklahoma City and Tulsa, showing his appreciation for their service by giving them $500 gold Rolex watches. He had also given one of the watches to Spot Gentry. Now in the oil royalties business, Olson worked out of an office on the tenth floor of the Petroleum Building in Tulsa. Bryce received a check from him every month.

Bryce's business also included frequent trips to Amarillo, Texas. Retired OCPD Lieutenant Chris Walker, then a representative for Smith and Wesson, also had frequent business in Amarillo and ran into Bryce there on a number of occasions. Bryce always had Shirley with him on those trips and he and Walker developed a habit of meeting for coffee on the mornings they were both in town.

Bryce was beginning to show his years but some things never changed. He was always armed, still carried a pump shotgun in the trunk of his Cadillac and always sat with his back to a wall facing doorways. He was also still a snappy dresser. One morning, out of curiosity, Walker asked him how much he charged for his private investigations work. Typically, Bryce replied "If they have to ask the price, they can't afford me." In spite of his terse speech that sometimes bordered on sarcasm, Walker still described him as "a super gentleman."

Leon Cleary occasionally helped him with his private investigations and still shared a fondness for Cadillacs with his old friend. When they traveled together, Bryce usually still had Cleary drive because he was "tired of driving so much."

Bryce also still did some work for the FBI, albeit very quietly. In the early 1960's, Bryce spent at least three months working on the case of Billy Sol Estes, the multimillionaire Texas swindler who was making allegations of connections between Vice President Lyndon Johnson, several murders and an agricultural swindle.

Johnny and Jelly Bryce, mid-1960's. (photo courtesy of Agnes Tichy)

On the home front in the Spring of 1963, Johnny Bryce graduated from Mountain View High School thirty-seven years after his father. He had been a member of the local Future Farmers of America chapter for all four years as well as the Farm Shop Team. He had served on the Office Staff his sophomore year, the Dairy Judging Team his final two years and was in the Junior class play. His athletic participation was more sporadic. He had played basketball and football his freshman year but only returned to football during his senior year. He was a guard on the Tiger football team that finished the year with a 5-4 record.

The Mountain View school system had naturally grown since Jelly Bryce's day. It now contained almost 500 students but one yearbook still contained them all. Alphabetically, Johnny Bryce was listed first of the 34 seniors in the yearbook. All of the 14 senior boys but one had been on the football team.

Johnny's parents were hoping to have their son grow up fast, at least the father was. Maybe too fast. Jelly was trying to play match-maker for his son. Although Johnny was barely past his eighteenth birthday, Jelly apparently hoped that marriage would have a settling and maturing effect on the boy.

A girl with old family connections, Marsha Tate was a grand niece by marriage of Smokey Hilbert, the daughter of Jewell Hilbert's nephew. Petite at barely five feet tall, she was exactly seven months older than Johnny. On her eighteenth birthday, Jelly Bryce gave her a present of eighteen silver dollars. In his inimitable style, he casually took one of the silver dollars back from her, said "you don't need this one", threw it up in the air and shot a hole through it with a pistol that suddenly appeared from his pants pocket.

Prior to his marriage to Marsha, Johnny had spoken to others about the fact that he didn't want to get married yet. Understandably, only months out of high school, the young man still had some wild oats to sow. But his parents had their expectations. They wanted him married so married he was.

On February 7, 1964, John Fel Bryce and Marsha Annette Tate applied for a marriage license in Oklahoma County. He was 18, she had just turned 19. Delf Bryce signed the application and consent affidavit as his father. Johnny's father's former position and connections continued to benefit him.

J. Edgar Hoover sent a personal telegram congratulating them on their marriage. Percy Wade, longtime owner of Cattlemen's Café, made their wedding cake. For decades, Cattlemen's has been the 24-hour-a-day steakhouse in the Stockyards area of Oklahoma City. Years after her infamous husband's death, Pretty Boy Floyd's widow had been a waitress there. Always open, it is a rare law enforcement officer over the last several generations who hasn't eaten at Cattlemen's. Associates say that Jelly Bryce ate lunch at Cattlemen's virtually every day he was in Oklahoma City, usually having the calf fries, one of the restaurant's specialties.

If he had hoped that his "wild boy" was settling down and their

relationship might improve, Delf Bryce was destined for another dis-
appointment. Johnny had grown up but apparently not in every way.
At 6'4" and well over 200 pounds, he was a giant compared to his
diminutive father. Admitting he was "a big good-looking kid", some
considered him to be "conceited—he couldn't pass a mirror without primping his hair." Virtually all considered him "immature" and
"never taught responsibility." Johnny had always been close to his
mother but his father had frequently been gone during his youth, always working for the FBI. When he was around his son, as we shall
see later, unfortunately it wasn't what you would call "quality time."
Family friends and relatives are consistent in their descriptions of
the tensions between father and son—"Jelly and Johnny couldn't get
along for fifteen minutes without getting in an argument."

To all outward appearances, Jelly bent over backwards to do for
the boy. Too far backwards, by all accounts. Others consider that
"Jelly spoiled the boy rotten—always throwing money at him."
Johnny lived rent free on the Ponderosa and Jelly gave him money

*Marilyn, Delona and Johnny Bryce with FBI Director Hoover while Johnny was an
FBI clerk in Phoenix, AZ. February 28, 1968. (photo courtesy of D.S. Bryce)*

every month. One remembered a constant presence of uncashed checks lying around from his father. In his defense, maybe the boy had never gotten what he needed from his father. Witnesses say that Johnny couldn't seem do anything to please Jelly. On one visit to The Ponderosa, Jelly found the house in something of a mess. As with his personal attire, Jelly always demanded a neat, clean house. Seeing the disorder, Jelly immediately began criticizing his son, his daughter-in-law and the house's condition. Even considering that they were living in Jelly's house, it apparently wasn't handled very diplomatically.

Bryce continued to bend too far backwards for his son. He rented him an apartment in Oklahoma City and handled all of his finances for him rather than forcing him to learn it himself.

Under those conditions, it isn't surprising that the marriage failed rapidly. After barely fourteen months, on April 29, 1965, Johnny and Marsha were divorced. There were no children.

Things still didn't stabilize. Through his connections with the FBI, Jelly got Johnny a job as a clerk in the Oklahoma City FBI office soon after he graduated from high school, perhaps with some hope that the boy might become interested in a career as an agent. When the boy was little, in a throwback to his own youth, Jelly had occasionally removed the firing pins from some of his guns and let the boy play with them. Apparently it didn't take. Witnesses say that Johnny became a pretty good shot with a rifle but was lousy with a pistol.

Any hopes for a new career interest were not to be, either. The chief clerk in the office at that time was Pat Hammersberg, the wife of an OCPD officer. She and the office's agents soon recognized that Johnny wasn't cut out for that line of work, as clerk or agent. He was a good worker but very "task-oriented." Given definite tasks, he completed them promptly and correctly but showed little imagination or individual initiative. Jelly periodically asked the supervisors how his son was doing and told them "If Johnny's giving you trouble, let me know. Don't let him get away with anything." To his credit, Johnny Bryce himself asked the supervisors to correct him if he did anything wrong because he said he didn't want to embarrass his father.

Johnny was outspoken about having no interest in going to college which obviously limited his career opportunities in the FBI. The Bureau was long since out of the business of hiring gunfighters without college degrees, not that Johnny would have qualified anyway.

The four-year degree requirement was universal now. Several of the agents and clerical supervisors tried to stimulate his interest in college but he said he didn't want to go because his father "interferred with everything he tried." Johnny told them that he could have had a football scholarship to college but if he had taken it, "Dad would be there coaching."

He told them that while he was playing football in high school, his father had always been on the sidelines complaining to the coach about their handling of his son. When he entered animals in 4-H exhibitions, his father was always there trying to influence the judging. If Johnny didn't win a blue ribbon, Jelly would complain that the judging was bad or fixed.

When some of the clerical personnel suggested that he solve the problem with distance by attending a college in Montana or Washington, he said that his father "would probably cut his allowance." Not wishing to embarrass Jelly Bryce any more than absolutely necessary, the FBI office personnel began a clandestine campaign to encourage Johnny to quit the FBI and join the Marines. That worked—and not.

Shirley and Delf Bryce in their living room in Mountain View. The magic shows. (photo courtesy of D.S. Bryce)

Johnny was edged out of the FBI and joined the Marines. One of Bryce's close friends in the office, Special Agent John Rice, personally took Johnny down to the Marine Recruiting Office but that union wasn't to be any more successful. After only a few months, as they said, "Jelly got him out of that, too." It seemed that Jelly was continually bailing his son out of one mess after another. When he worked, the boy couldn't seem to hold a job for long either.

After leaving the Marine Corps, Johnny tried being a truck driver in Binger, then a night watchman in Mountain View—Jelly fretted about that one openly with friends. For as long as it lasted, Jelly was worried that "some character could take that gun away from him and he wouldn't have a chance." He needn't have worried for too long. That job also went by the wayside.

On May 9, 1967, Johnny Bryce married for the second time. The ceremony took place in his parent's house west of Mountain View. The bride was Marilyn Watkins. She was 17, he was 21. Her introduction to the family and friends would be gradual and peripheral. She would meet Smokey and Jewell Hilbert on their farm near Harrah but never saw Jelly Bryce shoot.

The marriage was more successful than the first, at least initially, and it produced two children. A daughter, Delona Sue, named after Shirley's mother, was born in early 1968. A boy, John Fel Jr., followed in 1970. Johnny worked as a FBI clerk in the Phoenix, Arizona, field office and his father's connections still benefited him. A month after Delona was born, the family had a photo taken with FBI Director J. Edgar Hoover, who personally inscribed and signed it. That privilege was not extended to every 22-year-old FBI clerk. Nevertheless that job didn't last. Neither did one as a Phoenix police officer and the family moved back to Mountain View.

Marilyn's impressions of her in-laws were that "they were not a very close family—they were distant with most people." That apparently also extended within the family. Fel and Winnie adored their great-grandkids and Marilyn felt they were "great people." Whenever the kids visited their great-grandparents, they always left with a present or something to play with, whether it was a few strands of leather from Fel's whip-making shop or Winnie's ceramics. Jelly and Shirley, on the other hand, were kind to their grandkids but were not nearly as doting as Fel and Winnie. That attention level dropped even more as the grandkids got older.

For most of the past three decades, Shirley Bryce had been the center of attention in her husband's world, having only the FBI for competition and that had ended with his retirement. She had gotten used to it and liked it. Now she became visibly jealous when attention was diverted from her to the grandchildren.

Even though Johnny's second union was longer lived than the first, it was to end infinitely worse.

In the same year his grandson was born, 1970, Jelly Bryce moved into a new brick one-story house. Purchased and built in Amarillo, he had it moved to a lot in Mountain View. Once again he wanted his

192

back against the wall. He had the home placed on a lot at the end of a dead end street at the address of 600 South Fourth Street. It was almost a family compound. His father and stepmother lived one block east of him in a small white frame house at 502 South Third Street. The house had a large basement where Fel Bryce did his leather work and Winnie worked on her ceramics. Fel raised sheep in a pasture behind the house. Bryce's sister Lila Bryce Dawson and her husband Elmer lived in a house directly across the street from Fel and Winnie at 521 South Third.

On May 2, 1972, J. Edgar Hoover died from a heart attack in his home in Washington, D.C., eight days short of his 48th anniversary as Director of the FBI. Interviewed by an Oklahoma City paper, Jelly Bryce lauded his former friend and boss. He called him "one of the great Americans of all time" and said "he was the only person I've ever known who never made the same mistake once."

During the winter of 1973, Shirley Bryce's health began to fail. Her diagnosis was troublesome and confusing. On March 23, she was admitted to St. Anthony's Hospital in Oklahoma City. She was eventually diagnosed with what was then and continues to be a very rare blood disease, almost as hard to understand as it is to pronounce.

Thrombotic thrombocytopenic purpura involves a deficiency in the platelets, one of the three types of cells in the blood. Red blood cells carry oxygen and white blood cells fight infection. Platelets are the smallest cells in the body and their primary function is to allow blood to coagulate and clot, preventing the body from losing too much blood during injuries. When the platelets don't do their job, blood can seep through the permeable blood vessels, causing many small hemorrhages and bruises under the skin or, in worse cases, serious internal bleeding.

There is a family legend that during her course of treatment in the hospital, a doctor recommended that one of Shirley's legs be amputated. Perhaps the internal hemorrhaging had so depleted the blood supply to the limb that it was dying. Jelly Bryce allegedly responded in a fashion that would have been expected. The legend is that he pulled a gun on the doctor and told him he'd kill him if he cut her leg off. No amputation was performed.

It didn't help. After lingering for slightly over three weeks in the hospital, Shirley had a heart attack on the afternoon of April 16. Treatment was unsuccessful and she died at 6:10 P.M. Her immediate cause of death was listed as a myocardial infarction with the blood disease as a secondary contributing factor. She was seven months short of her sixtieth birthday.

She was taken home to Mountain View and the funeral was held the following day at 2:00 P.M. with Marland Mason officiating. Following services in the First Methodist Church, she was interred in the Mountain View Cemetery. Jelly's old friend and employer, Tulsa oilman Arthur Olson, paid all the expenses by giving a blank check to the Dodd Funeral Home.

On May 4, 1973, less than three weeks after his wife's death, Jelly Bryce was to be honored as a lifetime member of the Oklahoma Sheriff and Peace Officers Association. Bryce had been a member of the organization since the days when he served with the OCPD. He was to be presented with a plaque by Association President O.K. Bivins at Adair's Cafeteria in Midwest City, a suburb of Oklahoma City. Also being honored was Tulsa County Sheriff Dave Faulkner, a retired OHP trooper.

Bryce asked Leon Cleary to attend with him. When he picked him up in the big Cadillac, he was running late but insisted Leon drive, as usual. Seeing how short their time was, Leon told Bryce he was skeptical they could make it to Oklahoma City in time. Undeterred, Jelly told him to just "put the hammer down."

Leon assumed Jelly was counting on the fact that the highway to Oklahoma City would be patrolled by a contingent of friendly OHP troopers, all of whom knew Jelly Bryce. They all knew Jelly Bryce, all right. They were all in Oklahoma City for the ceremony. Bryce and Cleary didn't see an OHP cruiser all the way to the city. They made it on time.

Bryce didn't do much after Shirley's death, primarily working around his acreages and raising his black angus cattle. In a rare outside job, he worked as security for an Elvis Presley concert in Oklahoma City and talked Leon Cleary into working it with him. Leon felt a little out of place but went along with his friend, more for companionship's sake than anything else.

Backstage, he asked Bryce what he should do if something happened. Bryce reached under his coat and handed him a pistol. Leon didn't want to take it because he had no law enforcement training or status, either active or retired. Bryce pushed the gun into his hand, telling him not to worry about that, "Just take it. I'll cover you."

Still, death—Shirley's—had become the overwhelming center of Bryce's life. Friends said her absence "just took the heart out of him." He smoked too much, wasn't eating right and didn't rest well. He was aging rapidly.

194

Northeastern Oklahoma's Grand Lake of the Cherokees is one of the state's reactions to the droughts of the Dust Bowl era. More familiarly known to locals simply as Grand Lake, it was created in the late 1930's with the construction of the Pensacola Dam across the Grand River. Almost a mile long, it is still the world's largest multiple arch dam. One of the state's top tourist attractions, the lake now covers 60,000 acres and has 1,300 miles of shoreline.

One of the main attractions of the area is the Shangri-La Resort. A combined resort, conference center and country club, it occupies 650 acres on the shores of Grand Lake. Featuring a 400-room lodge, two lush golf courses, indoor and outdoor tennis and racquetball courts, restaurants, lounges and a waterfront marina offering all types of water sports, it also offers some 80,000 square feet of space for conferences and meetings. Surrounded by expensive condominiums and private residences, it is situated at the southern end of Monkey Island. Not actually an island, Monkey Island is a peninsula of land extending south into the lake between the small towns of Bernice and Grove in Delaware County.

A reunion of former Special Agents of the FBI was scheduled in the Shangri-La conference center for the second weekend in May of 1974. Jelly Bryce, naturally, was planning to attend. The night before the reunion, Bryce had a dinner of mountain oysters in Gotebo with his old friend, Leon Cleary. He told Cleary that he was very tired and just "didn't feel good." Leon told him he should skip going to the reunion and rest up instead but Bryce said he really wanted to go. Cleary tried to talk him out of it but Bryce insisted.

Bryce did attend the reunion and took Shirley's 12-year-old small brown poodle, named Tequila, with him. Since his wife's death, the dog went virtually everywhere with him. People remarked that the man and dog were inseparable, almost like it was a palpable reminder of his departed spouse.

Leon Cleary describes the dog as "real smart, small but Jelly had it trained as a guard dog. The dog would raise hell whenever anybody came around. It was little but it'd go right after them." It was also "very much a one-man dog. The dog and Johnny hated each other." In fact, other than its owner, the dog would tolerate only Leon Cleary and his wife around it.

There was to be no shooting demonstration this time, just a relaxing weekend of camaraderie with old friends and colleagues. Although he undoubtedly enjoyed the company, the reminiscing and the war stories, he remarked to one of the former agents that he had never felt so tired in his entire life. Early Sunday evening, May 12, he went up to his room and went to bed.

The next morning, Bryce was not at the morning breakfast and coffee session. Habitually an early riser, his presence was naturally missed but his remarks about how tired he was were recalled and it was assumed he was catching up on his missed rest. He still didn't appear during the lunch hour. About noon, a housekeeping maid was going down the hall when she heard the muted sounds of a dog whining from one of the rooms. After no response to repeated knocks on the door, she entered the room with her passkey. If one of his colleagues had been there, there would undoubtedly have been some conversation about not wanting to surprise a man like Jelly Bryce in his sleep but this time there was no danger.

Bryce was lying in bed and the poodle was astride his body, barking furiously at the intruder. The maid went for help and returned with several of the former agents. One of them threw a bedspread over the dog and it was removed to a pen so they could check the welfare of its owner.

It was too late. Jelly Bryce was dead.

Susie Stephens was starting her third year working in the executive offices of Shangri-La and she still remembers the incident over a quarter of a century later. The Delaware County Sheriff's Office was notified and a local doctor from Grove, R.H. Bortz, was contacted. Bruce Duncan, the chief of security at Shangri-La and his assistant, John Bennett, were notified. So was Sam Harris, the local District Attorney. Jarvis Littlefield, the Delaware County Sheriff at the time, recalls that Deputies Johnny Johnson and Tom Price went out on the call to investigate but no one found anything to indicate other than a natural death. The doctor indicated that it appeared he may have passed away almost 24 hours earlier.

Some relatives and friends have heard rumors and others believe that his true cause of death was suicide by gunshot and it was covered up by all or some of his FBI comrades present at the reunion. Presumably due to despondency over the recent loss of his wife.

This is what I know.

Bryce was undoubtedly despondent and irretrievably saddened by the loss of Shirley. She was the love of his life and the mother of the only son he got to raise. After 29 years with her, he lived only 392 days without her, undoubtedly grieving every one of them.

There is a high rate of suicide among law enforcement officers due to, among other factors, the stress of their profession, the atten-

196

dant stresses this transfers to their social and marital lives, and their ready access to and familiarity with firearms.

Similarly, Jelly Bryce made enemies in the course of his profession. On more than one occasion, his life was threatened and he was known at various times to wear a bulletproof vest or travel with what his friends termed "bodyguards." That Jelly Bryce ever needed a bodyguard is probably ridiculous on its face but it isn't unreasonable that a man in such a position would take comfort from the presence of old friends who happened to be almost as good with a gun as he was, men he could count on in a pinch. No man is an island.

But the official manner and cause of death listed on his death certificate, Oklahoma State File Number 09276, Local Registrar's File Number 393 in Delaware County, Oklahoma, is "Natural death-Myocardial infarction." A heart attack. There was no autopsy performed and no visible causative injuries were observed on the body.

This is what I believe.

I have no doubt that criminal conspiracies occur daily in this country, some of them quite sophisticated. In general, the more conspirators or witnesses there are to them, the more likely they are to come unraveled.

Some suicides are tampered with to make them appear to be something other than what they are, usually unsuccessfully. Ditto with some homicides doctored to appear as suicides. I have been involved in some of those investigations. It is much more difficult to fake these things than the entertainment media would lead you to believe.

Many people still consider the suicide of a family member a stigma to be avoided at all costs if possible. From what I have learned about Jelly Bryce, if he decided to end his own life, I find it hard to believe he would commit suicide by any means other than a single gunshot wound to the head. I find it equally hard to believe that, with his sense of self-preservation and the natural paranoia of a man with dangerous enemies, a contract killer or old enemy could slip into his hotel room and assassinate him, making it look like a suicide or

D.A. and Shirley Bryce's gravestones in Mountain View, Oklahoma.

natural death. The problem of avoiding a small, noisy animal without harming it would have made it doubly difficult. Surely that possibility occurred to some of his FBI colleagues who would have made certain any such suspicions were thoroughly investigated.

I have found it possible to enjoy many television shows and movies without investing a lot of credibility in them. I find it virtually impossible to believe that a resort full of former FBI agents, hotel management, housekeeping personnel, local law enforcement officials and a local physician would or could successfully conspire to cover up a suicide, regardless of how esteemed the victim was. Nor do I believe they could do it successfully and maintain the coverup for more than a quarter of a century. Eradicating the physical evidence alone would be an almost insurmountable obstacle even with 1974 technology. Believe me, Hollywood's portrayal of CIA "Clean Up Teams" don't really address the reality of the circumstances. I won't even go into myriad flights of fancy such as he could have been drugged or he could have been clandestinely injected with ricin poison and so forth and so on, ad infinitum.

As impossible a task as it would be more than a quarter of a century later, I could try to locate and interview all the surviving former FBI agents who attended that reunion. I could try to interview legions of their relatives and friends to verify their version of what happened that weekend. I could try to locate and interview all the housekeeping personnel, management and residents at the resort that weekend.

As I said in the beginning of this book, it has been an investigation but it hasn't been a homicide investigation and I have found absolutely no reason to treat it as such.

Jelly Bryce died alone, in bed, in his room, from a heart attack, just like his mentor J. Edgar Hoover had two years earlier.

One of the former agents (he doesn't remember the name) contacted Leon Cleary and told him of his old friend's death. He also told him about the attack poodle they had corralled outside. Knowing of the dog's anti-social tendencies and Bryce's wishes, Cleary drove all the way from Mountain View, picked it up and took it home with him. Tequila lived another six years with his family before it passed away after a healthy span of 18 years.

On Wednesday, May 15, 1974, the Oklahoma Sheriff and Peace Officers Association held its annual ceremony at the Department of Public Safety Headquarters in Oklahoma City to honor all the peace officers slain in the line of duty in Oklahoma. Even though Jelly had died a peaceful death in bed and not in the line of duty, Johnny Bryce was invited to attend. He did and a photograph of him standing next to the Peace Officers Memorial was printed in the Association's magazine, The Peace Officer, in the July issue. Exactly one year earlier, they had published one of the last photos of Jelly Bryce on the occasion of his OSPOA life membership award. Leon Cleary had brought Johnny to Oklahoma City and bought him a new suit for his father's funeral.

The myriad of obituaries spread through newspapers throughout the state and were universally glowing in their praise as well as continuing and expanding some of the legends.

Former reporter Bob McMillin said "he was an enigma, really—very seldom talked about himself or anything he ever did. He was credited with being one of the people who got Pretty Boy Floyd. He never admitted it, but he never denied it, either." But he got it right when he said that Bryce "thought the sun rose and set in J. Edgar Hoover."

Former FBI Agent Spot Gentry gave one of the more understated and factual interviews by saying Bryce "was one of the best all around shots the Bureau ever had, if not the best" and described some of his firearms feats. In one column that credited Bryce with involvement in the killing of Pretty Boy Floyd, Gentry corrected the reporter by saying that Bryce was not involved in Floyd's killing but "was involved in aspects of the Floyd case as a police officer when Floyd was making his forays around Oklahoma."

Old friend Smokey Hilbert said "No doubt about it, he was the best. Before the age of computers, Bryce was the kind of guy who could just sit down and figure things out." Hilbert might have gone a little too far by alleging that Bryce "had personal knowledge about everything going on in the United States in the way of law violations."

An associate who preferred to remain anonymous said "Jelly would only drink with certain trusted people, but after a few nips, he liked to harmonize on some good old barbershop singing." The most often repeated story in the eulogies about his nickname credited it to a drunk that Jelly put in jail early in his career with the OCPD.

At 10:30 on Thursday morning, May 16, 1974, Jelly Bryce was laid to rest in the largest funeral Mountain View had ever experienced. Tom Bright and Reverend Robert Barr officiated at the services in the United Methodist Church of Mountain View. A contingent of the OCPD Honor Guard attended to render honors to one of their own. Two of the pallbearers were Bob Wilder, now a Major with the OCPD, and retired Special Agent Spot Gentry. Among the mourners were Bryce's father and stepmother, 90 and 78 years of age respectively. The burial was in the Mountain View Cemetery next to Shirley's grave. Befitting his status in the small community, his grave is in the central roundel near the flagpole in a direct line with the cemetery's main entrance. As with Shirley's funeral, all the expenses were paid by Tulsa oilman Arthur Olson who wrote a personal check to the Dodd Funeral Home for $2,193.23.

Family controversies didn't stop after Jelly Bryce's death. There was a small luncheon after the funeral. Some of the people attending to pay their respects to the family said they didn't see Johnny Bryce there but several others did. None thought he portrayed a grieving son. One said he didn't eat but sullenly stood by the entrance door the entire time. Another heard that Johnny had met his half-brother, Bill, for the first time that day. Two others said they thought Johnny was drunk and heard him grousing because he didn't get his father's diamond ring.

On the day of the funeral, the Oklahoma State Legislature drafted Enrolled Senate Concurrent Resolution Number 165, sponsored by 97 State Senators and 101 State Representatives. The Resolution commemorated "the career and life of the late D.A. "Jelly" Bryce, public servant and lawman; tendering heart-felt condolences and sympathy to the bereaved family; and directing distribution." It further read;

"WHEREAS, on May 12, 1974, the people of the State of Oklahoma suffered a great loss with the death of D.A. "Jelly" Bryce' and

William Delf Bryce, 1985. (photo courtesy of D.S. Bryce)

WHEREAS, D.A. "Jelly" Bryce, one of the nation's most flamboyant lawmen, was a special agent in charge of the Oklahoma office of the Federal Bureau of Investigation in the 1930's and 1940's; and

WHEREAS, D.A. "Jelly" Bryce was involved in solving the famous Urschel kidnapping and helped capture some of the nation's worst criminals, including John Dillinger, Machinegun Kelly, Mad Dog Coll, the Karpis and Ma Barker gangs; and

WHEREAS, following his retirement from the FBI, Mr. Bryce

was an Independent candidate for Governor of Oklahoma in 1958.

NOW, THEREFORE, BE IT RESOLVED BY THE SENATE OF THE 2nd SESSION OF THE 34th OKLAHOMA LEGISLATURE, THE HOUSE OF REPRESENTATIVES CONCURRING THEREIN:

SECTION 1. That we hereby express profound sorrow and regret at the demise of D.A. "Jelly" Bryce.

SECITON 2. That we hereby recognize and acclaim the outstanding contributions of this dedicated public servant,

SECTION 3. That we hereby express our most sincere and heartfelt condolences to members of his bereaved family as we and the people of this state share their great loss.

SECTION 4. That duly authenticated copies hereof be prepared and forwarded to the following members of the family of D.A. "Jelly" Bryce as an expression of the esteem of the Oklahoma Legislature:

John Bryce, his son;

John Bryce, Jr., his grandson;

Delona Sue Bryce, his granddaughter;

Mrs. Lila Dawson, his sister; and

Mr. and Mrs. F.A. Bryce, his father and stepmother."

It was signed by John R. McCune, the acting President of the Senate, Bill Willis, the Speaker of the House and certified by Lee Slater, the Secretary of the Senate. The Resolution was adopted by the Senate that day and by the House on the following day.

XIV
Legacy

Not only did the controversies surrounding Jelly Bryce not end with his death, they intensified. When probated, his will proved to be a unique document. It had only existed for ten months, created with an attorney in Hobart on July 11, 1973, three months after Shirley's death. He named his niece, Delf Ann Dawson, Lila's daughter, as his executrix.

His first bequest was to direct the payment of his debts and funeral expenses although Arthur Olson's generosity made the latter unnecessary. The next paragraph started pointing out how unusual the document would be;

"I leave nothing and exclude from participation in my estate a child, WILLIAM DELF BRYCE, who was issue of a prior marriage of the testator (D.A. Bryce) to Maxine Bryce, and make mention of him in this my last will and testament, but leave him nothing."

The next bequest was to his granddaughter, Delona Sue Bryce. He left her Shirley's elegant wrist watch which was encrusted with 96 diamonds. The watch was to be given to her when she graduated from high school. He also bequeathed her a three and one-half carat diamond ring to be given to her at the time of her marriage.

All the rest of his property and possessions he divided into two trusts with Delf Ann Dawson as trustee with a cousin, Margaret Meek, to succeed her if Delf Ann died before the will was enforced.

The majority of his property was placed in Trust I. It consisted of all of his real estate, livestock, farm machinery, jewelry and firearms, to be held in trust for his son, John Fel Bryce. Should Johnny decide to operate the property as a lifetime estate, he was to receive all the profits as well as all the obligations (taxes, upkeep, repairs, insurance) such operations entailed.

Even in Bryce's posthumous benevolence, there was criticism—and control. Bryce said his intent in this first trust was to provide Johnny with a lifetime income. But he also said "it is also my intention that he (John) shall not become vested with the corpus of any trust property—the final decision and management of any trust property shall be at the sole discretion of my trustee—to the end that the corpus of this trust estate—shall not be dissipated or encumbered

202

In any manner—during the natural lifetime of the said JOHN FEL BRYCE."

If Johnny decided not to operate the ranch, farm and real estate, the trustee could rent it and apply the rent to Johnny's income. Delf Ann Dawson was empowered to lease the property for agricultural purposes or oil and gas leases but could not sell, mortgage or borrow against it.

Johnny was also left the house at 600 South Fourth in Mountain View as well as all of its furnishings and contents but would have to pay the taxes and insurance. Fastidious even beyond the grave, Bryce also said his son must "—keep the same in a state of good repair—." BUT if Johnny failed to occupy the residence for more than three months, it was to be sold to the highest bidder and the proceeds placed in Trust II.

Bryce had apparently acquired some vindictiveness about Johnny's second marriage. He finished the bequest by saying Johnny's right to occupy the house would "—immediately terminate in the event he should remain married to Marilyn Bryce by terminating or dismissing presently pending divorce proceedings, or—in the event of their remarriage to each other."

Trust II contained Bryce's savings, stocks, bonds and unencumbered life insurance policies. Johnny was to receive the interest from these investments. The body of this trust was intended for his grandchildren but he specifically defined that as John Fel Bryce's children born in wedlock, "—it being my specific intention of excluding herefrom any heirs—by blood or otherwise of my child, William Delf Bryce—."

Just as Bryce's personal fastidiousness intruded upon his will, so did his personal feelings about his own limited education. He gave his trustee the same powers over Trust II but with exceptions. The first exception was that any of his grandchildren (by John) would receive all the higher education they wanted "—even to the invasion, if necessary, of the entire corpus of this trust—." Only the real estate was excluded.

Trust II was to terminate when Bryce's youngest grandchild reached the age of 25. Should the trust outlive all children, grandchildren and great grandchildren, whatever was left would be divided between his sister Lila and Ardell Bloodworth, the widow of Shirley's brother, William.

Jelly could have left out the clause about Johnny and Marilyn. Their divorce was finalized not long after the will was completed and they did not remarry.

After the funeral, Johnny Bryce lived in his father's house for a while. He got married for a third time to a woman whose name began with an "M", this time Mary. After a while, the couple moved and disappeared. Fell off the face of the earth, is more like it. Before Johnny left, he piled some things on the floor of the kitchen and burned it. If anyone knows what he burned, they're not saying and neither is he.

At the insistence of Bryce's attorney, a small stipend (less than $200 a month) awarded to Johnny in the will, was diverted to Marilyn Bryce for the support of her two children. After two years, this stopped and no more child support payments were made. Delona Sue Bryce grew up with only dim memories of her father and her brother had no memory of him. Marilyn Bryce remarried and that man became a true father to her children. The main memory Delona cherishes of her famous grandfather (she was only six when he died) was of him taking her into Chickasha, Oklahoma, and buying her a pair of white zip-up boots not long before his death. She loved those boots. As she grew up, she had to learn about the fame of the man she fondly remembered as "Grandpa" from others, not her father.

Delona Bryce received Shirley's diamond watch when she graduated from high school and the ring when she married. Approaching her majority, Delona decided to try to find her father. Bill Bryce, Delf Ann Dawson and other relatives professed no knowledge of his whereabouts. With his disappearance so complete, he could have been dead but his half-brother, Bill, felt he was alive somewhere. Delona eventually tracked him down in 1988. When John Jr. called him on the telephone, his father informed him that he "had no son." When Delona called him, he initially denied his identity to her but finally admitted it. Gradually the details of his life since his father's death came out. The third wife, Mary, had come and gone with no children. With another failed marriage behind him, he was living with his fourth wife, Susan, and they had a daughter in 1991. More jobs had gone by the wayside and a cousin had bailed him out of some gambling debts.

Delona and Johnny slowly formed the beginnings of a relationship but it has never blossomed into what it should have been. The Ponderosa and its 160 acres, where she had spent part of her childhood when they were a whole family, was the only part of Jelly Bryce's estate that meant anything to Delona. Johnny promised it to her verbally but reneged and sold it. The proceeds were divided into equal fourths between Johnny, Delona, John Jr. and Johnny's other daughter.

Although she eventually received a portion of her share of Jelly Bryce's estate, Delona's relationship with her father remains tenuous. To this day, she "wouldn't trust him as far as I could throw him" and, in some ways, wishes she had never sought him out. She was even unsure as to where he had been born, having never been able to get a consistent answer from him on the subject.

Apparently, John Bryce's relationship with his father has colored his entire life and the relationship never improved. Multiple requests of John Fel Bryce for cooperation in the preparation of this volume were refused. The last thing he said to this author on the subject was "Let's just say that the man you know is not the man I knew—or the man my father was." The bitterness in his voice was almost palpable.

On August 11, 1975, a correspondent for Time Magazine named Martin O'Neill sent a letter to FBI Director Clarence Kelley. He wrote that he had interviewed Bryce at the time of the Dale Maples case, the American soldier who had assisted German POW's to escape in World War II. After an introduction condemning the current fashion of exposing the nation's covert operations, O'Neill professed to be a great fan of Bryce. He claimed he had seen Bryce encourage a confession from Maples by jamming his revolver under Maple's chin and snarling "Listen, you son of a bitch, I'm fighting a war—". He also said that when the investigation was turned over to Army Intelligence, a frustrated Bryce blurted "I told them if they'd give me fifty men who could piss hard against the ground, I'd—". At that point, O'Neill supposedly reminded Bryce that he was a journalist, whereupon Bryce leaned close to him and threatened to kill him if he told anyone what he'd told him.

The upshot of the letter was that O'Neill was asking for Bureau cooperation on substantiating or disproving some of the Bryce legends because he was working on a movie proposal about the Bryce/ Maples incident titled "The Little Known Soldier." Among the questions he had were how many men Bryce had killed with the OCPD, how much he paid for his diamond ring and "where the hell did Bryce get a nickname like 'Jelly'?"

On August 29, a form letter was sent to O'Neill under Kelley's name. It said that the FBI didn't have the information he requested and suggested he contact Bryce's family. They included two of Bryce's obituaries from Oklahoma newspapers.

The movie was never produced.

In the fall of 1983, Hollywood came beckoning again for the Jelly Bryce story. This time, they went straight to the top. On September 26, a man named Robert H. Forward wrote directly to Attorney General William French Smith. The letter was on Mr. Forward's letterhead for his own Hollywood production company.

Addressing the Attorney General familiarly as "Bill" and signing it "Bob", Forward recounted some of his experiences writing for the television police show Adam-12 and working with Jack Webb. Basically he asked if enough material was available through the FBI to produce a screenplay or documentary about Jelly Bryce. He mentioned that he had met Bryce once during World War II at the Army Air Corps Base in Albuquerque. He described Bryce as "Indian, all or a good part, had coal-black eyes that burned holes through you, along with shivers down the spine. I thought to myself, 'Thank God he's on our side'."

The letter was sent down the chain of command and, unfortunately, met with much the same fate as Martin O'Neill's inquiry eight years earlier. On December 1, Mr. Forward got a reply from a FBI Assistant director. The reply gave some basic biographical information and pledged their cooperation, although saying that their files "do not reflect the minutiae of Mr. Bryce's career with the FBI, such as all the specific cases on which he worked as investigator or supervisor." Several articles from a FBI magazine and other sources were included.

Apparently it wasn't enough information for Forward Productions. Again, no production was forthcoming.

Epilogue

On November 5, 1975, Bryce's old boss and friend Clarence Hurt died in McAlester, Oklahoma. After retiring from the FBI in 1955, Hurt had moved to McAlester and been elected to two terms as the Sheriff of Pittsburg County. He was buried in McAlester.

On February 6, 1976, Fel Albert Bryce died in Hobart, Oklahoma, a month short of his ninety-second birthday. Two days later he was buried a few yards from his son in Mountain View Cemetery, next to Delf's mother, Maggie. As had been said of Fel Bryce more than half a century earlier, "the number of his friends is limited only by (the number of) his acquaintances."

On January 16, 1988, Winnie Bryce died in a Mountain View Nursing Home nine days after her ninety-second birthday. She was buried next to her husband in Mountain View Cemetery.

In her eighty-ninth year, Lila Dawson lives in a nursing home in Mountain View, Oklahoma.

During the process of trying to get to know Jelly Bryce during the research for this book, I remembered reading a biography of Audie Murphy, World War II's most decorated soldier. I was struck by some of the parallels between these two extraordinary men despite the 18-year difference in their ages.

Both were featured in stories in Life Magazine four months apart at the end of World War II although Murphy was actually pictured on the cover due to his combat achievements.

Both were small men, even by the standards of their day. When Murphy first tried to enlist in the military, he was half an inch under 5'6" and weighed 112 pounds. Although his later Hollywood press releases listed his height at 5'10", he probably never topped 5'7" or 170 pounds. Bryce's FBI physical exam measurements from ages 28 to 52 vary from 5'7" to 5' 8 3/4" and from 151 to 174 pounds. One officer who worked with him described him as "almost fragile" in appearance compared to other officers. His colleagues soon revised their initial estimate of him.

Both were scrappy despite their modest physical size. Much larger men did not intimidate them. Murphy once manhandled a much larger Assistant Director who had yelled at him on a movie set. In an early road rage incident, Murphy confronted two men who were driving recklessly. When they tried to beat him up, Murphy beat the men, "both twice his size" according to a witness, unconscious. One can't help but recall Bryce's incident with Jack Garrette's extra large drunk.

Both had phenomenal eyesight, immeasurably better than 20/20 and never needed glasses throughout their lives. Their reflexes and eye-hand coordination also far exceeded those of most other men. Both learned to shoot with .22 rifles at an early age and developed into prodigious marksmen. To feed his family during the Depression, Murphy shot rabbits on the run 40 miles south of the Oklahoma line in northeast Texas and Bryce burned up enough ammo to train a small army less than two hundred miles away in western Oklahoma. Both would use these talents to save their lives numerous times. Both would also turn their talents with firearms into factors in their "second jobs", Murphy in his acting and Bryce in his firearms demonstrations for law enforcement officers.

In his biography of Murphy, author Don Graham includes a chapter titled "Quick-Draw Audie." In it, he writes "In the late forties and fifties, when every actor had to prove his manhood by making a western, there was a kind of fast-draw culture that pitted earnest would-be Hollywood gunslingers against each other." One can't help but wonder if that was influenced by the widely publicized Life article on Bryce.

Murphy naturally became very proficient at the fast draw and was a member of what was called "the half-second league", a small group of fewer than half a dozen western actors who could draw and fire in that length of time. That is one-tenth of a second slower than Bryce's timed four-tenths of a second with real ammunition.

Murphy's and Bryce's experiences of risking their lives and taking others, in war in Europe and enforcing the law on America's streets, formed them into something extraordinary recognizable among other men. As a result of those experiences, both men always kept guns nearby for the rest of their lives. Murphy had a large collection of guns, wangled both official and complimentary concealed weapon permits from several law enforcement agencies and usually carried his .45 automatic pistol. Friends said he never felt really secure unless he had a gun close at hand at all times. Bryce naturally felt he had untold enemies from his many arrests and was always armed, even years after his retirement. After his death, relatives found a sawed off shotgun concealed behind the night stand next to his bed.

Both men were known for their unflappable "unearthly calm." The kind of self confidence that only close brushes with violent death can bestow. The kind of unselfconscious, unwavering gaze of a predator that unsettles the meeker animals. The eternally tired but observant look of eyes that have seen so much to be feared that they are wary of everything but fear nothing anymore.

Murphy's biography recounts an incident where the baby-faced actor was confronted by a much larger, intimidating man in a public place. When the larger man looked down into the eyes of the man who had recently killed over 250 German soldiers in the process of winning the Medal of Honor and almost every other award for combat valor his country could bestow, he meekly and rapidly walked away. One Hollywood director even altered camera angles to avoid close-ups during movie scenes where Murphy was portraying anger to keep from terrorizing audiences. He said Murphy had "frightening eyes."

Bryce's eyes also made a lasting impression on everyone who looked into them. Even when Bryce was relaxed among friends, Bob Wilder said his eyes were "a clear, vivid blue but cold...hard...they'd cut right through you." Doug Hilbert, a nephew of Smokey Hilbert who worked with Wilder as an FBI clerk when Bryce was SAC in Oklahoma City, said he had "the aura of a killer."

Murphy's biographer related several examples of his finely honed automatic survival instincts, exemplified by a dislike of being touched by strangers, especially unexpectedly. Hilbert has a similar memory about Bryce. When Bryce was SAC in Oklahoma City, a new agent reported to the office and was seated in the boss's office waiting to meet him and formally report for duty. As Bryce walked in, the agent stood up behind him and, to gain his attention, the new agent reached out and touched his coat sleeve. Before the man could blink, Bryce instinctively whirled and the agent had a .44 revolver firmly planted against his forehead. The man allegedly resigned that day, evidently deciding he was not meant for this line of work.

Both Bryce and Murphy were outspoken, blunt, direct, forceful men in their speech, men who didn't often soften their words or spare others their opinions. Having been put closely in touch with their own mortality seemed to have shortened their patience with the niceties or political correctness of cafe society conversation.

Both had wide circles of acquaintances whom they were on good terms with but kept a very small, select group of close friends. Both gave their trust and true friendship grudgingly but, once given, were extremely loyal.

Both had trouble sustaining successful family relationships, either as a result of their professions or the violence in their lives.

After all the violence in their lives, both men died in unexpected ways but, in the old western vernacular, "with their boots on." Murphy died in a plane crash in 1971 and Bryce from a heart attack two years later.

Murphy's later career as an actor in 44 movies and his status as World War II's most highly decorated soldier insured his lasting fame. He wrote his autobiography, To Hell And Back, and starred in the movie made from it.

Even today, his gravesite in Arlington National Cemetery is a tourist attraction second only to that of President Kennedy. A veterans hospital are named for him in his home state of Texas and the Internet hosts dozens of sites concerning him.

Jelly Bryce is little known outside of law enforcement circles and even then mostly in Mountain View, Oklahoma City and Quantico, Virginia.

Following the attacks on the World Trade Center, the FBI's priorities were realigned to terrorism and homeland security. The September 2002 issue of American Heritage magazine featured an article titled "The FBI Driscoll, Barbara M.Driscoll, Barbara M.and its ever-changing targets." On the cover was a photo of an FBI agent drawing a revolver, anonymously titled "Agent In Action-1945." Apparently someone thought this dated photo was still universally representative of a fearless, iron-jawed Federal agent bringing America's enemies to justice.

It is one of Life Magazine's stroboscopic photos of Jelly Bryce.

The walls of the Oklahoma City Police Department's headquarters building are lined with framed enlargements of many historical photos of the OCPD's history. One of them hangs on the wall in the reception area of the Investigations Bureau, the old Detective Division. People waiting to see detectives sit under it and dozens of OCPD officers and detectives walk by it every day of every year. In the old black and white photo, three hard-looking men in 1940's-style business suits are leaning on a counter, the glass behind it riddled with bullet holes. They are Delf Bryce, Mickey Ryan and Smokey Hilbert.

We remember.

The End

Bibliography

BOOKS:

Carmichel, Jim, *Book of the Rifle*. Outdoor Life Books Inc., New York, N.Y. , 1985.

Edwards, Jim, and Hal Ottaway, *The Vanished Splendor, Volume* I. Abalache Book Shop Publishing Company, Oklahoma City, OK., 1982. *Volume* II, Abalache Book Shop Publishing Company, Oklahoma City, OK, 1983 and Mitchell Oliphant, *Volume* III, Abalache Book Shop Publishing Company, Oklahoma City, OK, 1985.

Faulk, Odie B., Laura E. Faulk and Bob L. Blackburn, *Oklahoma City, A Centennial Portrait*. Windsor Publications Inc., Northridge, CA, 1988.

Franklin, Jimmie Lewis, *Born Sober, Prohibition In Oklahoma, 1907-1959*. University of Oklahoma Press, Norman, OK, 1971.

Graham, Don, *No Name On The Bullet*. Viking Penguin Books, New York, NY, 1989.

Jinks, Roy, *History of Smith and Wesson*. Beinfeld Publishing Inc., North Hollywood, California, 1977.

Jones, Leroy, Editor, *Mountain View*. 1899-1999, *The First 100 Years*. Schoonmaker Publishers, Weatherford, OK, 1998.

Nash, Jay Robert, *Bloodletters and Badmen*. M. Evans and Company, Inc., New York, NY, 1973, 1995.

___ *Encyclopedia of World Crime*. Crimebooks Inc., Wilmette, Ill., 1989/90.

Ottenberg, Miriam, *The Federal Investigators*. Prentice-Hall Inc., New York, NY, 1962.

Owens, Ron, *Oklahoma Justice: The Oklahoma City Police, A Century of Gunfighters, Gangsters and Terrorists*. Turner Publishing Co., Paducah, KY., 1995.

Shirk, George H., *Oklahoma Place Names*. Second Edition, University of Oklahoma Press, Norman, OK, and London, UK, 1965, 1974.

Sifakis, Carl, *The Encyclopedia of American Crime*. Facts On File Inc., New York, NY, 1982.

Smith, Jack H., *Oklahoma, A Land and Its People*. The Vestal Press Ltd., Vestal, NY, 1989.

Society of Former Special Agents of The FBI. Turner Publishing Company, Paducah, Ky, 1996.

Stewart, Roy P., *Born Grown, An Oklahoma City History.* Fidelity Bank N.A., Oklahoma City, OK., 1974.

Theoharis, Athan G., Editor, with Tony G. Poveda, Susan Rosenfield and Richard Gid Powers, *The FBI, A Comprehensive Reference Guide.* Oryx Press, Phoenix, AZ, 1999.

Unger, Sanford J., *FBI.* Little, Brown and Company, Boston and Toronto, 1975, 1976.

Wallis, Michael, *Pretty Boy, The Life and Times of Charles Arthur Floyd.* St. Martins Press, New York, NY, 1992.

Welsh, Louise, Willa Mae Townes and John W. Morris, *A History of The Greater Seminole Oil Field,* Oklahoma Heritage Association, Oklahoma City, OK 1981.

NEWSPAPERS:
The Daily Oklahoman
The Luther Register
The Mountain View News
The Mountain View Times
The Oklahoma City Times
The Oklahoma Journal
The Osage County News
The Seminole Producer
The Shawnee Morning News
The Tulsa World
(All in Oklahoma)

MAGAZINES, JOURNALS AND OTHER SOURCES:
Callahan, Clyde, *Pioneering In Kiowa County, Volume 3.* Kiowa County Historical Society, Hobart, OK., 1978.

Cartledge, Rick, *The Guns of Frank Hamer.* Oklahombres Newsletter, Spring 1993.

Chaffin, K.B., *Jelly Bryce, The FBI'S Legendary Sharpshooter.* Oklahombres Newsletter, Spring 1993.

__, *Jelly Bryce, Fast Gun of The FBI.* Handguns Annual, 1994.

__, *The Most Dangerous Gun,* Oklahoma Today, Oklahoma Tourism and Recreation Department, Oklahoma City, OK., November/ December 1998.

Federal Bureau of Investigation, Personnel File 67-38692, *Delf Albert Bryce.*

___, various publications, Research Unit, Office of Public and Congressional Affairs.

Jones, Sandy and Bob Fischer, *It's Death To Bonnie and Clyde,* Oklahombres Newsletter, Winter 1999.

Koch, Michael J., *Tri-State Terror, The Sage of Wilber Underhill In Oklahoma.* Oklahombres Newsletter, Winter 1994, Spring 1994, Summer 1994, Fall 1994.

Life Magazine, November 12, 1945 issue, ime. Inc., Chicago, Ill., 1945.

Markardt, Special Agent Stephen P., FBI Office of Public Affairs, *An Evening At The Bio.* The Investigator, July/August 1990.

Mattix, Rick, *Bonnie and Clyde In Oklahoma.* Oklahombres Newsletter, Winter 1991.

Mattix, Rick, *Southwestern Lawmen Slew Dillinger,* Oklahombres Newsletter, Fall 1994.

Maxwell, Gloria, *The Kansas City Union Station Massacre,* Oklahombres Newsletter, Spring, Summer and Fall issues, 1991.

McBride, Mrs. Gertrude, *Mountain View, Pioneering in Kiowa County, Volume I.* Kiowa County Historical Society, Hobart, OK, 1978.

Oklahoma City Police Department. 1928 Annual, 1929 Annual and various personnel files.

Oklahoma Department Of Wildlife Conservation. Biennial Report, 1992-1994.

Peace Officer Magazine. Various issues, Oklahoma Sheriff and Peace Officers Association, Oklahoma City, OK.

R.L. Polk City Directories, Oklahoma City. various years.

Wagner, Steve, Editor, *Outdoor Oklahoma.* Oklahoma Department of Wildlife Conservation, Oklahoma City, OK, January/February 1994.

Personal Interviews and Correspondence:

As listed in the Acknowledgements.

Afterword
A Special Plea to the Federal Bureau of Investigation
and the Freedom of Information Section

I remember reading an amusing parable once. A little bird was flying south for the winter but had started very late in the season. As a result, he got caught in an ice storm and landed in a barnyard. As he was shivering on the ground, a cow walked by and stopped over him. The next thing he knew, he was completely buried in a pile of fresh, warm cow dung. A few minutes later, a chicken came by and, noticing movement in the pile, started scratching at it. In a few minutes, the chicken had scratched away all the dung and freed the little bird. As the bird was cleaning his feathers off, a hawk flying above saw him on the ground, swooped down, picked him up and ate him. The morals of the story were:

Everyone who craps on you is not necessarily your enemy.

Everyone who takes crap off of you is not necessarily your friend.

When you're warm and safe in a pile of crap, changing the situation may not always be in your best interests but it does deserve some consideration.

I would like this section read with all that in mind.

Also please bear in mind that I have had a career in law enforcement that has made me privy to a lot of confidential material over the years so I am not approaching this from an excessively naïve viewpoint. I fully realize some secrets have to be kept and why. The OCPD doesn't know if Oswald really acted alone or the names of our deep cover agents in foreign countries but some of our confidential material does have some things in common with the confidences in FBI files. Some of it could have ruined businesses, reputations and lives at one time—if made public within a certain period of time. But most of it, if released after the passage of a couple of generations and printed, might garner no more than a "Gee, how about that?" from readers.

Conducting the research for this book was my first experience with seeking information through the Freedom of Information Act. I approached it with much trepidation. I had heard a myriad of horror stories about government red tape and two-year waits for files so heavily redacted as to be rendered virtually useless. I expected the worst, especially considering that I was trying to gain access to personnel files of retired FBI Special Agents. When I became acquainted with the reality, I was surprised, pleasantly for the most part.

The red tape was minimal, the responses prompt, professional, courteous and helpful. The results, while much better than expected in my ignorance, were far from perfect but this isn't Utopia and never will be. We are all human beings and fallible in judgement and performance to one degree or another. Nevertheless, a constant striving for improvement is one of the hallmarks of our species which I suppose is one of the reasons we control this planet instead of the elephants, tigers or insects.

I'm not enough of a megalomaniac to believe for an instant that anything I say here will change the policies or procedures of the Federal Bureau of Investigation or their Freedom of Information Section. Nevertheless, this nation has gotten more mileage out of people thinking differently and speaking out than any other in the history of the world so why not? Someone told me once that if you don't have a solution, don't bitch about the problem. In that light, I have some suggestions and thoughts on the matter.

1. When I received Delf Bryce's personnel file, it was redacted but not especially heavily. The reasons for that will become more apparent under Number 2.

2. I'm not a lawyer but after more than thirty years as a law enforcement officer, I've spent a lot of time around some very good ones. As a result, I do know a few things about the law. One of them is that it is not legally possible to invade the privacy of deceased persons nor is it possible to libel or slander them.

Some of the redacting is patently unnecessary and some approaches the ludicrous. The initials of someone who wrote a memo sixty years earlier is hardly a matter of national security. Redacting the name of a person who was old enough to be a Chief of Police 72 years ago in a matter that is preserved somewhere on the microfilmed front page of an obscure newspaper is relegated to a matter of inconvenience rather than any reasonable right of privacy the person should expect or have any right to expect.

The release of the files is presupposed on the fact that someone isn't dead until it can be proven they are or a century has passed since the incident. This timeline even predates the existence of the FBI or any of its predecessors.

Less than one ten-thousandth of one per cent of our population lives to be 100 years of age or older. And it is particularly difficult to prove someone is dead when you don't know who they are! Some of this falls under the governmental Catch 22 of "If I knew the answers to the questions you're asking, I wouldn't need the information I'm asking you for because I'd already have it."

In all fairness, when I filed an appeal for the release of some of the redacted information, it was granted and I received the information promptly. My point is that the appeal shouldn't have been necessary and the redaction violated common sense in the first place.

3. When I received Delf Bryce's personnel file, it consisted of 262 pages. What was frustrating and, I believe unnecessary, was the fact that 469 pages had been removed and destroyed within four years of his death. Many of those pages covered the earliest and most active years of his career with the FBI during the gangster era of the 1930's.

Many of the most important details of the history of law enforcement's struggles against gangsterism in that decade reside in FBI files. What was gained by destroying those 469 pages? Two inches of filing space? Even multiplied by the thousands of current and former FBI agents, and hundreds of thousands of cases the Bureau has investigated in the last three-quarters of the Twentieth Century, we might have to build a few more storage buildings for government records but look at the National Archives, the Smithsonian, the Library of Congress, etc. etc. Our government has never been shy about building more storage space.Surely we waste more tax dollars than that on the infamous $600 hammers and $1100 toilet seats supplied by alleged lowest bidders on some government contracts.

Lastly, an intellectual appeal. This isn't just paper, this is history. The history of a relevant period in our country's formation. History that is available from no other organization. A history many people worked very hard to compile. Some of them died, were crippled or maimed in the process. It deserves to be treated with respect, preserved and, in many cases, publicized. Please.

216

INDEX

219